PRINCE
CHARLES EDWARD STUART

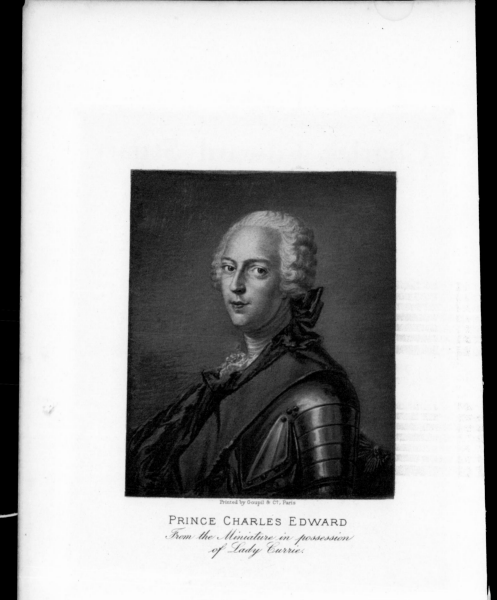

Printed by Goupil & C⁹, Paris

PRINCE CHARLES EDWARD
*From the Miniature in possession
of Lady Currie.*

Prince
Charles Edward Stuart

THE YOUNG CHEVALIER

BY

ANDREW LANG

AUTHOR OF 'THE MYSTERY OF MARY STUART' ETC.

NEW EDITION

LONGMANS, GREEN, AND CO.
39 PATERNOSTER ROW, LONDON
NEW YORK AND BOMBAY
1903

First published by Messrs. GOUPIL & CO. *in August* 1900, *with numerous Illustrations.*

New Edition March 1903.

TO

ELSPETH ANGELA CAMPBELL

———

Tha bradan tarra-gheal 's a choire gharblaich,
Tha tigh 'n o'n fharige bu ghailbeach tonn,
Le luinneis mheamnach a' ceapadh mheanbhchuileag,
Gu neo-chearbach le cham-ghob crom.

PREFACE

THE following Life of Prince Charles is longer than other biographies prepared for the same series. The Author's excuse must be that in this book, for the first time, by the gracious permission of her late Majesty, Queen Victoria, it has been possible to use the whole Correspondence (1720–1786) and other MSS. of the exiled House of Stuart, now at Windsor Castle. Some of the Cumberland MSS., too, were consulted.

The State Papers in the Record Office have also been used.

I have to thank the Marquis d'Éguilles for procuring a transcript of the 'Mémoires' of his ancestor, who represented the French Government in the Prince's camp (1745–1746). M. d'Éguilles also drew my attention to a tract on the mission of his ancestor, by M. Lefèvre-Portalis, a most valuable essay based on French State Papers. Some transcripts from these Papers were made for me in Paris.

These are the chief sources in manuscript, though various private collections of contemporary letters have been perused. Other documents I have read, for example, in a collection of printed family papers by the Duke of Atholl, which his Grace kindly permitted me to study for my book 'The Companions of Pickle.' The 'Memorials of Murray of Broughton' (edited by Mr. Fitzroy Bell for the Scottish History Society), and 'The Lyon in Mourning,' printed for the same Society, have been most serviceable. To Mr. Blaikie's admirable 'Itinerary of Prince Charles,' published by the same Society, I am especially indebted. Other useful papers are given in the last edition of the 'Histoire de Charles-Edouard' (1845–1846), by M. Amédée Pichot.

To Mr. D. Stewart I owe permission to read a curious Manuscript Diary of 1745–1746, by a Professor in the University of Edinburgh. The learned Professor, however, rather heard of, than looked on, events of importance.

In contemporary printed books, I have read, I think, most that has been published ; the names of the works are cited in the course of the narrative.

Considerable study of the pamphlets of the period was rewarded by little of value. These tracts are usually ignorant, or mendacious, or satirical. The 'Scots Magazine,' which summarised the newspapers, and was conducted with laudable impartiality, has been of service.

After the illustrated edition of this book had been printed, I became aware, through the kindness of Mr. F. H. B. Daniell, that certain bundles of undated Stuart Papers had escaped my notice at Windsor Castle. Some of them deal with the Prince's obscure years, between 1749 and 1752. These letters do not add much to what is here stated in Chapter V., and with more detail in 'Pickle the Spy.' One note signed 'T.' (Madame de Talmond) and undated, introduces Mademoiselle Luci, and accounts for that cypher-name. The writer speaks of a Madame de Morslains, or Monstains, who seems to have been one of Charles's Parisian friends. She is now married again, and is Madame de Luci. In writing to her the Prince may address her 'chez une femme qui fait mes commissions . . . cette femme se nome M^{dlle} La Marre.' *Cette femme* is clearly Mademoiselle Ferrand des Marres, the friend of Madame de Vassé, and to her, as a cypher-name, is transferred that of

'Luci.' Her address, as given by T., is *chez M. Lecuyer, Tapissier, Grande Rue Garonne, Faubourg Saint-Germain*. To this address Charles wrote to Mademoiselle Luci, on October 20, 1750 ('Pickle,' p. 113).

He had noted the address of Mademoiselle Ferrand as early as March 1749 : the confusion between Ferrand, La Marre, and Des Marres is puzzling, but these names all appear to refer to the lady who is generally styled 'Mademoiselle Luci.' I think that the undated note is of March 1749.

Goring calls her 'Mademoiselle Lucy.' The following letter of Goring's to Charles is in the undated parcel, and may be of 1750 :

Goring to Charles.

[UNDATED.]

S^r. . . . I find by ye Ladies here and what they hear from L. S-dw--h (Sandwich) that Monsr de Ville has a great mind to see you and by all appearance is in some impatience for it. . . .

I was told yesterday by Mad^{lle} Lucy that a foreign Minister named the place you are in actually, in a publick assembly, after which you are best judge if you should continue there or remove. You are offer'd by ye Ladies the château you know of, which by the description is a lonely solitary place, if you think it safe to make the journey : for if it should ever become publick where you are, or if it were suspected, it would be almost impossible to remove and at the same time dangerous to stay.

. . . Lally has entertained Ld Bath and by indirect discourse and grimace gives to understand he knows where you are, and that he has great share in all your proceedings, not to say more. He has not been at Rome but made a private journey to ye End that people might think he went to meet you in secret. . . . The Ladies by way of discourse asked me if you was in want of money, upon which I replied I was not enough acquainted with your affairs to know how that matter was, but I did not believe you were in distress, they told me that when you were with them they had often a mind to speak to you on that subject, but were affraid you would take it ill, to whom they sayd they could speak with more liberty, to propose it to you, I told them it was an affair too delicate for me to medle in without your orders, I thought however it was my duty to acquaint you with the generous sentiments and ye noble friendship of the two Heroines for such they are. . . .

P.S.—If I dare be so bold I would beg my respects to ye Goddess of ye residence. (*Perhaps Madame de Talmond.*)

It is probable enough that the two heroines (Madame de Vassé and Mademoiselle Ferrand) did lend money to Charles. Another bitter letter of Goring's is concerned with his refusal to take part in conducting Miss Walkinshaw to the Prince, whose conduct he severely criticises. ' I will not act a low part in your pleasures. My desire of not living with you, when accompanied by my utter dishonour, is

not what you can in justice condemn.'   Many Jacobite
papers, I learn through Monsieur Kerallain, are preserved in the archives of the town of Quimper ; they
are the documents of Warren, who carried the Prince
to France in 1746.

Information has been kindly given by the
Duchesse d'Albe et de Berwick, by Lord Braye,
and by the Baron Tanneguy de Wogan ; while
Mr. Harold Tinson has obliged me by carefully
reading and correcting the proof sheets of the first
edition.[1]

Finally, I have to express my vast debt of gratitude to Miss Violet Simpson, who aided me in
making researches and transcripts at Windsor Castle,
at the Record Office, and at the British Museum ;
and my thanks to the Duc de la Tremoïlle who presented me with the printed Jacobite correspondence
of the Walsh family, and to Mr. Hussey Walsh, who
kindly sent me a transcript of the cypher key to
that correspondence, found at Windsor Castle by
Mr. F. H. B. Daniell.

ANDREW LANG.

[1] Messrs. Goupil & Co. 1900.

CONTENTS

PRINCE CHARLES EDWARD

CHAPTER I

THE PRINCE BEFORE 1745

A wonderful star broke forth,
New-born, in the skies of the North,
    To shine on an Old Year's Night.
And a bud on the dear White Rose
Flowered, in the season of snows,
    To bloom for an hour's delight.
Lost is the Star from the night,
And the Rose of an hour's delight
    Went—where the roses go ;
But the fragrance and light from afar,
Born of the Rose and the Star,
    Live through the years and the snow.

THE eighteenth century, in its moments of self-consciousness, wrote itself down unromantic. It was the age of good sense, of moderation, of the estimably commonplace ; not conversant, not anxious to be conversant, with great adventures. Looking back, we see it with other eyes as an age, like all ages that have been and shall be, not destitute of forlorn hopes, and desperate enterprises, and high devotions.

B

Among all these enterprises, none was so gallant in
defiance of time, and chance, and force as the adventure of Prince Charles Edward Stuart.   The last of a
princely lineage whose annals are a world's wonder
for pity, and crime, and sorrow, Prince Charles has
excelled them all, save Queen Mary, in his share of
the confessed yet mysterious charm of his House.
He is the best remembered, next to the Queen, of his
Royal line : as each generation grows up, he takes
young readers captive : no hero has been celebrated in
songs so many, so spirited, and so tender.   Yet Charles
had not the intellect of the first James, the poet and
statesman.   His was not the unflinching courage of
the fourth James, who died far in front of the fighting
line at Flodden, within a lance's length of the English
commander, Surrey.   In domestic conduct and
loyalty to a creed he does not compare well with
Charles I.   He had not the brilliant wit of the second
Charles ; nor that geniality of his which covered so
many sins.   Far from him was the literary skill of
James II. : and the keen sense of honour, the undeniable dignity, and the Christian stoicism, of his own
melancholy father, James III., ' The Chevalier de St.
George.'   Of Mary Stuart he lacked the redeeming
steadfastness to loyal friends ; but he somehow rivals
Mary Stuart in his inexplicable hold on the sentiment
of his adorers.

Old men, known to Sir Walter Scott, had seen

the Prince, and could not speak of him without tears ;
and Scott tells us that Donald Macleod, Charles's
pilot in the stormy western seas, never mentioned
him without tender emotion. After years of bitter
quarrels, and many more years of separation and
silence, the Princesse de Talmond still acknowledged
her affection for the Prince. Even to-day hearts
are stirred when the band plays ' Will ye no come
back again ? ' in assemblies of the Kirk at Holyrood ;
parties held in that long bare hall where Charles lived
his little hour of royalty. Like his fair unhappy
ancestress, who sinned with such a heavy heart,
Prince Charles has his devotees. ' If he came again,
I would go with him,' enthusiasts say, even to this
hour. Why would they go with him, why is his
memory loved ? Unhappily it is not possible for any
writer who places historical truth above sentiment to
represent Charles as ' a very perfect gentle knight.'
His figure is beheld in a lustre not its own : in the
splendour of the love and loyalty that gave themselves
ungrudgingly for him and for his cause, that cherished
his memory, and even now hold it a kind of treason
to tell the truth as far as the truth can be known.
We are unable to find in Prince Charles the shining
figure that bewitches our fancy in our childhood.
But we can at least discern, clearly enough, the circumstances which made the Prince other than we
would believe him, we can estimate his temptations

and unravel the complex net of events, trials, betrayals, disappointments, and insoluble perplexities, which thwarted, blinded, perverted, and finally ruined a gallant heart, and a nature kindly but never strong. We are compelled to judge him, though, as Monsieur Coppée says :

L'Écosse ne peut pas te juger, elle t'aime.

Scott speaks of a gentleman of the name of Stuart who, in 1788, was seen in mourning, and was asked for what relation he wore it. 'For my poor Chief,' he answered ; and it is in the spirit of this reply, and with this pardoning pity, that all who have a heart to care for a ruined cause, and a brave man undone, must think of the Prince. He failed utterly, failed before God and man and his own soul, but, if he failed greatly, he had greatly endeavoured. Charles is loved for his forlorn hope : for his desperate resolve : for the reckless daring, the winning charm that once were his : for bright hair, and brown eyes ; above all, as the centre and inspirer of old chivalrous loyalty, as one who would have brought back a lost age, an impossible realm of dreams.

Romance was in Charles's blood. '*His* kingdom also,' said a French lady, speaking to Madame d'Aiguillon (who wore Charles's miniature, with that of Christ, in a bracelet), 'is not of this world.' Of this world his kingdom never was, and could not be ;

but he was and is lord of the region of dreams and desires. He was born of desire and dream : of high hopes unfulfilled. His father, the unhappy White Rose Prince of Wales of 1688, was a character with much less of appeal to the imagination than himself. But James, in youth, had been brave and eager, had charged the English lines, again and again, with the Maison du Roi, at Malplaquet : and James had boldly passed, disguised and unhurt, through the armed myrmidons of Stair. From the 'Jamie the Rover' of the old song, Charles inherited his passion for wanderings that were distasteful, at last, to the elder and wiser exile.

From his mother, Maria Clementina Sobieska, Charles drew the fitful energy which, in the famous John Sobieski, the deliverer of Christendom from the Turks, had leaped into a light that dazzled Europe. Adventure had been the Prince's mother's portion in her girlhood : she had run strange risks for the dazzle of an airy crown. In 1718 the Chevalier (James III.), a man of thirty, an exile in Italy, found it desirable to wed. The enterprise of 1715 had failed utterly, but George I. was hardly yet secure on his throne. Atterbury, Oxford, Lansdowne, Orrery, and others were conspiring : Ormond was young, and ready, with his fellow exiles, Keith, later Frederick's field-marshal, and his brother, the Earl Marischal, to lead in a new exploit. Spain, under Alberoni ;

Sweden, under Charles XII., were friendly to the cause : in brief there were hopes, to be shattered by the death of Charles XII., and by ' the Protestant wind,' that ruined the Spanish fleet and the attempt of 1719.

Therefore, lest his line should fail, James must take a wife. The Duke of Ormond and Charles Wogan of Rathcoffey, early in 1718, were sent to sue for the hand of a Russian princess. The mission of Ormond failed ; but Wogan went round the Courts of Europe looking for a lady to be Queen of England,— over the water. He was a man of ancient family : the Wogans went, with Maurice Fitzgerald, from Pembroke to Ireland in 1169. In 1295, under Edward I., John Wogan was Justiciary of Ireland. ' Mr. Thomas Wogan,[1] a very beautiful person of the age of three or four and twenty ' (says Clarendon), was the hero who led a loyal troop of cavalry from Dover to the Highlands, where he died of a wound, in 1655. Charles Wogan, the early friend of Pope, and the correspondent of Swift, had lived, like Pope, in the little Catholic colony of Windsor Forest ; till with his brother Nicholas, a boy of fifteen, he took an energetic part in the rising of 1715.[2] Nicholas was

---

[1] Edward, not Thomas, seems to have been the real name of this gentleman.

[2] Charles himself, according to the dates in the French History of the Wogans, was very young ; only about nineteen in 1715.

captured and pardoned for his gallantry in rescuing
a wounded Hanoverian officer out of a cross-fire at
Preston. There was no pardon for Charles, but he
made a romantic escape from Newgate, and entered
Dillon's regiment in French service. He was very
accomplished, and wrote English, French, and Latin
(verse and prose) with equal fluency and felicity.
Such a wooer, gay, witty, brave, and handsome,
might well have made love for himself, as King
Mark's envoy, Tristram, did to Iseult ; but Wogan
sought a heart for his master. Conceivably he was
not so remote from the fortunes of Sir Tristram.
Half a generation later, when Clementina had died
after an unhappy wedded life, James reviewed the
past, and suddenly conceived the idea (he expresses
it in a letter) that Charles Wogan, innocently and
unintentionally, had been the earliest cause of the
disunion between his bride and himself. Accustomed
to the gay and resourceful chivalry of Wogan, good
at need, Clementina may have been disappointed in
her grave, patient, and laborious lord.

Of all this Wogan could not dream, when, visiting
Prince James Sobieski in the course of his matrimonial mission, he found the usual three daughters
of fairy tale ; Casimire, ' bristling with etiquette, and
astonishingly solemn ;' Charlotte, ' beyond all measure gay, free, and familiar ;' and the youngest, the
fairest, Maria Clementina, ' sweet, amiable, of an even

temper, and gay only in season.' Alas, the even temper was to become petulant and sullen ; the round glad girlish face was to be drawn and melancholy, peaked and wan, yet resigned and sweet, before all was done.

Wogan chose Clementina as the best bride for the mournful King.

He then returned from Silesia, to Urbino, where James was captivated by his account of the chosen bride, and wished to send the Irish envoy back to complete the arrangement. But instantly arose, as it rose daily, the spectre of Jacobite disunion. More than once James might have 'sat in Geordie's chair,' if he would have abjured his religion. On this point he was honourably firm, which made it certain that there could never be a Stuart Restoration. But, as if this bar were not enough, those about James took every opportunity to quarrel among themselves. There were Scottish, English, Irish, Protestant, and Catholic parties in the faction of the Jacobites, at home and abroad. So James was not allowed to send Wogan back to finish the marriage negotiations.

Wogan was, like the bride, a Catholic, also he was Irish. This was enough to rouse the hostility of James's chief minister, that Earl (or, by James's patent, Duke) of Mar, whose incapacity had ruined the Rising of 1715, and whose treachery or folly later secured the condemnation of Atterbury. In place of Wogan, Murray, son of a Jacobite mother, a Scot and Protestant, was sent to Prince Sobieski. This was the beginning of evils. Murray was brother to Lord Mansfield, later so well known, and he came to be distrusted and disliked by almost the whole Jacobite party. Except the Earl Marischal they would probably have disliked and distrusted any minister whom their King preferred. In later days, Clementina herself hated both Murray and his brother-in-law, Hay, brother of Lord Kinnoull, and on these reefs the domestic happiness of the father and mother of Prince Charles was shattered. For the moment, probably not by Murray's fault (though of course he was blamed), the marriage scheme was ruined. The secret had leaked out : England threatened the Emperor (the cousin of Clementina) with a breach of the Quadruple Alliance, and it was plain that Clementina would not be allowed to travel from Silesia to Italy through the Imperial territory.

Knowing nothing of this, James sent Hay to escort Clementina, but she, with her mother, was arrested by Imperial decree, at Innsbrück in the Tyrol (September 1718). Hay returned to James at Bologna, and Wogan found himself fitted with an adventure to his taste. He determined that he would rescue his future Queen. He hurried from Urbino to seek James, who had gone to Rome, and received

full powers to treat with the father of Clementina.[1]
If he failed in his forlorn hope, an Austrian prison or
an English scaffold would be his reward. Disguised as
a travelling merchant he made his way to Clementina
and her mother at Innsbrück : who welcomed his
romantic resolve.   Then he sought Prince Sobieski at
Ohlau in Silesia, who at first laughed at his ' Quixo-
tade,' but was won over, by the gallantry of Wogan,
and came into the plot.   After delays many, Wogan
early in 1719, visited Dillon's Irish regiment, at
Schelestadt, near Strasbourg, and enlisted his Three
Musketeers, Gaydon, Misset, and the huge blue-eyed
O'Toole, the Porthos of the party. Mrs. Misset,
though soon about to be brought to bed, and her
maid, Jeanneton, were to act, the first as chaperon,
the second as substitute for Clementina.   Meanwhile
James was in Spain, in connection with the enterprise ruined at Glenshiel. But, on April 26, the
venturous little party crossed the Rhine, ' and declared
war on the Emperor.'

The plan was to smuggle Jeanneton into Clementina's house ; to take forth Clementina, disguised as
the maid, while the maid, as Clementina, should keep
her bed under pretence of illness.   Jeanneton was
with difficulty brought to accept her *rôle*, but finally
all succeeded to a wish. From the hotel at Innsbrück,

---

[1] The romance of *Clementina*, by Mr. A. E. W. Mason, adheres
closely to actual history.

in a fearful night of snow and rain, Wogan led
Jeanneton to Clementina's house (it still exists) and
came forth with Clementina dressed as Jeanneton.
The Princess began by falling into a gutter, and
time was wasted in getting her dry clothes. Her
only baggage was an apron with pockets full of books,
and a black parcel containing James's present; no
less than the crown jewels of England! The parcel,
as the party set forth from the inn, was casually left
behind, Clementina and her friends drove off in a
berline: 'Where are my jewels?' she asked, and
O'Toole had to ride back, force the hotel gate by
sheer strength, find, and restore the jewels. Never
was a worse quarter of an hour of anxiety, for the
jewels, if discovered by the people of the hotel, would
reveal the plot. But O'Toole was lucky, and the
long drive over the Brenner began. Till they crossed
the frontier they lived in terrors. The Princess was
gay, laughing like the lively child she was, at the
precipices, the breakdowns, the fears of Mrs. Misset
and her own fall into a flooded stream. Almost
without food, except for a few eggs, and tea made in
a vessel that had been used to store oil in, the
Princess kept up her heart, 'sleeping like an angel.'
in garrets of bad inns, or in the jolting country cart
that replaced the broken-down *berline*. They were
delayed by the Princess of Baden, who was travelling
in front, and had secured all the post horses. Mean-

while, at Innsbrück, Jeanneton lay abed, and declined, in the character of Clementina, to see the magistrate on his daily visit. This device saved twenty-four hours, and when a hurrying courier was at last sent, O'Toole waylaid and entertained him at an inn, leaving him dead-drunk under the table. The flying party reached Bologna, where the bride visited the Palazzo Caprara. Her purpose was to see the portrait of a young lady of the House, who had been 'talked about' with James. On beholding the portrait she 'flushed vermilion,' says Gaydon, in his account of this exploit. Apparently she was of rather a jealous temper. On May 8 Murray arrived, James being still in Spain, and soon a proxy marriage was performed. On September 2 James had returned from his futile Spanish journey, and the wedding was duly celebrated. A medal with Clementina's head was struck : on the obverse we see her driving a chariot into Rome. Clementina had brought to James her beauty, youth, and wealth, including the Sobieski rubies, and she received the right to sign herself 'Clementina R.'

The Four Irish Musketeers were made Senators of Rome, and Wogan was created a Baronet, and, appropriately, was appointed to the Governorship of La Mancha. 'If he dies there, it must be allowed that he dies at his post,' wrote Sir Charles himself in 1744. The others were knighted by James. Jacobites now waited hopefully for the birth of a Prince of Wales ; the offspring of fair Clementina. It was on an Old Year's Night, 1720, that their hopes were fulfilled. In the presence of Cardinals and noble ladies, Charles Edward Louis Philip Casimir Stuart saw the light.[1] The last Birthday Ode for the infant then born was destined to be sung by no Cibber nor Pye, but by Robert Burns. But for the first Birth Night a laureate was not wanting :

> A radiant Host round the Eternal stood ;
> An Host solicitous for human good :
> To whom th' Almighty — 'Seraphs guard my care,
> Protect the Infant, and preserve the fair ! '

A new star was said to have appeared on the Prince's birth night, and, later, was introduced on one of his medals. The English agent in Rome, Walton, reported that the child was so ill-fashioned that he would never be able to walk, and that his mother could never be a mother again. These were un-fulfilled prophecies. An account of the exiled Court is given in a letter which exists in a thin quarto pamphlet. The author (said to be Lord Blandford), visiting Rome, is astonished to find that James has an Anglican chapel for his Protestant adherents. It was always James's attitude to be thoroughly tolerant : to his own creed he must cling, but never would he

---

[1] He had a few other names, as his baptismal certificate proves.

do other than protect the religion of his subjects.
The letter of 1721 speaks of two Anglican chaplains,
Cooper and *Berkeley*. Later (1747), the author of
' Genuine Memoirs of John Murray of Broughton '[1]
names Cooper and *Bartlett*, the latter dismissed
by order of the Pope, for a polemical sermon. The
same writer says that when Charles and his brother
Henry were ' at their devotions ' in this Anglican
chapel, ' a small piece of the ceiling detached itself
from the rest, and a *Thistle* fell into the lap of the elder,
on which he started, and looking up, a *Rose* fell
immediately after : this, together with a Star of great
magnitude which the astronomers pretend appeared at
his nativity . . . might have had some share in exciting him to his rash enterprise.'

The early troubles of James's married life were
partly due to his attitude of religious toleration
(which did not suit Clementina), and to the difficulty
of combining Protestant with Catholic tuition for his
son. The letter writer of May 1721 says ' the
Princess observed to us that as she believed he was
to live and die among Protestants, she thought fit to
have him bred up by their hands, and that, in the
country where she was born, there was no other
distinction but that of honest or dishonest.' These
did not continue to be Clementina's sentiments, and

[1] These are not Murray's *genuine* Memoirs which have but recently
been published.

probably the letter is a mere Jacobite tract. The following note from James as to a governess, Mrs. Sheldon, is highly characteristic of the Chevalier. The lady was 'bigg enough' to prove a firebrand in the family.[1]

From Kg. James to Duke of Mar.

Rome, April 1st /21.

You know that I have sent for hither Mrs. Sheldon but I am engaged to nothing with her more than to keep her when here. If I find her fitt to put about my son I am always master to do it, but whether she should be fitt or unfitt, it would be a satisfaction to me to have some persons in my view equall to such a trust. The qualities of a person for so important a charge are obvious. The better born she be, the better, but what is above all requisite is prudence, a reasonable knowledge of the world, *and a principle of obedience, attachment and submission to me*, which may put her above private envies or factions. I know by experience these qualities are rare, but without them all things will not be right managed and without the last the case might happen the child might personally suffer by it. Till he is a year old our Englishwoman will do, and she doth mightily well, but after that she will not be bigg enough, I mean of too low a rank.[2]

James wanted to be King in his own house ! Alas, obedience and submission to him were what

---

[1] When no other source is cited the letters and notes are from the Stuart MSS. in the Royal Library at Windsor Castle.

[2] Apparently 'our Englishwoman' is not Mrs. Sheldon, but Mrs. Hughes.

he could not win, either from mother or child. As early as February 20, 1722, we find Hay writing to Mar that 'Peter' (James) 'is resolved to meddle no more in these matters'—matters of the nursery. Hay has 'a notion of the impossibility of women's ever agreeing together.' Trouble had obviously begun around the cradle. James, in fact, was a man indifferent to society, and the pleasures which a pretty bride like Clementina has a right to expect. He was poor, for he made great efforts to provide for his impoverished adherents, and even a large pension from the Pope went to aid his exiled friends. He was immersed in business, absorbing if futile, and mainly conducted his own immense correspondence. Left much alone, Clementina was thwarted in her desire that her child should be entrusted only to Catholic hands. Her lord was much in the company of Hay and Murray. She disliked Murray, and hated Hay, who is accused of insolence to his Queen. Her son, even now, was the centre of conspiracies. Layer, an English barrister, afterwards hanged for his share in a side-branch of Atterbury's plot, was intriguing with Mrs. Hughes, the Prince's Welsh nurse, while the Guards of George I. were to be corrupted (so Layer planned), and Ormond was to invade London, the populace was to rise, and the Royal child was to be carried to the Highlands and head the Clans! Such, if we may believe the Report of the Lords' Committee on Layer's case, was the scheme of that English lawyer, and of the Welsh nurse. It was to be financed by a Lottery!

By July 10, 1723, Hay wrote to our friend Gaydon that 'the Prince is the finest child in the world, healthy and strong, speaks everything, and runs about from morning till night.' In January 1723 steps were taken to secure the presence at Rome of the learned Chevalier Ramsay, like James himself the friend of Fénelon, as the Prince's tutor. But there were mysterious difficulties. Was not Ramsay of the party of Mar, who was now in disgrace for his conduct towards Atterbury? Mar's letters had led to Atterbury's conviction for treason; he had, or was said to have, a pension from George I., and thus the party was again rent by suspicions of treachery. Hay was sent to Paris to seek out a tutor, and generally to observe the situation. James wanted Ramsay, 'as a pedagogue,' but had uneasy suspicions that he was coming as an agent of Mar. Hay thought Ramsay the best man for the post. Finally, Hay and Ramsay reached Rome, after Ramsay had suffered an upset on the way. 'The King was mightily pleased with him' (February 1724), as he admitted to Atterbury, now in exile, and acting as James's manager in France. All desired to keep Ramsay to his pedagogic duties merely. Perhaps already he found the Prince rather too robust a pupil. 'He is a great musician,' writes Hay, 'and plays on his violin continually : no porter's child in the country has stronger legs and arms, and he makes good use of them, for he is continually in motion. . . . You may easily imagine what amusement he gives to his Father and Mother ; *and indeed they have little other diversion.'*

In politics there was no glimmer of hope, and poor Clementina, her gaiety finding no outlet, was beginning to be wretched. Of her husband she probably saw little ; he was labouring all day, like a secretary, at his immense and futile correspondence. Meanwhile there are traces of secret dealings that had passed between Mar, Ramsay, and the Regent Orleans. In the autumn of 1724, Ramsay insisted on returning to Paris, to relieve three friends there from a mysterious calumny, probably connected with the charges of Atterbury against Mar, whom the Bishop regarded as a paid agent of England, and his own betrayer. 'Ramsay is a creature of the Duke of Mar's,' writes Hay. 'Two glasses of wine unhinges him,' and 'he is not capable of sincerity. . . . He was *called* here for one purpose, and *sent* here for another.' Thus the internal factions of the party deprived the Prince of a most distinguished tutor, and, in his place, James nominated Murray, and Tom Sheridan, a left-handed cousin of his own, who làter landed with Charles in Moidart. Meanwhile Hay (Lord Inverness) acted as James's chief minister. The notorious

Duke of Wharton, the profligate and witty defender
of Atterbury, now himself an exile, approved of
Murray's appointment (October 13, 1725). ' Make
my compliments to him, and desire that he will not
only train the Prince to glory, *but likewise give him
a polite taste for pleasurable vice !* '

At this time (March 6, 1725) Clementina bore
her second son, Henry Benedict, Duke of York, and
there was some talk of carrying him away to Spain.
But this was naturally opposed by Clementina. The
poor lady's sorrows had fairly begun. She disliked
both Murray (created Lord Dunbar) and Hay.
Lockhart of Carnwath speaks (in the Lockhart
Papers) very bitterly of Hay, as treacherous, insolent,
avaricious, and uncultivated ; but one observes none
of these bad qualities in Hay's MS. correspondence.
He had no desire to oust Mar, and succeed to his
unenviable position. It was forced upon him by
James. The Queen is also said to have been jealous
of Mrs. Hay (though we find them at one time on
friendly terms), and James's character therefore
suffers. But, in fact, James was not, and had never
been, amorous or profligate. As a young man, residing at Bar-le-Duc, he undeniably kept a mistress.
But a pamphleteer of 1716 rails at him for his
continence, and 'cruelty' to the Caledonian beauties.
After his death, when there was some talk of a
bastard of his, those who had known him best in

Rome averred that the story must be false. Yet the King, in *Esmond*, appears as a reckless profligate, his character, and his situation in the novel, being obviously, though unconsciously, adapted by Thackeray from those of Charles II. in *Woodstock*. James merely stood by his chosen servants, who were probably the best within reach. He appointed Murray, as we saw, to be one of Charles's tutors, though Murray was a Protestant, simply as a part of his usual policy. Yet this gave deep offence to the devout Clementina. Her friend, Mrs. Sheldon, was removed (or rather, James gave orders for her removal), and, early in November 1725, Clementina retreated to a convent. James wrote to her on November 9 (when she had probably retired to her own suite of rooms), complaining of her conduct ; of the threats levelled at him ; and of ' the public insult of your retreat.' He feels no resentment, but suspects that the intrigues of his enemies have incited Clementina. ' I will be master in my own affairs and in my own family.' ' Return to reason, to duty, to yourself, and to me, who await your submission with open arms, and am eager to give you peace and happiness as far as depends on myself. I conjure you once more, my dear Clementina, to reflect seriously,' (I translate the French of the original MS. at Windsor Castle.) On November 10 Hay wrote thus to an unnamed correspondent :

Rome, Nov. 10, 1725

It is manifest that this foolish affair is the consequence of an old project hatched elsewhere, but put into circulation here without the least prudence or good conduct. Mrs. Sheldon's behaviour and the continual instances she gave the King of her irritating the Queen on every trifling occasion, obliged the King to discharge her his service and it is evident that it has been by her means that this affair has been conducted. The King ordered she should be furnished with every thing necessary for her journey into France, and a gentleman to conduct her, but she took the party to retire into a convent, I suppose not to leave the main view unexecuted, which at last has been effected.

Thus Mrs. Sheldon (in the strong position of nurse of a first-born child) was at the bottom of the royal quarrel which scandalised Europe, broke the hearts of the Jacobites, and prejudiced Lockhart of Carnwath, James's Scottish agent, against his King. On one side was a pretty lady, on the other a melancholy husband, actually desirous to be master in his own household ! The husband *must* be in the wrong : so the world, as usual, decided. The inner politics of the case are stated by James : Mar is the secret source of the mischief.

He writes to Princess Constantine Sobieska, December 1, 1725 :

She has listened neither to reason, duty, nor interest, and has fallen headlong into the trap which our enemies have laid ; consulting neither her father, nor, I believe, any of her relations, she has entered a convent, following a lady whom I had dismissed for good reasons. If, instead of listening to bad advice, she had reciprocated my tenderness for her, she might have been happy.

In the same strain James wrote to Atterbury in France.

On other occasions James urges that Cardinal Alberoni (who had been disgraced at Madrid, and was now in Rome) is the chief instigator of Clementina. The royal quarrel was caught into the wheels of dim ecclesiastical intrigues of Rome, and the politics of the Vatican. Clementina behaved with hysterical passion. The English agent, Walton, writes that the disturbance began among the women (Mrs. Sheldon and Mrs. Hughes), who had previously been intrusted with the care of the child, and now were jealous, like other nurses. He makes Clementina withdraw to her convent on November 15, but James, on November 9, speaks of her 'retreat,' perhaps merely to her own apartments. 'I know from a brother of one of the nuns,' says Walton, 'that the Princess wept freely, and used very exaggerated language, in her first explosion of anger : 'her husband,' she declared, 'wished to bring up her boys as heretics, and rather than permit such an infamy, she would stab them with her own hand,' like a Polish Medea. 'Such speeches, and her declamations against Mr. and Mrs. Hay, filled the convent with alarm.'

The devotees and bigots were of Clementina's party. According to Walton, the Pope accused James of immoral relations with Mrs. Hay (never alluded to in the correspondence), and Alberoni envenomed the dispute ; brought the old charge about the Protestant education of the Prince : talked of removing the children from James's care, and listened to the suggestions of Walton himself. For her part, Clementina ascribed her behaviour to the 'insolence' of the Hays, who 'tease the King to part with his best friends,'—probably Mrs. Sheldon. For six years, ever since her bridal day, she has been subjected to affronts. James, like Byron, protested that he knew of no offence given by him to Clementina : he kept asking his dear wife to return to his arms. Nothing is said, on any side, by the principals, of a flirtation with Mrs. Hay : that is only gossip, which flew everywhere, and greatly harmed James's cause.

The probability is that the natural gaiety of Clementina was soured in her gloomy home, and by the society of her melancholy laborious husband, for ever writing letters to all Europe in hopes of an alliance. Then came the real issue, the jealousies of her women, and the half Protestant education of Charles. Murray, says Walton, had been seen to pick the child up, and place him in his carriage when the bells rang for the *Ave Maria*, and all Rome was on its knees. Things like this, and the dismissal of Mrs. Sheldon, irritated Clementina : the Hays, with or without reason, she detested : bigots and clerical intriguers fanned the flame : James, usually reasonable, had not the art to manage an excited wife ; and the Queen flew into a passion and a convent. Europe, and her sisters, took her side : James now indiscreetly appeared with Mrs. Hay at the Opera, probably as a protest against intimidation.[1] The Queen of Spain assailed James in a furious letter : Lockhart of Carnwath wrote in severe terms : in brief, as usual, every one was on the lady's side. Meanwhile a Mr. O'Rourke, at Lunéville, wrote the following simple philosophy of the case to Hay. James, like Dickens in a domestic quarrel, took the public into his confidence, publishing his extremely reasonable letters of remonstrance. The publication was an error, as O'Rourke observed :

O'Rourke to Inverness.

From Lunéville, Dec. 8, 1725.

. . . All Europe thought his Mj. happy in a wife, and soe many excellent things speak aloud in favour of the Queen yt. his friends thought to have as much ocason to rejoice as his enemys to repine at soe happy an union : . . . Men's reasoning will be various upon the subject, a very few will descend into particulars, and such as may, will be always apter to follow their own judgement of things than

---

[1] Walton, Feb. 16, 1726, not January 26, as in Mr. Ewald, i. 29, note.

those reasons alleaged of either side. It is the common fate of such dissensions to be attributed rather to the humour or temper of persons, than to real causes, the publick (tho' aften divided into partiality) generally concure in one thing, wch is to condemn both partys, and in this very case, tho' all mankind will blame the Queen for running into that extremity, most people will say yt. a tender way of proceeding and a judicious complaisance (wch is the great delight of her sex) might have prevented that melancholy scene, and it is certain that women of all sorts (unless it be one in a thousand) are incomparably better governed by a reasonable fondness than by reason itself . . . If I dare offer my humble sense I would not judge it very suitable to the King's dignity to make much use of the two letters whereof you sent me copys. It will look odd to all people yt. such an affair should have been treated by letters betwixt the King and Queen within the precincts of their own house . . . the next is that he enters upon certain particularitys of his kind usage to the Queen, wch is noe better than to justifie himself from being a very bad husband, a point noe body (I suppose) accuses him off, not even the Queen herself, at least as to her liberty and expenses, &c . . . he ought never to descend soe low as to justify himself of wht he is not capable, wch is to lay such particular hardships upon the Queen his spouse as would appear not only unusuall but odious to all reasonable people. The goodness and sweetness of his nature free him from such insane censures, and therefore it were to be wished such points were not handled at all in letters to be produced for to justify the choice and continuation of his minister ; and some things that he is accountable for to noe body upon earth, and that certainly offer such strong arguments after

the Queen's retreat as will make all Europe blame her, and
nothing can excuse that unhappy stepp but her being mis-
led by some people who followed rather their own passion
than any enmity to the King . . . In my weak notion of
matters the King may, and perhaps ought, for to steer
right, use many condescentions, and shew much confidence
to the Queen, without being governed by her, *this medium,
if he can only hitt upon it, is the perfection of marriage.*

'This medium' is not so easy to 'hit upon,' and
was never hit upon by James. He meant to retire
to Bologna, but three Cardinals called on him, and
lectured him in the name of the Pope (September
1726). Now the Pope held the purse-strings. On
September 10 James took the poor boy Prince
Charles to see his Holiness, and say his Catechism.
His Holiness was pleased: the boy had 'a good
sprag memory.' James, however, did retire to
Bologna, telling Lockhart (July 20, 1726) that reason,
of all things, will never influence his wife. He ought
never to have tried reason!

Through the spring of 1727 every endeavour was
made, by a friendly Cardinal and others, to mollify
her Majesty. All manner of stories circulated; for
example that she accused James of striking her (this
was said, on hearsay, by her sister, the Duchesse de
Bouillon), and vowed that Hay would poison her
if she returned! A wilful woman must have her
way, and, by the end of March 1727, James and

Inverness, with deep regret, had to make up their minds to part, James retaining his esteem for his unfortunate servant. The little Prince must have been puzzled by his mother's absence, but managed to amuse himself. The Duc de Liria, son of the Duke of Berwick, writes :

The Prince of Wales was now six and a half, and, besides his great beauty, was remarkable for dexterity, grace, and almost supernatural address. Not only could he read fluently . . . he could ride, could fire a gun ; and, more surprising still, I have seen him take a cross-bow and kill birds on the roof, and split a rolling ball with a bolt ten times in succession. He speaks English, French, and Italian perfectly, and altogether he is the most ideal Prince I have ever met in the course of my life.[1]

By August the Royal pair had been reconciled, but James was now at Avignon, on political business of the usual helpless kind. George I. had died, and James pressed for a rising in Scotland, to no avail. He wanted Clementina to join him at Avignon, but, for several reasons, she declined. The real reason was her apprehension that Hay might again be forced on her. At this time Lockhart of Carnwath preached a long and verbose epistolary sermon to James, who replied briefly, but with perfect good temper. Lockhart was violently prejudiced against Hay, who may have been all that Lockhart deemed him. We can

[1] Documentos Inéditos, xciii. 18.

only say that, on the existing evidence of Hay's and
James's letters, nothing justifies all the Jacobite fury
against either the servant of the King, or the King
himself.   Hay was hated just as Walpole was hated :
James was condemned just as George II. was condemned, for attachment to an ' unworthy favourite.'
Jealousy was the main motive for the attacks on the
King, and the Minister, *de jure*, and *de facto*.   Even
Lockhart could never find a trace of evidence for the
slanders about James and Mrs. Hay.   Her husband
and the Chevalier had all the troubles, without one
of the compensations, of a reigning monarch and a
valued minister.   Finally, James returned to Rome,
and Clementina to her husband.   Her hysterical
behaviour, aided by clerical intrigues, had made
James the talk of Europe, and, naturally, the little
Prince's education must have suffered during these
disputes.   We have this picture of him in a letter
from J. E. (James Edgar ?) to Graeme, written on
March 22, 1727 :

The eldest improves daily in body and mind to the
admiration and joy of everybody. As to his studies he
reads English now correctly, and has begun to learn to write.
He speaks English perfectly well, and the French and
Italian very little worse.   He has a stable of little horses
and every day almost diverts himself by riding.   Chevalier
Geraldin is his riding master.   He is most alert in all his
exercises, such as shooting, the tennis, shuttlecock, &c.
And a gentleman in town has prepared a Caccia of pigeons

and hares to be shot by him this afternoon. You would be surprised to see him dance, nobody probably does it better, and he bore his part at the balls in the carnival as if he were already a man.

Here we may print Charles's first letter, written before James's return from Avignon. The large clear hand promises well, but the spelling was probably corrected in a draft, which the child would copy out fairly. Charles was the very worst speller of his century : except Lady Mackintosh.

DEAR PAPA,—I thank you mightily for your kind letter. I shall strive to obey you in all things. I will be very dutifull to Mamma, and not jump too near her. I shall be much obliged to the Cardinal for his animals. I long to see you soon and in good health.

I am, dear Papa,
Your most dutifull and affectionate son,
CHARLES P.

The Queen's nerves must have been shattered indeed, when her son had to promise not to 'jump too near her.' At this time he was a pretty boy, with large brown eyes, and a smiling, happy, mischievous face as in contemporary portraits. Clementina's own letters of this period are affectionate, devout, and wholly devoid of other interest. Again was Ramsay suggested as a tutor for the Prince, but James thought him indiscreet, and others (probably erroneously) thought him insincere. In October 1728 a Mr. Stafford was entrusted with the care of Charles : he remained attached to the Prince till long after 1745. Two dozen shuttlecocks and two racquets were ordered in Paris for the boy. His 'favourite diversion' was 'the Golf,' and Sir James Hamilton is told that 'it would very agreeably surprise you to see him play so well at it.' His grandfather, James VII., had been one of the best golfers in Scotland. 'They are of mighty different tempers,' says James to Father Innes (of the Scots College at Paris) writing about his two sons. Even the letters written in French by Charles, at this date, are correct in orthography. He was learning Latin, and spoke Italian fairly well. But his education had (as all his later letters prove) been entirely superficial. Later, at the age of thirteen, he 'got out of the hand of his governors,' so the Earl Marischal wrote from Rome, and spelling he ceased to trouble himself about. In fact he was a strong, spirited, lively lad, excelling in every sport and athletic exercise, but with only the faintest care for literature. In July 1730 he had a slight attack of smallpox, which did not disfigure his pretty complexion.

Meanwhile Clementina's own health had broken down : her temper had not improved, and, by October 1730, James only wished that he could find some 'prudent means of separation.' But, in January 1731, Clementina resigned herself, poor lady, to see

Hay, and treat him with civility. She had become extremely devout, and aimed at the saintly life of austerities and meditation. Ever since their reconciliation James had been working for this recognition of his authority.

James's attachment to the absent Hay begot abundant trouble with the exiled Earl Marischal (a strange mixture of Republican and Jacobite), and with one Ezekiel Hamilton, a turbulent tedious Jacobite. They all had little secrets from each other, and James wrote to Hay about Clementina's temper in a style not chivalrous. One knows no real harm of Hay, but James's affection for a servant who divided the family, and the party, was certainly indiscreet. To abandon him was what James, naturally, could not endure : to retain him was to alienate most of his adherents. ' How hard it is for a King to be a friend ! '

The effect of all these Court and family squabbles on Charles must have been pernicious. We have seen that, in 1733, the Earl Marischal, writing to his brother from Rome, said that the Prince ' had got out of the hands of his governors.' Now, in October of that year, Walton wrote that Charles uttered violent threats against Murray, and had been put under ward in his rooms, while weapons were placed out of his reach. His conduct may have been exaggerated (as we shall find later, he was occasionally placed ' in penance'), but it corresponds with the brief remark of the Earl Marischal, who was fond of the younger brother, the pretty little Duke of York. From the Earl's letters we learn that the exiles had amused themselves by forming an Order del Toboso, the Princes being the patrons. From this Order, with its badges, Murray was excluded, and Ezekiel Hamilton's letters are full of attacks, usually spiteful and petty, on James's minister, and Charles's governor. The boy would . imitate the Knights of Toboso in his dislike of Murray, and it seems probable that he did shake off his tutors. In later life the Earl Marischal (who now left Rome in disgust, and presently proposed to send Charles to Corsica, of all places) was always unfriendly to Charles.

The Prince's brief boyhood and scanty period of education were practically ended at thirteen. We have seen him as the pretty, fair-haired, brown-eyed child, the golfer, the violinist, the noisy, cheery, active little fellow, already distraught between two religions. Then comes a kind of revolt against teaching and teachers, and we find him the handsome, petulant lad (as in several portraits) who is to see war at Gaeta.

By June 4, 1734, James was on the best terms with Clementina, who showed him a witty and malevolent letter of Ezekiel Hamilton's, calculated to revive the old quarrel. ' She did what was like herself, and what I took very kindly of her,'—but health was failing. On June 18 the Duke de Liria, son of the famous Duke of Berwick, was inviting Charles to join the Spanish forces which were besieging the Imperial troops in Gaeta. 'He is to be absolutely incognito,' writes James, 'under my old name the Chevalier de St. George' (July 24). So now the boy is 'The Young Chevalier' of Scottish song! The Pope was *attendri* when Charles took leave, 'but gave me' (James) 'no money on this occasion.' Unhappy King! Rome was his paymaster, but his residence in Rome offended his English partisans, and they wished him to retire to Switzerland. Charles left, with his suite, on the 27th, and James (July 30) sent 'my blessing, with all the tenderness I am capable of,' and with hopes that he 'may one day be both a great and a good man.' Murray and Sir Thomas Sheridan accompanied the Prince, and on August 5 Murray wrote a long letter to James, full of the 'compliments' which the boy had made and received. The Spaniards thought it a pity that two friars were with him, as the Dutch and English papers were certain to be severe on this unusual part of his retinue, probably sent to please Clementina. The Prince was teasing the Duke to let him go into the trenches: but the difficulty was that the King of Naples (Spanish) had never chosen to run the risk himself. However, Charles did enter a position

D

whence the besieging generals had retired under fire of artillery.

By August 11 Charles and Murray were in Naples. The boy had gained golden opinions for his address and pluck from all conditions of men. The Duke de Liria applauded his fearlessness, and he was popular with the soldiers. The Duke had fallen in love with Charles as a child of six : 'in his very countenance I discover something so happy that presages to him the greatest felicity.'[1] Charles himself wrote two copies of a brief note to James ; the rough copy has 'grese' for 'grace,' 'umbly' for 'humbly,' 'cuntinu,' for 'continue,' and 'my' for 'me.'   In the second copy the spelling is correct; probably Murray or Sheridan marked the original and characteristic blunders, from which the Prince never emancipated himself.   Sheridan, indeed, asked James to speak to Charles about the nature and exceeding shortness of his letters.   Amused and caressed by all the nobles at Naples, he was averse to the labour of correspondence.   On September 3 James hinted that Charles (who had been ill) might be 'more temperate in his dyet.'   A boy in a camp is hardly tried.   By September 14 Charles had re- joined his father at Albano.   He appears to have been lectured for the brevity of his letters, and to have shown temper.   'He was in penance again yesterday, but things went better to-day.'   While

[1] Ewald, i. 48.

even Walton admitted that Charles returned with glory, and with plenty of pocket money, and that he would be more dangerous to England than his father, we note that he showed wilfulness of a rather distressing kind on his return.

Meanwhile James and Clementina were, at last, on the most loving terms. But in January 1735 James had to report to his Paris agent, O'Brien, that the Queen's health grows 'worse and worse, as she is now at the last extremity.' Since her reconciliation she had lived an ascetic life, wholly occupied with prayer and good deeds, and the results as to her health were fatal. 'The Queen received the *viatique* this morning,' James wrote to Hay on January 12. 'She is perfectly in her senses, and dies with a tranquillity, a piety, and a peace which is, with reason, a great comfort to me in my present situation.' He nearly fainted after long praying in her chamber, and both princes, writes Murray, were almost ill with weeping and want of sleep.

Poor Clementina died at 5 P.M. on January 18. Her married life had been one long misery, till she yielded all points at issue with James, and betook herself to religion.

In quarrels of husband and wife the truth is hard to discern. Clementina had been passionate, both were obstinate, both unhappy. Long afterwards miracles were said to have been wrought for persons

who appealed to her saintly spirit. She had been
drawn into the coil of the Stuart sorrows, and her
heart broke. Such was the pathetic fate of the gay
and charming girl who used to call Charles Wogan
her 'papa Warner.' Her letters to Charles are brief,
pious, and tender ; indeed, as parents, both she and
James were most gentle and affectionate. Even now
James could not forget : but he tried hard to forgive
the two persons who, in his opinion, had ruined his
peace. He wrote the following highly characteristic
letter to Hay on April 4, 1735 :

I thank God there is not only the appearance but a great
reality of forgiveness in me towards Mrs. Sheldon and
Cardinal Alberoni. The first I really believe did not faill
in anything essential and as for the Cardinal my only view is
to defend myself agst any future practices he might use agst
me, and to do all the justice I can to others, both which ends
I think are answered when his bad conduct comes to be
known, and that can easily be the case without my publishing it with affectation which I have no thoughts of doing.
Mrs. Sheldon has made many submissions to me, but as
Cardinal Alberoni does not seem to retract or repent, there
is no room for exercising either forgiveness or generosity
towards him. . . .

James was convinced, by certain evidence, 'of the
uprightness of the Queen's intentions, and the wicked-
ness of Alberoni's conduct : ' so he wrote to Colonel
Cecil. And yet he writes to Ormond about Clemen-

tina's desire *to repair her past conduct*, by leaving a
gift to the Hays. The conduct had been most unfortunate, but James ought to have forgotten the past.
His fault was a desire to be always, and always to be
acknowledged to be, in the right; *d'avoir toujours
raison.* The same temper wildly indulged was to
ruin Charles.

As to Charles, a marriage proposal for an Infanta
of Spain was bluntly refused; and the Prince, says
James, ' continues wonderfully thoughtless for one of
his age.' But the age of fifteen is seldom very
thoughtful. He had become a mighty sportsman,
and capable of enduring much fatigue. The little
Duke of York (who was hurt at not being permitted
to go to Gaeta) is reported ' more thoughtful ' than
his elder brother. James believed Charles to be
'very innocent, and extreme backwards in some
respects ' (Wharton's ' pleasurable vice ') ' for his age.'
Charles, in truth, had little of that ' weakness for the
sex ' which, in ' Esmond,' Atterbury excuses in his
father, who had none of it. Neither man was a
Charles II., or James V.: Charles was often the
pursued, never the pursuer. Lord Elcho found him
shy and awkward with women.

James thought that travel would not injure his
backward boy's morals, and might wean him from
' little childish amusements.' In short, Charles, care-
less, rather selfish, without ' application,' merry, pas-

sionate, and devoted to exercise, was a very common type of the human boy. James had at first thought of sending Charles to see his grandfather in Poland. But he contented himself with an incognito tour as 'Count of Albany,' through the great Italian cities from Florence to Genoa and Venice. (May, June, 1737.) Murray accompanied Charles, with Mr. Strickland, who was to superintend his writing. James later came to think that in Strickland he had given his son a misleading companion. Henry Goring, son of Atterbury's accomplice, Sir Harry, now entered on his long and faithful and ill-rewarded period of service. Meanwhile Murray sent ecstatic descriptions of the splendid receptions and glittering company in which his heart delighted. 'A noble dinner' was the tutor's joy. He cared less for the effusions read by poets, to which Charles listened with becoming gravity. The Prince was to ask permission to serve as a volunteer in Hungary, but there was no chance that the offer would be accepted. It would sound well in England, Murray thought.

There is now no interest in these 'noble dinners,' 'compliments,' and dances. We casually learn that Charles wore curl-papers in the morning. Murray asked Captain Redmond, who saw the royal hair in curl-papers, not to mention it at Dublin, where these artifices might be thought effeminate. 'Had I soldiers,' said Charles, ' I would not be here now, but

wherever I could serve my friends.' In Venice
Charles was received with royal honours, which
England resented by dismissing the Venetian resident
at St. James's. At Florence the English envoy
checked these manifestations of hospitality. While
the Prince's manners were excellent in public, Murray
writes ' I cannot but tell Your Majesty that in private
we might make the same exceptions as formerly, and
that he gives us rather more uneasiness when he
travels. But this is only a trouble to his own people,
and particularly to me who go in the chair with him.'
Murray hopes that these faults (whatever they were,
probably rudeness) may be amended. As usual,
Charles left off writing to James, who says, ' Don't
forget a father that loves you better than himself '
(June 21, 1737). Charles returned to his father,
elated no doubt with all the fine things he had seen,
and the fine speeches he had heard. He had watched
and enjoyed the glories of actual royalty : had
beheld the splendour of that gilded *papier mâché*
Italy ; the brilliant, fading, and fated sunset of
the Venetian Republic. He must have wearied the
more of the ' moth-eaten hangings and outworn
furniture of the Palace of the Apostles in Rome, and
disliked the more a city of priests and of curious
English tourists. Ambition had awakened : he
longed to be in action. To his great joy his long
hair was now cut (the operation was on August 3) and

he was equipped with a wig. On his next birthday he was shaved for the first time.

This manly ceremony offers a proper conclusion to the chapter of the childhood and boyhood of the Prince. Hard would be the heart that criticised severely the early years of Charles. Yet we cannot but recognise that his qualities were showy, rather than solid, even in these early years. Physically he was strong, a good pedestrian, and fonder of long wintry walks with his gun than of the Opera. He had spirit, personal courage, and, when he chose, an accomplished address and distinguished manners. But these were for the great world ; in private, it is plain, among his 'servants,' he caused 'uneasiness.' This heralds his behaviour to the devoted Henry Goring, about 1750–1754. Considering the affectionate letters of his father and mother, his own silence speaks of rather more than the usual boyish dislike of letter-writing. Except in music and military matters (we hear of his erecting mimic fortifications) he had no 'application.' He was spoiled, in short, by the deference of his little court of tutors, and gentlemen such as Stafford, Strickland, and Goring. His shining and popular qualities were superficial, though his Highland distresses later showed that, in more wholesome circumstances, he had the elements of a manly character. The disadvantages of his perturbed childhood must never be forgotten : for these, and their consequence, he was in no way responsible. But a man worthy of his position would have risen to it, in the matter of education.

We all are, it seems, what we are born to be. Our characters are innate, and in the later Charles Edward of history we readily recognise the spirited spoiled Charles Edward of the days of boyhood. Misfortune was to sour and not to strengthen a character which was never strong : always self-centred and petulant, though adorned with certain attractions of audacity and of bearing. Italy was an excellent school of manners, but Charles wore them as he wore the brilliant court suits or uniforms in which he is usually painted, 'with all the orders.' Among his 'people' he took his manners off, he was unkind and rude, at least according to Murray, the chief sufferer. In religion his mixed education made him a cast-away. He scouted the priests, in whose society his brother already delighted. He had no love for friars who accompanied his military jaunt. There are signs that at this time James was contemplating the chance of Charles's turning Protestant : if called to England. But to this the King could never really reconcile himself. The step would alienate any possible Catholic ally : would stop supplies of money from Rome, and, moreover, James was honestly devout. Thus Charles's religion, by stress of circumstances, 'was still to seek,' as was said in 1745 ;

while, unfortified by religion, he had no strong sense, as his father had, of duty.

In all this we see the germs of his brief success, his audacity being boundless, and his charm, when he pleased, irresistible ; while the elements of the final failure and misery, selfishness and self-indulgence, are no less conspicuous. The letters of Gray, the Poet, and of the President Desbrosses, show that Charles impressed casual observers as enterprising, fascinating, and courteous. Lady Mary Wortley Montagu was in Rome in the February in 1741, and she wrote to her husband : ' I never saw the Chevalier during my whole stay at Rome. I saw his two sons at a public ball in masque ; they were very richly adorned with jewels. The eldest seems thoughtless enough, and is really not unlike Mr. Lyttelton ' (later Lord Lyttelton, Fielding's patron) ' in his shape and air.' Charles's ' people ' knew him in a worse light, though his father's secretary, James Edgar, an accomplished scholar and immaculately honest man, always spoke of him, even in evil days, with sincere expressions of love. To Edgar, though one of ' his people,' Charles must have displayed himself at his best, perhaps because both were the keenest of sportsmen. To Sheridan, also, he later showed singular consideration in Scotland, and it is probable that Murray, generally unpopular, beheld him in the worst light. Still, that

light was not wholly fallacious. The Charles of late
life is but a thwarted and embittered child of the
boyish Charles who hated letter writing, was wilful,
obstinate, and harsh to his tutors. Yet the seduc-
tions of Italy were lost on him : he never dallied in
Armida's gardens, but loved the wintry woods, hunting, shooting, walking stockingless, all to harden
himself for the campaigns that lay before his imagination.

The years 1737–1743 were important in the
history of Charles, because, on all hands, matters
political and personal were converging to the point
at which his chance of action arose. In the Courts
of Europe the Jacobite cause had long been neglected.
While France and England were on peaceful terms,
while Spain was decadent and almost bankrupt, the
Jacobites could not serve the only purpose for which
foreign diplomacy employed them, that of hampering
England. But the death of Friedrich Wilhelm of
Prussia introduced the disturbing element of his son's
ambitious genius, while the death of the Emperor
Charles VI. (October 1740) soon let Frederick's
ambition loose on the province of Silesia. On all
hands attacks were urged against the loosely connected provinces of Maria Theresa. France took
part against her : England was in sympathy with
her struggles : and Sir Robert Walpole had already
begun to reap the harvest of long accumulated

grudges. The old Jacobite motto, ever since the Revolution of 1688, had been ' Box it about, it will all come to my father.' In England parties and politics were being boxed about.

Walpole had been for nearly twenty years in power : this was good reason why he should not be popular. A pamphleteer compared him to Cochrane, the favourite of James III. of Scotland, who was hanged over Lauder Bridge. In 1738 a great English outcry was raised over Spanish interference with our commerce and our mariners. One Jenkins, seven years before, had been mutilated of an ear by the Spaniards, he said : he lost it on the pillory, said others. In any case ' Remember Jenkins's ear ' was a useful cry, and the pacific Walpole was hard pressed by Pulteney in the Commons : by Carteret and Chesterfield in the Lords. Walpole patched up a Convention with Spain in January 1739; Pitt denounced it as a ' Convention of national ignominy.' Walpole survived the storm, but was at length compelled to choose between war, which he hated, and the loss of office, which he still more detested. He chose war (October 1739).

Just before this date Walpole had actually opened communications with the exiled head of the House of Stuart ; that House which he always professed to fear and hate. His emissary to James in Rome was Carte, the historian. Mr. Carte, long before, had

been Atterbury's secretary, after the arrest of George
Kelly.   Long after Culloden, Carte was still engaged
in dark and desperate intrigues.   This was the man
whom, in 1739, Walpole sent with a *verbal* message
to James.   The English Minister declared his attachment to the Cause, but desired to know the Chevalier's intentions as to the Church of England and the
persons of the Hanoverian dynasty.   On July 10,
1739, James wrote a letter to Carte, which Carte
handed to Walpole, who preserved it, endorsed in his
own hand, among his papers.   It is extremely probable that Walpole, as Lord Mahon suggests, showed
the letter to George II., and acted with his connivance.   He would thus secure himself against the
results of a discovery.   He had ' hedged ' in the case
of a Restoration : he ran no risks (if he had taken
George into his councils), and he probably expected
James to bid the Jacobite members of Parliament
vote for him in the case of a division.

But James was not entrapped.   He merely bade
Carte refer Walpole, as far as the protection of the
Church of England went, to his reiterated promises.
Should the Princes of the House of Hanover fall into
his hands ' I shall certainly not touch a hair of their
heads.'   Walpole had also been intriguing with
Colonel Cecil, of the House of Salisbury, a Jacobite
organiser in London.   He may have surprised some
valueless secrets in this way.   Early in 1740 Colonel

Brett went to London from Paris, to consult the leaders of the English Jacobites. They were the Duke of Beaufort, who was succeeded by his brother in the spring of 1745, Sir Watkin Wynne, Lord Barrymore, Dr. King of St. Mary's Hall, in Oxford, Sir John Hinde Cotton, M.P., and other broken reeds. Lord Sempil (not, of course, the Whig lord of that name) was one of James's managers in Paris, and wrote in a sanguine way about the English Jacobites. But, on March 23, 1740, James confided his own ideas about Walpole to O'Brien at Paris, in a letter which escaped the research of Lord Mahon. ' It does not seem to me that Walpole has any serious intention of help-ing the Cause, unless he is forced to do so in his own private interests, and the less the subject is worked on the better. It is not worth while to approach Cardinal Fleury in the matter.' In March 1740, from Madrid, the Earl Marischal thanked James for a commission as Commander-in-Chief in Scotland, and Murray of Broughton's Memoirs prove that Macgregor of Balhaldy was then talking of an expedition to be commanded by the Earl. He was consulting with Ormond, and, on the Spanish side, with Montemar. But the Spanish army, he said, was ' naked and starved.' The very officers are ' starving and begging.' James thought that the ' disgrace ' of the Duke of Argyll and his bad relations with George II. might prove serviceable to Jacobitism.

.Now (June 11, 1740) comes a singular letter from
the Earl Marischal. 'Timothy' (James Keith, the
Earl's brother, in Russian service) was secretly in
London, sounding the Duke of Argyll. ' He had
more civility from Julius' (Argyll) 'than from any
one else, but Julius never would give him any en-
couragement to converse of your Majesty's affairs.
They were together when Julius got a message that
vexed him : he said, on reading it, "Mr. Timothy,
fall flat, fall edge, we must get rid of these people,"
which might imply both man and master' (George
and Walpole) 'or only the man. Timothy resolved
on this to speak freely to him, but I much fear he
has had no success.'

In Lady Mary Coke's 'Journal and Letters'
(privately printed, 1. xl–xli) will be found, as reported
by Lady Louisa Stuart, the family account of the
Jacobite attempt to tamper with the Duke. Lord
Barrymore thrust into his hand a letter from James,
of May 22, 1741. There is a draft of the letter in
the Stuart Papers for that date. James says that he
is far from approving the mistakes of former reigns.
' I see and feel the effects of them, and should be void
of all reflection did I not propose to avoid them with
the utmost care, and therefore I do not entertain the
least thought of assuming the government on the
footing my family left it.' He will maintain the
Church of England, and tolerate Dissenters. ' I have

ever had the greatest abhorrence of all dissimulation,
and will certainly never promise anything during my
exile but what I shall perform after my restoration.'
This is a circular letter, and, contrary to Lady Louisa
Stuart's story, contains no special allusions to Argyll.
But there may have been two letters.   Argyll 'instantly sent the letter to the King' (George II.) and
felt 'wounded to the very soul.' If then he did
converse with Keith, it was probably on general
matters. Lord John Drummond also mentions Keith's
visit to London.

I am unable to believe that Argyll, ' Red John of
the Battles,' the hero of Malplaquet, ever compromised
himself with the Jacobites.   It was probably curiosity
that induced him to meet ' Timothy,' James Keith,
when that hero risked himself in England, after
recovering from his wound received at Oksakoff.   It
is true that, in 1740, Walpole induced George II. to
deprive Argyll of his offices, and the notification
may have reached him when Keith was present, as
Lord Mahon supposes.   But Lord Mahon could not
find the Earl Marischal's letter, just cited, about his
brother's interview with Argyll, and relied on a
copied extract.   ' I much fear Timothy had no
success,' says the Earl.   When Walpole later resigned
(February 11, 1742) the Opposition met at the
Fountain Tavern, and Lord Mahon, on the authority
of a pamphlet by Lord Perceval, represents Argyll

as 'the leader more especially of the Jacobites in Parliament,' at the tavern conference. If so, with Walpole approaching James privately, and with Argyll leading the Jacobites, things must have seemed hopeful to James. But he was not hopeful. Argyll died in 1743, being succeeded by his brother, Lord Islay ; so, whatever were Red John's intentions, Clan Diarmaid was secured for the Government.

The Forty-Five was not really due to these English intrigues, nor to the action of great European statesmen, at least in the first instance. It sprang from the energy and ambition of a small Lowland laird, John Murray of Broughton in Tweeddale ; and from the address of a Highland laird of no higher position, Macgregor, or (the clan name being proscribed) Drummond of Balhaldy. Murray's first connection with the Jacobite Court of Rome leaves no mark on the Stuart Papers. His action has been misunderstood, because wrongly dated in the pamphlet falsely called his 'Genuine Memoirs' (1747) which is followed by Mr. Ewald. The Memoirs really genuine have now been published (1898) from the manuscripts, by the Scottish History Society. Murray was but twenty-two when, after studying at Leyden, he visited Rome in 1737. He said later, when acting as Evidence or Informer, that, while in Rome, he never was introduced to James. He was in the Jacobite set,

E

however, and was admitted to their Masonic Lodge.
He probably met Charles, and, if we may trust a
letter of his published in the Memoirs of 1747, fell in
a deep admiration of his person.   A snuff-box set with
diamonds, once in his possession, contained an enamel
miniature of the Prince (now in the author's hands),
of the apparent age of fifteen.   James's secretary,
Edgar, spoke to the King about Murray as likely to
prove a useful correspondent in Scotland : in 1740
he was officially recognised in that capacity.   In
1741 Lovat, Traquair, Balhaldy, and others formed
a Jacobite association, with Balhaldy as chief agent,
and Murray was joined with them in their intrigues.
From the first he was jealous of and distrusted
Balhaldy, whose promises far outran performance.
Murray kept working at the Jacobite organisation,
where we may leave him for the moment.

Among all these intrigues the Earl Marischal
found the Spanish Court impotent to help, and withdrew to the country.   He resigned, and hoped James
'would allow him to live quietly with a great Plutarch,
in the way I wish.'   He thought Lord Sempil, one
of James's Paris agents, was not to be relied on, nor
was Cardinal Fleury, the French Minister ; Sempil
giving, as he often did, sanguine accounts of Fleury's
intentions.   February 1741 found Charles occupied
in his old way, as Edgar's letter sets forth :

To M. Waters (*the Paris Banker*).

Feb. 9, 1741.

As the Prince's parties of shooting are now over, his present diversions are those of ye Carnival in which he takes a great share, last night, H.R.H. went, after ye Opera, to a publick Ball, masked in a fine complete Highland Dress, wch become him very well, and did not return home till day light ; we have all the comfort that no fatigue, and no exercise does H.R.H. any harm, on the contrary he is always ye better for it.

By July 1741 James was hoping that Charles might have a chance of a French campaign, but not at that moment. 'We are entirely in Cardinal Fleury's hands.'

James was convinced that France's policy towards him would depend on war or peace with England. Fleury had detected the jealousies among the Jacobites, and it was no fit time to solicit him.

Meanwhile in England the combined but distracted opponents of Walpole had driven him from office, and were at feud about places. According to Lord Mahon, the Duke of Argyll had insisted on an appointment for Sir John Hinde Cotton, the leading Jacobite member of Parliament. Sir John later received a place, and, in 1745, France insisted that he should resign it, as a proof of his Jacobite sincerity. But to resign would have meant imprisonment in the Tower. Argyll himself took a seat in the new

Cabinet, and, of course, was suspected of Jacobitism by Walpole, who thought others like himself.   Argyll presently resigned over George's refusal to accept Sir John Hinde Cotton at that moment, and death soon ended his stormy political career.   Meanwhile James was enlisting a fatal recruit.   In May 1742 we find him promising to assist Young Glengarry 'in applying close to all gentlemanly learning, at the Scots College in Paris.'

The eldest son of Glengarry was unhappy at home, where his step-mother, a daughter of Gordon of Glenbucket, ruled his weak and shifting father. As a spy, in later days, Glengarry speaks of his old friends at the Scots College.   His learning, as time was to show, did not make him a perfect gentleman. On October 1, 1742, James gave Balhaldy, or Edgar gave in his name, an account of Charles, who is named 'Mr. Fisher :'

To Balhaldy.

October 1, 1742.

. . . It is a very sensible mortification to me that the worthy sages should be kept so long in expectation and suspence, but I would fain hope that the time is near when they will have occasion to try and show their skill, wch I cannot doubt that they will do to good purpose. *Mr. Fisher* told me t'other day that he longed to be with them, for that he was quite wearied of this country. I don't wonder at it, for his sole amusement here is to go out a Shooting, to wch he has gone every other day during all this season before daybreak, whether fair or foul, and has killed a great dale of game, such as this place affords. He fatigues at that diversion so much that nobody here can keep up with him, even a servant or two, that are clever fellows have more than enough to do to do it, and if he were where we wish him, I doubt if I could find many that would not tyre with the constant fatigue and exercise he takes, his Brother takes a great dale of exercise also. Sometimes he goes out a shooting, but has not such delight in it as Mr. Fisher, and sometimes he takes the air on horseback at night after a day's strong fatigue. Mr. Fisher sits down and diverts himself with musick for an hour or two, as if he had not been abroad, and plays his part upon the Bass Viol extremely well, for he loves and understands musick to a great degree, his Brother does not understand it so well, but he sings, when he pleases, much better. Were their Friends to see them either at home or abroad, they could not but be infinitely charm'd with them both : tho' of different characters and tempers, they agree very well together, and love one another very much ; were I to enlarge upon their different good qualities I would never had done . . .

Physically, Charles was all that could be desired. Meanwhile Marischal was at Boulogne, 'waiting,' he said, 'for the Angel to stir the Pool.' A letter to the Earl shows Charles practising what he was later to perform in the way of endurance :

To Marischal (from Edgar ?)

May 9.

. . . Their R.H.H. went on Monday to Palo, the Prince that he might not lose a whole Day's Shooting, after supper on Sunday night made put on his Garters, and in his riding coat slept in a chair till after one o'clock, and went away at two, they are to return here next Monday. What a pleasure would it be to see better game than shooting of quails. . . .

By the end of June 1743 Cardinal Tencin, who owed to James his Hat, and had now succeeded Fleury as Minister, was proposing that Charles should visit France, and James was weighing the proposal. Ways and means were discussed in September ; a land journey by the Prince would mean detention in a Lazarette, delay, and discovery. The French Court must be made to speak clearly and positively. While James and the French were thus engaged in diplomacy, the Jacobite party in Scotland and England was practically broken up, and quite disorganised. John Murray's account is, in essentials, corroborated by contemporary letters. Cardinal Fleury had died on January 29, 1743, leaving, as we saw, Tencin as his successor, while Amelot also listened to Jacobite envoys. Murray left Scotland for Paris, on the news of Fleury's death, and visited Balhaldy. He was disgusted with the coldness of Amelot's and Tencin's reception, and convinced that Balhaldy had been giving exaggerated accounts of the readiness and numbers of the Jacobites. The Earl Marischal saw as clearly through Balhaldy and Sempil, who now attempted to make the Earl un-

popular, calling him 'an honourable fool.' Returning
with Balhaldy to England, Murray found Colonel
Cecil (of the Salisbury family) disgusted with the
conduct of affairs. Balhaldy went about among the
English Jacobites, and was satisfied with vague and
scanty support. The chiefs, already mentioned, were
the Duke of Beaufort, Lord Orrery, Sir Watkin
Williams Wynne, who had no ready money, Sir John
Hinde Cotton, representing the City, and Lord
Barrymore (died 1747). None of these men, of
course, ever struck a blow for the Cause : and, as
they only sent oral messages, they leave little trace
on the Stuart Papers. They always refused to put
hand to paper till France should send a large
force, and this France would never do till these
English Jacobites committed themselves. In Lancashire, on the English Border, and here and there
in the South, as at Arundel, there were Jacobites by
sentiment. A little money they may have given, but,
except for a few recruits in Lancashire, no man was
to stir in England.

Murray, returning to Scotland, told Lochiel and
Traquair about the falsehood of Balhaldy's brags.
The death of Lord Kenmure cut off the chance (such
as it was) of raising the Cameronians of Galloway
and Ayrshire under Gordon of Earlstoun, a descendant of the famous covenanting ' Bull of Earlstoun.'
Traquair, a vain and veering featherhead, intercepted

a letter of Murray's, warning the Earl Marischal, superfluously, against Sempil and Balhaldy. These men were trusted by James, and thus it is plain that, at the end of 1743, the Jacobite party was a mere chaos of suspicion and contradictory counsels. Lovat was playing for a Dukedom ; Murray, though clear-sighted and then in earnest, later showed his real nature, and, in the North, only Lochiel was at once trusted and loyal. But in Paris the sanguine Balhaldy had now got leave to go to Rome, and bring the Prince to France, which meant war with England.

The countries were already on bad terms : England, in 1742, had subsidised Maria Theresa in her struggle with so many enemies, and had sent troops to loiter in Flanders. George II., in the interests of Hanover, was hiring Hessian and Hanoverian troops. Pitt was declaring that England 'is considered only as a province to a despised Electorate,' and that the Hanoverians were hired 'only to drain this unhappy nation of its money.' Squire Western could not have spoken more bluffly ; the Opposition was, so far, at one with the Jacobites. Charles had such reasons as these for calling his country 'enslaved,' a circumstance which really seems to have weighed on his mind. With Pitt to back him in these opinions, the Prince's enterprise may seem by no means one of mere personal ambition.

But, in England, George II. had recovered his popularity by his courage at the battle of Dettingen, in June 1743, and Cumberland had also distinguished himself. Toasts of ' No Hanoverian King' might still be drunk, 'even in loyal companies,' but Parliament now passed a bill of Attainder against Charles and his brother Henry, and against even the posterity of their adherents, if the Princes should land in Britain. Barrymore and Cecil were arrested, laws against Catholics and Nonjurors were put in force. In fact the country, while it flattered James and Charles in toasts and sentiments, was entirely resolved to have a Protestant on the throne, even a Hanoverian Protestant. The exiles might be sanguine, owing to English discontents and French demands for the presence of Charles, but the religious objection was insuperable, and James probably knew it.

On December 4, 1743, James wrote thus to Sempil in Paris :

James to Lord Sempil.

Dec. 4.

I am impatient for Balhaldie's safe arrival to show the practicability of the road for another person [the Prince] and feel the importance of the secret, and of the making the enterprize by surprize, tho' I fear we should venture losing more than we should gain by such a surprize, if, for the sake of it, the affair should be undertaken without either mine or the Prince's presence, but I would fain hope some expedient may be fallen upon to avoid so great an inconvenient ; and I hope also that Balhaldy will bring me ample and particular information.

To Ormond he wrote, December 25 :

That the K. of France has determined to act in his favour, though requiring all for the present to be kept secret. 'You have already by you a Commission of Regency, in virtue of which you will act until such time as the Prince may join the Expedition, and then you will remain general under him.'

Balhaldy reached Rome safely, and a plot of great ingenuity was concocted, whereby Charles might reach France before it was known that he had left Rome or its neighbourhood. On January 2, 1744, James wrote to Sempil, praising the arrangements which Balhaldy had made on the road. Balhaldy himself returned to Paris. Despite the censures of Murray of Broughton, he had done his work well, and indeed, if he was the author of the history of the great Lochiel, he was a gentleman of sense and education. The Earl Marischal is found not to have distrusted him nearly so much as Murray declares. ' *Bar accidents* the Prince will probably be at Antibes about the 20th of the month,' writes James, using a phrase not merely modern. Charles was to leave Rome before dawn on January 9. 'A party of *chasse*,' such as the Prince was in the habit of making, was to be the pretext of his exodus. Charles was to remain incognito at Antibes till he received a message from Louis XV. On January 9 James wrote that his 'children' had departed before day-break. He was never again to see the face of his 'dearest Carluccio.' The pretended object of the journey was a shooting party at Cisterna, and even the younger brother, the Duke of York, was not admitted to the secret. This, as he wrote later, he did not regret, as he was apt to show his grief at the separation, and so give a clue to the secret. Of the complicated plan there is a record in a pamphlet: 'An Authentick Account of the Intended Invasion by the Chevalier's Son, 1744.'[1]

Walton, the English spy in Rome, also described the arrangements on January 28, and Lord Mahon prints a version of January 25. Walton was wrong in saying that James strongly opposed the adventure. After leaving Rome, Charles told Murray (his tutor) that he would ride, not drive, on account of the cold; and Murray pretended to oppose this design. Charles galloped off towards Albano, and the self-sacrificing Murray fell purposely into a ditch, to distract the attention of 'the people that were with him.' When out of sight, Charles changed his wig and coat: a companion carried the abandoned clothes to Albano,

[1] A contemporary owner of my copy notes that he paid 'eight shillings duty' on a tract sold at a shilling in London.

and thence went to Cisterna, where Henry, who left Rome later than Charles, had arrived. Charles made a detour, got post horses from Cardinal Aquaviva, with passports, and drove without pause through heavy snow to Massa, and so to Genoa. At Albano Henry stayed for several days, sending presents of wild geese, as from Charles, to friends in Rome. By the eleventh of the month Horace Mann, from Florence, was despatching a description of Charles to the Duke of Newcastle. Walton had not been long in the dark, but when he described Charles's eyes as 'blue,' Mann, unconsciously, made it impossible to identify the brown-eyed Prince. From the coast Charles took boat for Genoa ; thence to Savona, where he seems to have got into some difficulty ; 'locked up at Savona,' writes his brother Henry, 'and in a very ugly situation,' probably in quarantine. From Savona he sailed to Antibes, and there landed, not far from the place where Napoleon landed after his escape from Elba.

From Fogliano, where he was still keeping up the mystery, Henry wrote to James, and the letter may be worth giving as a proof of his amiable character, and of the loving relations which existed between the brothers till shortly before Henry struck a blow at the Cause by taking a Cardinal's hat :

The Duke of York to James.

Fogliano : Jan. 15, 1744.

Sir,—I am very much obliged to your Majesty for the honour of your two Letters, your goodness has really been very great in giving me reasons for not revealing to me sooner this Affair. You may be very well assured, Sir, that I can never be anxious to know any things but what you think fit I should know, and that also but when you please ; certainly the thoughts of such a separation could not but at first have some impression on me, but that lasted very little, for those very reflections which your Majesty put under my Eys in your letter, as also many other joifull prospects, immediately came into my mind, and not only put me at ease, but filled me with vast content and satisfaction so that the Road which of itself is very long and tedious, passed away without allmost my perceiving it. I have however had a good deal of anxiety whilst I was at Cisterna, for I really did not think it a good Air in the present conjuncture, but now that wee are, thank God, at Fogliano, as I think out of all harms way, and that I perceive by your Majesty's letter that all things continue quiet at Rome, I am very happy, but am at the same time very impatient to hear news of our Dear Traveller which news I do not doubt will be but good, for the hand of God seems to be remarquably upon him on this occasion. The pretence of staing on here longer is very naturall and easy, so that here I shall stay with a great deal of Pleasure as long as your Majesty will think fit, were it to be of any use, in this occasion I would really be locked up very willingly in the Old Tower till Easter. I am very much ashamed of myself for not having writt sooner to your Majesty as I have no good reason to give for my excuse I shall say nothing, but only aske your Pardon for my negligence. . . .

A letter of Henry's to Charles may also be read with interest :

Henry to Charles.

Rome : Feb. 6, 1744.

Dear Brother,—I really had not the heart to write to you before I heard of your safe arrival at Antibes, but as soon as I got that comfortable news, I have saised on the first occasion, for to return you many thanks for the great goodness you have showd me on this occasion. I can assure you, Dear Brother, that I am here without you like a fish out of water, the only thing which makes me bare our separation with patience and even with Pleasure is the reflection of its being at present so necessary for your honour, Reputation, and (I hope) Advantage, and besides all that, I hope in God it shall not be for long. I have allready thanked the King, and I also thank you particularly for not having told me the secret of your journey beforehand, for certainly the great love I have for you could not but have show'd itself may be imprudently on that occasion, the secret has been kept here much longer I believe than you expected, for it was the 11th day, before any Courrier went of ; I have already been upon thorns untill I heard you safely landed, and particularly whilst I heard you was locked up at Savona, for certainly you was there in a very ugly situation, but now I thank God, that Providence has freed you from all these Dangers. I am not sorry for them, for the manner in which you have made this journey will gain you a vast deal of honour all over the world, and I don't doubt but that you will daily increase it in all your future undertakings. I wish you cou'd see all the content and satisfaction my heart feels every time I hear anything that can redound to your honour and Glory, and that I am sure proceeds from the Respectuous love and tenderness I have for you, which, I can assure you, Dear Brother (were the King but to permit me) wou'd make me fly through fire and water to be with you . . . I have nothing else to say to you, Dear Brother, at present, but waiting very impatiently for that happy Day in which wee shall meet again, whenever it be : am with all respect, Your most loving Brother   HENRY.

Charles had distinguished himself by secrecy, rapidity, and endurance. For the first five days of his expedition he neither went to bed nor changed his linen. A gentleman had met him on the way, and took part in his perils, a Mr. Graham, or Graeme, who later shared the misfortunes of the servants of the Stuarts. ' He has been very careful of me and done everything with great affection,' Charles wrote to his father, after his arrival in Paris, on February 10. ' Both he and the two servants suffered by my impatience to arrive at the end of my journey. I gave them little or no rest, and if I had been to go much further I should have been obliged to get them ty'd behind the chase (chaise) with my portmantle, for they were quite *rendu*. I have met with all that could be expected from the King of France, who expresses great tenderness, and will be careful of all my concerns.' Yet it was asserted later, by Æneas Macdonald, that no notice was taken of the Prince by Louis or his ministers.

Now we are to mark quite a new Charles, manly, not without humour, careful to keep his father well informed, and brimful of energy. His wish was to see a campaign. Till hope deferred put him on a desperate resolution, Charles figures in an amiable light. He was born for action, and now the path towards action seemed to lie open, and his faults were lost in his new happiness. Given employment that he could understand, Charles rose gaily and strenuously to the needs and duties of the hour. Unoccupied, he relapsed into the bitter gloom of his long years of later life, and fell back on the stimulant that was his ruin. But now he had hopes and happiness.

Charles, as we saw, was satisfied by the kind treatment of the French King. Not so was James. Long taught to shun self-deluding dreams he looked on politics less in the spirit of an exile's dreams than with a sad lucidity. The measure of support which France would give was absolutely limited by what she expected to get in return. James writes to Sempil (February 13, 1744): 'Your letter of January 27 gives me no small astonishment and concern. The promises of France are not to be reconciled with her negligent and indifferent behaviour to the Prince,' who, says James later, has never seen the King. He was obliged to be incognito : he was not royally received. The Prince himself answered, under the

cypher name (he wrote ' Sifer ' usually for ' cypher ')
of Malloch.   Now Malloch was the cant name of
Macgregor of Balhaldy, in the correspondence, just
as it was of the father of Mallet, the poet, himself
one of the proscribed Macgregor clan.   In this letter,
which is partly in Scots, Charles poses as a serving
man.   He makes no complaint and says that ' little
intrigues are going on for Mr. Fisher's amusement,'
that is, in his own interest (February 17).   On
February 24 he declares that everything goes to a
wish.   Steps were really being taken at Dunkirk,
under Marshal Saxe, for the despatch of a French
invading force, which Charles was to accompany
to England.   Clearly the French had been persuaded
that the English Jacobites would rise, which it is next
to certain that they would not have done.

England had been warned by a dispatch of Mr.
Thomson, at Paris, to the Duke of Newcastle
(February 25).   He had remonstrated with Amelot
about Charles's presence in France, a breach of treaty.
Amelot answered that England had taken the
initiative.   Captain Ridley, master of a packet boat,
announced the French naval and military preparations.
On February 25 Parliament assured George II. of their
loyalty, and Sir John Norris was ordered to Spithead with twenty ships of the line.   On February 28
it was ordained that oaths of allegiance should be
taken from Papists and Nonjurors, who, on refusal,

F

should be sent ten miles out of London. Their
horses and arms were to be confiscated. Arms in
great numbers were seized at Plymouth and in the
Belle Sauvage Yard, on Ludgate Hill. Colonel Cecil
and Carte, the historian, were placed in custody, with
Lord Barrymore. The City and the Universities
presented loyal addresses. Meanwhile the English
Jacobites were drinking healths in private. Charles
went secretly to Gravelines, while the Earl Marischal
was at Dunkirk. Holland was sending 6,000 men to
England. But the tempests of the last days of
February 1744 made help for England unnecessary.
Papers of the French Marine, recently published by
Capitaine Colin, give the details and prove that invasion was seriously intended, on a large scale, without
declaration of war. Roqueville, commanding the
French Marine, had found no ships at Spithead, and,
supposing the English fleet to be in Portsmouth,
bade Saxe and Charles set forth. Seven thousand
troops were embarked, the Prince and the Marshal
were at sea ; Roqueville, however, was driven away
by Norris, and the transports were shattered by a
tempest. Saxe was sent to Flanders ; all was over.

Yet Charles lingered at Gravelines : he would
not despair. On March 5 Marischal tells Charles
that his solicitations of the French Court are hampered
by his own entire ignorance of James's schemes.
The Earl had not been trusted, and, if not lukewarm,

he was aggrieved. It was necessary that a larger sum of money than Charles had calculated must be demanded from France. He admired Charles's 'noble and generous sentiments,' his design to go alone to England. The English ('Lord B.' probably Barrymore) insist, by word of mouth as usual, on an expedition of 12,000 French. 'To go single, unless you are invited by the principal peers (of England) both for credit and good sense, would be for ever the destruction of the Cause.' Thus early the Earl foresaw the desperate resolve of Charles, to fling himself, alone and uninvited, on his country: thus early he predicted the inevitable end. On March 6 Charles wrote from Gravelines to James :

The little difficulties and the small dangirs I may have run, are nothing, when for the service and Glory of a Father who is so tender and kind for me, and for the service of his countrey who is so dire to him. Thank God I am in perfect good health, and every thing goes well, as to particulars as I have no sifer, Lord Sempil will enform you. I hope in a few days to date my letters from a place which will shew of itself that all is finished. When I left Antibes there was such a rumour that I was there that I durst not write in my own hand, for fear the packet might have been opened, and by consequence confirmed what was as yet uncertain, but I left particular instructions to the Governor to make my excuses, and to express the whol, but it seems he has not understood me, otherwise your Majesty would approve of the caution. I have every day large packets to answer,

without aney body to help me but Malloch (Balhaldy).
Yesterday I had one that cost me seven owers and a
half.

P.S.—Tho it was fore a clock before I could get my
dinner by being busy yet I could not resist writing to my
Brother reflecting that it was his Birthday. . . .

Writing to Marischal, on the same day, Charles
asks for Buchanan, an agent of Æneas Macdonald,
the Paris banker of the Kinlochmoidart house, a most
shifty personage. 'Wogan is not available,' that is,
Nicholas Wogan, brother of Charles, the gayest and
most intrepid of Irishmen. The messenger, Buchanan,
was to report in England (or Scotland?) that Marshal
Saxe (who was to command the expedition) had had
orders to return, 'if not joined' by English adherents,
'at the Hope.' Balhaldy had asked Andrew Cockburn, in London, to send pilots to meet Saxe, and
to Cockburn the Earl Marischal promised to despatch
Buchanan, with Wogan, if possible. But Cockburn
was perfectly incapable : Murray of Broughton found
that he often left the key to the Jacobite cypher on
the window seat of the parlour! Such were the
futile Jacobites of England, but Murray adds that
Balhaldy had given no explicit orders as to where
the pilots were to be sent. The pilots were not
despatched, whether by fault of Balhaldy, who was at
Gravelines with Charles, or of Cockburn and, had
Saxe's expedition approached English shores, it must

merely have sailed back again.   What could France
do with such imbecile allies ?

Charles, by promises from France, was kept
hanging on at Gravelines and elsewhere, in disguise,
'eating his own heart, avoiding the path of men.'
The deferred hope, the long delays of France, the
disunion of his adherents, drove him, after fifteen
months, to take his own headlong course, and force
the game in his own way.   On March 11 Charles
wrote to the Earl Marischal.   The end of their
correspondence was a coldness, the Earl thinking
Charles a hot-headed young fool, and Charles dis-
covering that the Earl was no man of action, but a
humorous and upright philosopher, who could not
serve his turn.   The Earl had a habit of seeing things
as they were ; and steadily declined to ruin loyal
Highlanders by putting them on a hopeless enterprise.
Nor would he wrong France by such sanguine and
futile encouragements as Balhaldy and Sempil plied.
Thirty years earlier the Earl might have been
Charles's man, but he now was wise with the wisdom
of age and humour.

Meanwhile d'Argenson, the French minister, told
Saxe that Charles had better withdraw, incognito, to
a villa of the Bishop of Soissons, with the Earl for
his chaperon.   The Prince declined, and wrote to
Sempil that '*if he knew his presence could be of service
in England*, he would venture thither in an open

boat.' On April 5, or 6, he was reported as lurking in Paris.[1] On March 26 Charles told James of his forlorn position, and asked for the company of Sir Thomas Sheridan, his cousin and old tutor. ' I have learned from you to bear with disappointments, and I see it is the only way, which is to submit oneself entirely to the will of God, and never to be discouraged.' The poor lad was endeavouring to be wise. On April 3 he writes :

The situation I am in is very particular, for nobody nose where I am or what is become of me, so that I am entirely Burried as to the publick, and cant but say but that it is a very great constrent upon me, for I am obliged very often not to stur out of my room, for fier of some bodys noing my face. I very often think that you would laugh very hartily if you saw me goin about with a single servant bying fish and other things and squabling for a peney more or less. I hope your Majesty will be thoroughly persuaded, that no constrent or trouble whatsoever either of minde or body, will ever stope me in going on with my duty, in doing anything that I think can tend to your service or your Glory. . . .

April 10.

. . . Whether I am free from company or diversions, its all alike to me for I can think of nothing, or taste nothing but your service, which is my Duty. . . .

James bids him ' avoid precipitate and dangerous measures, some rash or ill-conceived project, which

---

[1] This intelligence is from papers in the French Foreign Office, in Mr. Fitzroy Bell's appendix to *Memorials of Murray of Broughton.*

would end in your ruin, and that of all those who
would joyn with you in it.' Sheridan and Stafford
were setting out to join him, and Charles is adjured
'to behave to them in a proper manner.' James
supposed that the Prince would make a campaign
with the French army, but, much to his chagrin, the
Earl Marischal rendered this impossible. Charles
was urged to be economical, as he was supported
by the King of France (April 3). On April 24 he
replied that he was in strict retirement : his retreat
unknown, reading hard. On May 11 he was certainly in Paris, and attests the tenderness of Louis XV.
Yet Louis would not see him. He remarks with
some humour on the Earl Marischal's behaviour. He
will certainly see a campaign, if Mr. Isham (Lord M.)
does not prevent it, ' for he dose all that lise in his
power to hinder it, and the commission yr Mty has
given him makes what he sese of some impression,
he tells them that my serving in the Army in flanders,
it would disgust entirely the English, by serving in
the same Army that is to fite against them, and so
forth. He has don all this without telling me anything of the matter or consulting me about it. When
I was at the seaside after the storm I rit to him to do
all that was possible for to encourage the People that
the Expedition should not be stopped, but he did
quite the contrary, by seing things that discouraged
them to the last degree : I was pleaged with his

letters *which were reather Books, and had the patience
to answer them article by article* striving to make him
act reasonably, but all to no purpose. Your Majesty
may judge how busi I was.'

Charles adds that Balhaldy and Sempil advise
him to take George Kelly as a companion. The
Rev. George Kelly (born 1688) had been Atterbury's
secretary ; then he lay fourteen years in the Tower :
escaped very ingeniously, and joined the Duke of
Ormond at Avignon. His departure now was ' very
agreeable to the Duke, because that he was a great
constrent on his amoors.' The Duke, who had served
with Marlborough, was indeed a veteran amorist.
Kelly remained true to Charles, despite the later
efforts (about 1751) which the Earl Marischal made
to remove him, for a time with success. He was
learned, discreet, witty, brave, and a general favourite
with men and women. The Kelly who loved the
bottle too well was a Catholic priest of the same
name : Charles's confessor at this date.[1] From the
hour of his return to Paris, in April 1744, Charles's
experience was purely heart-breaking. First he was
practically a prisoner in his little house near Montmartre. Next it was impossible to extract the

---

[1] I have not made use of the Examination of Æneas Macdonald,
when a prisoner in 1747. He appears to have been with Charles at
this time, and especially blames Balhaldy and Sempil for misleading
the French Court with false intelligence. But he was far from being a
truthful witness.

money for his pension (5,000 livres a month) from the French Minister of Finance, though Sheridan journeyed, in bad health, to the King in Flanders. Again the Scottish Jacobites sent Murray to warn Charles against Sempil and Balhaldy ; while Sempil tried to undermine his faith in Sheridan, and James was not only teased by the irreconcilable letters of complaint sent from all sides, but also by an anonymous epistle, accusing his younger son of being too devout. Hope or shadow of hope from France there was none, but Murray, in Scotland, was maturing the plan of a rising, against which, if unaided by a French force, James frequently expressed his decided opinion. It was this long protracted strain on his temper that drove Charles into the adventure of July 1745. He reckoned to force the hand of France, and to compel his own distracted party to unite.

The details of the many months of waiting, from April 1744 to July 1745, are copious but uninteresting. At first, France was full of promises ; later, Tencin told an envoy that Louis had never even sent for Charles. 'If he did not send for him, he received him,' was the reply. James thought that the Prince might as well be in Rome again, and Charles himself thought of retiring to Avignon. His debts amounted to 30,000 livres, and they were not paid till, in January 1745, he left Paris for St. James, the seat of his kind cousin, the Duc de Bouillon.

The weary details of the party intrigues of July-September 1744 are given at great length in Murray of Broughton's Memoirs. He left London in July, and met Balhaldy, who was not pleased with the encounter. Charles he met privately, behind the stables of the Louvre. He poured out his charges against Sempil and Balhaldy, which Charles heard ' with as much coldness, caution, and circumspection as the most experienced statesman.' He defended the accused, and finally, if Murray is to be believed, ' said that, at all events, he was determined to come the following summer to Scotland, though with a single footman.' Murray replied that he could not come too soon for his friends, but that he hoped a French force would accompany him.

Murray, in fact, never really opposed, but rather encouraged the desperate act, by inducing Scottish Jacobites to sign papers expressing their resolve to rally to Charles if be came alone. A few of these documents made it reconcilable to Charles's conscience to say that he had been ' invited ' to Scotland. The first result of Murray's visit was a serious break between Sheridan, Sempil, and Balhaldy, all of whom Charles had been commanded to trust. The severest criticism must confess that Charles, a young and inexperienced man, was now in a cruel position. If, as Murray declares, Balhaldy stole the Earl Marischal's baggage at Sheriffmuir fight (1715): if, as

Lord John Drummond vowed, Balhaldy left Scotland
in trouble about a fifty-pound note ; if he had pretended falsely to have bought arms in Holland, who
could trust Balhaldy ?   Yet James trusted him.   Of
how much confidence Murray was deserving appeared
on a later day.   Returning home, Murray undermined the faith of Lochiel and Traquair in Balhaldy,
while Balhaldy sent over Young Glengarry, then in
French service, to undermine faith in Murray.
'What a parcel of rogues in a nation !' as the old
song runs.   Murray was accused of bidding Charles
'seat himself on the throne, and leave the King at
Rome,' whereas, on August 11, 1745, James confided
to Louis XV. his own intention of resigning in favour
of Charles : subject to the French King's approval.
A Prince's party and a King's party were being
evolved.   The hopeless folly of the Jacobite leaders
makes it strange that, when the claymore was once
drawn, the clans gained their brilliant successes.

Leaving Murray to collect money, and enrol
adherents, and found 'the Buck Club' in Scotland,
we return to Charles in his hermitage at Montmartre.
His letters are many, and some, as to his devotions
and choice of Father Kelly (not George Kelly) as a
confessor, must have pleased James.   But the tone of
hope yields to that of anger, and, as far as France is
concerned, of despair.   Sheridan and he tell the tale
of the many splits in the party.   Sempil retorts with

counter charges. The Prince amuses himself by visiting the Opera : that diversion is then forbidden. For plate he had but 'twelve forks, spuns, and nives' (August 3). James (August 21) realised that he was 'more in Sempil's hands than in the King of France's,' and bade Charles show the letter to Sheridan. Who was to be trusted ? One or more cliques of adherents must be kept in the dark. Thus Charles was forced to secret ways, and to a measure of dissimulation.

The party was playing a game of blind man's buff, in which all were blinded. To cool reflection, it seems that the exiled family should simply have withdrawn from hopes and projects, and accepted a good pension from England, which owed them the dowry of the wife of James II. But James had no other profession than that of Royalty. No Court in Europe would have allowed Charles to put his sword at its service. He was bound beyond release to the fugitive hope, to the ominous eagle that flitted before his boat as he sailed to Eriskay. His weird was written, and strength, endurance, courage, charm were, from the first, under the shadow of doom. At a given point his character, never stable, must break down in moral ruin, but, looking at his temptations and his trials, and 'knowing all,' perhaps we ought to 'pardon all.' At this moment, with what sincerity he might, he fortified himself (as he often tells his father) by the exercises of his religion. He was assuredly making a moral effort to be strong, resigned, and dutiful. We, who have so often failed, cannot throw the first stone at one who did what he had the strength to do, and fell under temptations more subtle and terrible than ours, under stress of inherited character, evil training, and adverse circumstance. He strove to get clear of his 'imprisonment,' he writes on September 7, 1744, but the power of the French Court was too strong. He even defended Sempil against James's suspicions of sowing distrust between himself and Sheridan. The letters between the Prince and his younger brother, who had hoped in vain to fight in the army of Naples, declare an unbroken affection and sympathy. On October 12 he discouraged any rash movement in the Highlands. The following letter shows his attitude :

Charles to James.

Nov. 16.

I write to you this appart in answer to your in the same manner. Your Majesty may be assured that I will never faile (with the grace of God) to my dutys before God and men. I well no what one in my situation is obliged to, and what he has to answer, on all sides iff he dose anything wrong, you may judge by my being sensible of this, how much it engages me to be attention in everything that is my duty. At the beginning of this month I did my devotions, observing as much as possible, the doing of them as often as at Rome, and on the usual Holidays. I hope the Allmighty will have mercy on us at the laste, in the mene time I will always say *fiat voluntas tua* and I vowed to confess to Abe Sempill, ho to do him justice is a very exemplary and good Ecclesiastick, but since my being in Paris was *Le Scene de la Comedie* I thought it was better to do my Devotions in a Church and not in a Chappel as before, and by consequence, to go to a common confessor. I made good enquiris to go to one of noted character for lerning, and wright way of thinking, and have founde one to whom I go : he has all these Quallitys. He is called Kelly, of the same order of P. Francors, at the Convent here called La Grande Cardelie. He is releted to Kelly that is with me. I heve on all sides, of people that dose not no I go to him, a great Caracter of him. I reccomended to him to say to nobody untill I tell him otherwise that I confess to him, for only Sr. Tomas and Stafford nose.

At this time (November 16) Charles writes, 'As long as there is life there is hope !' He adds :

You may well imagine how out of Youmer I am : when for comfort I am plagued out of my life with *tracasyrs* from ower own People, who as it would seem would rether Sachrifise me and my Affairs, than fail in any private view. Lord John[1] is one of those that has been plaging me with complaints but I quieted him in the best manner I could, saying that whatever is sed of our own people, tho' never so well grounded, was cutting our own throts, at the same time I am plesed that people should spake freely to me. . .

The more I dwell on these matters, the more it makes me melancholy, for which I end.

On December 28 Balhaldy denounced Sheridan to James (who highly esteemed him) as 'pernicious

---

[1] Lord John Drummond, in French service.

and useless : ' he has deliberately put a stop to ' affairs.'
Whom was James, far from the scene, to trust ?
The imbroglio was inextricable.   Sempil (January 4,
1745) had described Sheridan to James as ' the
boldest adventurer I ever knew yet, or heard of.'
Marischal had told James that Lord Sempil and
Balhaldy ' impose, as far as they can, on all the world,
and conceal from your Majesty so great affairs '
(September 5, 1744).   The Prince now agreed with
the Earl : he detected Sempil and Balhaldy in lying
to himself, and, all through the spring of 1745, he
told his father, with glee, how he was pretending
to trust them, merely because he was afraid of the
mischief they might do, if neglected.   He raised
40,000 livres for the purchase of broadswords, the
hilts to be affixed in the Highlands.   He desired
James to pawn his jewels, which he would wear with
a very heavy heart on the wrong side of the water.
James reluctantly paid Charles's debt to Waters, the
banker, for the swords, but demurred to the pawning
of the jewels.   He warned the Prince that his dissimulation (inherited from James VI.) ' became
neither a Prince nor a Christian.'   He might have
guessed at Charles's design, but it came on him at
last as a complete surprise.   ' Our friends in England
are affred of their own shaddo, and think of little else
than of diverting themselves,' wrote the Prince.   Therefore Charles's designs clearly regarded Scotland.

Meanwhile communication with Scotland was rare. One Bleau, of Castle-hill, near Clackmannan, visited Paris in February 1745 with a scheme for taking Edinburgh Castle. 'He was hanged for murder in 1767, at the age of seventy-five,' says Mr. Fitzroy Bell. Sir Hector Maclean of Dowart (chief of Clan Gilzean) was nearly engaged in a duel with Lord John Drummond, who commanded a Scots regiment in French service. Drummond, to judge by Charles's reports, was almost insane, and to keep the men apart, or probably as an emissary to Murray, Maclean was sent to Scotland, where he was arrested just before the Rising broke out. All through April and May 1745 Charles was very secretly planning his expedition to Scotland. Neither James nor the French Court knew, or would have permitted the enterprise. The really important facts, in Scotland, in April and May 1745 were that Murray of Broughton was collecting subscriptions and promises, especially from the Duke of Hamilton, and Macleod. This great chief, among others, promised, in writing, to support Charles, even if he came alone.[1]

Murray's evidence tends in two directions. He wishes to exonerate Charles from blame because he set forth on the strength of such promises as Macleod's,

[1] See Mackenzie's *History of the Macleods*, p. 129. The correspondence of Macleod has disappeared from the family charter-chest.

which were not kept.   Again, he wishes to exonerate
himself from the charge (urged by Maxwell of Kirkconnell and others) of buoying up the Prince with
false hopes.   Thus he sent to tell the Prince that, in
a council, all but the Duke of Perth denounced his
adventure.   But Lord Traquair should have carried
that message and failed to do so.   Finally, Murray
sent a budget of advice by one Macnaughton, his own
footman apparently, but the advice not to come,
Murray admits, 'was in general terms, and might not
be sufficient to prevent his coming.'   In the end, an
obviously perplexing statement was entrusted to
Young Glengarry, for Charles, early in June 1745:
'too late to answer the end proposed.'   Glengarry
did not meet the Prince, and the last faint chance of
stopping him from setting out was lost.

Through the shuffling observations of Murray, it
is plain that he, and none but he, on the Scottish side
(with some aid from the delays of Traquair) was
responsible for exciting the hopes which led to the
adventure.   They did not amount to an 'invitation,'
but, with the English defeat at Fontenoy, and the
absence of troops from England, they decided Charles.
Even Glengarry's despatch included a request that
he would make Murray his aide-de-camp, if he *did*
come : the despatch, then, could not have contained
what was needed, a peremptory negative.   Meanwhile, after making his preparations at Fitzjames

G

and Navarre, Charles was in the hands of daring Irishmen : Sullivan, an officer in French service ; the 'boldest of adventurers,' Sheridan ; and George Kelly, a man habituated to every peril.   At this date Lady Clifford forwarded to James a remonstrance of her own.   She protested against the men who surrounded the Prince.   'Don't you see plainly that till the Prince has proper people about him, he maÿ go on years and ages in the same fruitless way he has passed days and months, since he has been in France. . . . The Kg. cannot be aware of it, nor kept duly informed. . . . That she does not wish to impugn the honesty of the people about the P. but they are *unknown, low-born, of no credit or weight, and so useless*.   That none is allowed by them to see the P. or have anything to do with him.   That Lord Marischal the "only man of quality" on this side, that could give credit to our Court here, is seen banished to Avignon.   That people won't pledge their lives at the bidding of the people now about the P.   That friends in England have just suppressed a Pamphlet called "The Conduct of a young Hero, his Court, and amusements."'

The lady's remarks are judicious : the English could not rely on unknown adventurers.   But, since 1715, the original exiles of birth and rank had been dying out.   Ormond was old, and on the verge of death.   The Earl Marischal was alienated ; and, as we repeat, the party was a chaos of cross-worked plots, and internecine quarrels. James could only ask for 'proper deference and confidence in his Majesty's conduct and judgment.' Meanwhile he warned Charles (as we saw) against the dissimulation of which he was boasting (his tricks on Sempil and Balhaldy), as to the last degree unworthy of a Prince or a Christian (June 26). And, even as James wrote, a letter of June 12, from Charles, was on the way to him, in which he acknowledged, tacitly, that for months he had been disobeying and deceiving his father. At Navarre, near Evreux, and at Fitzjames he had finally arranged, with his Irish friends, and with Routledge and Walsh (an ancestor of the Duc de la Tremoille), for a descent on Scotland ; that very rash resolve which James had so often deprecated and forbidden.

Charles's letter to James of June 12 was to go by a private and dilatory hand ; it was written in anticipation of movements which took weeks to mature. 'I have been six months ago invited by our Friends to go to Scotland,' he says. The successes of Murray with the Duke of Hamilton, Macleod, Stewart of Appin (who did not appear in the field), and the Duke of Perth, were all that Charles had, to our knowledge, as a basis for his assertion. Indeed, to do Charles justice, he adds that his friends 'have not said it directly,' have not explicitly promised 'to rise of themselves,' in despair of the French Court, which despair, he further adds, he tried to remove. But, if rise they must, he would conquer or die with them. A horse without spirit, he says, would find no purchaser : he must show his mettle, as James did in 1715. 'I have taken a firm resolution to conquer or to dye, and stand my ground as long as I shall have a man remaining with me.' Alas for the resolution ! He begs that his Sobieski jewels may be pawned : he never means to return. He explains that he has borrowed 180,000 livres from the Waterses. To Edgar he writes that he has purchased twenty small field pieces, 1,500 muskets, 11,000 broadswords, ammunition, ' durks,' and other supplies. He has 4,000 louis d'or. Routledge has lent a man-of-war, the *Elizabeth* (employed by him as a privateer), Walsh has a frigate, *La Doutelle*,[1] of 44 guns. He means to land on or near Mull. The French Court knows nothing of the affair.

Mr. Blaikie, in his valuable Itinerary, makes Charles sail from Belle Isle on July 5, Old Style. He wrote from Belle Isle on July 12, saying that he had just got his escort, a ship of 68 guns, and 700 men. His own vessel he calls the *Du Tellier*, usually written *Doutelle*. His companions, we know, were the Jacobite Duke of Atholl (who had been ousted by his younger brother, a Whig), Sir John Macdonald,

---

[1] This name is spelled in various ways.

Æneas Macdonald, Strickland (whom James greatly
distrusted), Sheridan, Sullivan, George Kelly,
Buchanan, and Walsh, the owner of the ship : ' old
allagrugous like fellows as ever I saw,' wrote Mr.
Bissatt, from Blair Atholl, to the Whig Duke, on
August 31. ' Allagrugous ' is interpreted to mean
' grim.'

The die was cast, the most forlorn of all hopes
was on its way to win a throne. How weak, how
distracted the party was ; how dark the machinations
which preceded the enterprise, has been made
sufficiently manifest. On no side was there a gleam
of promise, a single omen of good.

CHAPTER II

FROM MOIDART TO PRESTONPANS

The tartan plaid it is waving wide,
　　The pibroch's sounding up the glen ;
And I will tarry at Auchnacarry
　　To see my Donald and all his men.
And there I saw the King o' them a',
　　Was marching bonnily in the van,
And aye the spell o' the bagpipe's yell
　　Was, Turn the blue bonnet wha can, wha can !

JAMES HOGG.

BEFORE beginning the story of the Prince's campaign, it may be well to describe the then existing condition of the Highlanders, on whose hospitality he was to throw himself. Events since the union of the crowns in James VI. had entirely changed the old historical balance of parties, or rather of races, in Scotland. Between the time of the sons of Malcolm Canmore, in the twelfth century, and the accession of James VI. to the throne of England, the western Celts of Scotland had often been allies of England against the national monarchy, while the nation in general, the English-speaking Lowlands, and the

Court, had been allies of France against England. Now, in 1745, the Celts were, as against England, the allies of France. At various dates, up to Mary Stuart's reign, certain Highland clans had, indeed, been on the side of the central authority. Such were, for a few years, the MacIans (a Macdonald sept) of Ardnamurchan : such were the Mackays of Sutherland ; and, almost invariably, the Campbells of Argyll. But the great clan of the children of Somerled, the Macdonalds, whether under the half-royal Lords of the Isles, or under their descendants, the Chiefs of Clanranald, Glengarry, and Sleat in Skye, with the Camerons in Lochaber, Clan Chattan in all its septs, Clan Vourich (Macpherson), the Macleods, and Clan Gilzean (the Macleans of Mull and Morvern), with the dispossessed and lawless Macgregors, were usually opposed to the Stuarts, and to the Scottish crown. When, however, the religious troubles under Charles I. and Charles II. began, the Macdonalds and other Catholic or Episcopalian clans adopted the side of the Stuarts. To that Cause they remained loyal, as a rule, through the Civil wars, and at the Revolution.

Under Dundee, at Killiecrankie ; under Mar, at Sheriffmuir ; under Tullibardine, at Glenshiel (1719), the Celtic-speaking western tribes were Jacobite. But the Campbells of Argyll, the Munroes in Ross, and the Mackays in Sutherland remained, as a rule,

Whig and Protestant. The Sinclairs and Dunbars of Caithness for the most part held aloof. Between 1715 and 1745 much had been done to weaken the Jacobitism of the clans. The quarrels of James and Clementina had their effect. The roads and forts of Marshal Wade bridled the Celts as they had never been bridled before. A Whig Duke reigned in Atholl, where, as in Ross-shire, advancing civilisation lowered the old martial sentiment. In Ross, too, after 1730, there was a Whig Seaforth as chief of the previously Jacobite Mackenzies. The Jacobite ideas of the Frazers wavered with the incalculable veerings of the treacherous Lovat, who had adopted the Whig party in 1715. Clan Vourich was neutralised by the military commission held under George II. by Cluny. The chief of the Grants, the chief of the Mackintoshes, and the Cock of the North, the Duke of Gordon, were all, officially, anti-Jacobites.

Thus the clans from whom Charles had to expect assistance were limited almost to the Catholic Macdonalds of Moidart and Knoydart, to the remnant of the Macleans, almost dispossessed by the Campbells, to the Camerons, kinsmen of Lochiel, and to the Stewarts of Appin, Episcopalian in creed, and staunch to their chief, King James. Of these clans, some Macdonalds had kept up their warlike spirit by systematic cattle raiding, in alliance with the Rannoch men (Camerons), and the men of Rob Roy. They devastated the land from Sutherland to Menteith, and Lochiel had great trouble in winning his clan from this mode of life. The Macleods and the Skye Macdonalds were more than dubious allies, and their chiefs were destined to take the Whig side. Thus Charles could only rely on

A set of men whose worth was hardly known,

as the contemporary Jacobite poet sings, namely, the Macdonalds of the mainland, the Camerons, and the Appin Stewarts and Macleans, at all times the flower of his army. As the most remote and inaccessible of the Celts, they were most under the rule of Celtic ideas, fidelity to the chief and to the clan. Mainly pastoral in their life, and cultivating but a little grain, far from towns, and dwelling in small clachans, or villages, beside their scanty oatfields, they had much more of leisure than of employment. In their smoky huts, or in mountain shielings, poor and proud, their vigour was not undermined, or cramped, by labour. They were all sportsmen and gentlemen, except the almost servile septs, who were not of kin to the chief. These were but half armed, and their uncouth aspect amazed the Lowlanders. The spirit of the others was nurtured on ancient tales of war and Ossianic ballads. They thus formed an admirable militia, trained to the gun in sport, to the sword in private quarrel, and to long and secret marches, in the course of cattle-stealing. But it is improbable that the really devoted clans could bring more than 2,000 men into the field. Charles must depend on them for the steel head of his weapon, and on such other clans as might be roused by their example. The Lowland adherents were of much less value, while, among the less attached clans which later came forward, many men were 'forced out' by threats of fire-raising and mutilation of cattle.

The march of the clans with the gentry who had a right to the eagle's feather in their bonnets, and were each armed with an arsenal of gun, targe, pistols, claymore, dirk, and skene, 'all plaided and plumed in their tartan array,' must have been a gallant spectacle. But the long elf-locks and beards, the wild white hair of the aged warriors, the smooth faces of the boys, the Callum Begs of the host, and the ragged, unshod condition of the servile septs, could not conciliate Lowland or English waverers.

This rising, we must remember, sprang from no pressing popular grievance. Beyond sentiment and Presbyterian persecution, the Highlanders had practically nothing to complain of, as against the House of Hanover. They were only refused the free exercise of their religion. Otherwise they were left alone, to enjoy their ancient customs and their patriarchal condition of society. A few landlords were feebly trying to introduce leases and money rents, in place of a system which secured a croft for every swordsman by unwritten custom. This change was not popular, but it was not imposed by Government. The material trouble of the Highlanders—poverty caused by a population out of proportion to the opportunities of agricultural and other employments— merely provided active and idle men as recruits for Charles. The religious grievances—the persecution of the priests among Catholic clans, and the dis- abilities of non-juring Episcopalians, as in Appin and Glencoe—were not such as Presbyterian historians can regard as grave. The few Catholic clergy, however, proved to be useful recruiting officers in that ragged fringe of western coast from Knoydart to Lorne, which was the only home of enthusiastic Jacobitism.

Charles had been warned, if we can believe Murray of Broughton, about the true state of affairs. Doubt- less he had higher hopes, but the actual condition of his Celtic allies has been described. He wisely threw himself among his least uncertain friends, the Mac- donalds of Moidart, and of Clanranald's isles.

It appears, from a statement made by Scott in his journal of a Hebridean cruise (1814), that the Prince had been expected to land further south, in Morvern, or at Oban. By not doing so, he lost the Macdougals, but they were now a petty though very ancient clan : and in Moidart he was in the most favourable region.

The course chosen by Charles, in his long voyage to the coast of Moidart, led him round the Land's

End. From the very moment of his sailing from
Belle Isle, it is difficult to ascertain the real sequence
of events. The Jacobites wished to show him as a
hero in every circumstance : the Whigs, and alienated
friends, tried to prove him a coward. Thus, in a well-
known letter of David Hume to Sir John Pringle, it
is asserted that the Prince showed the white feather
at the last moment, and that his companions had to
bind him hand and foot, and carry him aboard the
Doutelle, or, as Charles writes it, the *Du Tellier*. This
anecdote Hume got, about 1765, from Helvetius, the
French *philosophe*, who declared that Charles at one
period lived in his house, and was much despised by
him. That Charles, about 1750–54, was in close
relations with some of the *philosophes* is certain ; but
I have found no trace of his sojourn with Helvetius.
In 1765, long after the Earl Marischal deserted the
Cause, he wrote to Hume thus : ' A propos of history,
when you see Helvetius, tell him I desired you to
inquire of him concerning a certain history. I fancy
he will answer you with his usual frankness.' This
must refer to the anecdote about Charles's alleged
cowardice. But had he really behaved as reported
by Helvetius, the Earl Marischal was better placed
to know the truth than was the *philosophe*, and the
tale is absolutely inconsistent with the Prince's
habitual audacity. Indeed, Æneas Macdonald, giving
information later to the English Government, said

that Charles declined, when remonstrated with, to abandon the expedition.

The chief incident in the voyage was a battle, many leagues west of the Lizard, between the *Elizabeth*, Charles's convoy, and the *Lion* (Captain Brett). The combat lasted for several hours ; both ships were crippled, and the captain of the *Elizabeth* was wounded ; was killed, if we believe Æneas Macdonald. According to Duncan Cameron, who was aboard, Charles entreated Walsh with the *Doutelle* to join in the sea fight, but Walsh refused, and said that he would send the Prince down to his cabin if he persisted. The Whigs, on the other hand, averred that Charles went below of his own accord. However the truth may be, the *Elizabeth* put back into harbour when the *Lion* drew off, and the *Doutelle* made her way westwards, escaped an English chase by her superior speed, and on July 23 (?) touched at the little low-lying isle of Eriskay. Coilleag a' Phrionnsa (The Prince's Strand) is still the name of the place where Charles first set foot on Scottish soil. A pink convolvulus, not elsewhere known on the island, is said to have sprung from some seeds that happened to be in the pocket of his jacket. Four hours before making land, ' an eagle came hovering over the frigate,' says Duncan Cameron, and the Marquis of Tullibardine welcomed the royal bird as a favourable omen.

Appearances were bleak enough on the little isle

which is still so remote from the modern world, and
so attached to ancient songs and to old beliefs in
apocryphal gospel sagas. 'They could not find a
grain of meal, or one inch of bread; but they catched
some flounders, which they roasted upon the bare
coals in a mean low hut they had gone into near the
shore, and Duncan Cameron stood cook. The Prince
sat at the cheek of a little ingle . . . and laughed
heartily at Donald's cookery.' Later he was to
instruct the Highlanders in the art of the *cuisine*.
Their host was one Angus Macdonald, and he was
annoyed by the Prince's inability to remain either in
the smoke of the central fireplace, or in the rain out
of doors. The cottage is a long low building, thatch-
roofed; the fire was in the centre of the room, the
chimney a mere hole in the thatch. Charles inspected
Sheridan's bed, 'to see that the sheets were well
aired,' and Angus announced that a 'Prince need not
be ashamed to lie in it.' Charles's rank was unknown : he had allowed his beard to grow, and, later
at least, was dressed as a clergyman in 'a plain
shirt, not over clean, a cambric stock fixed with a
plain silver buckle, a fair round wig, out of the buckle,
a plain hat with a canvas string, having one end fixed
to one of his coat buttons, and black stockings, with
brass buckles to his shoes.'

The Prince now sent for Macdonald of Boisdale,
in South Uist, the isle just north of Eriskay in the

archipelago of the Long Island. Boisdale advised him to return home. ' I am come home,' Charles is said to have replied, and mentioned Sir Alexander Macdonald of Sleat, and Macleod, as chiefs who would stand by him. Boisdale said that he feared they might even take the opposite part, and he was right. According to Murray of Broughton, and Maxwell of Kirkconnell, Sleat had never promised to rise, if Charles came unattended ; but Macleod had signed a promise to that effect. Charles probably knew this, from Murray's information. Macleod, in place of keeping his promise, informed the English Government, through Forbes of Culloden, of the Prince's landing, and when he raised such of his clan as would follow him, it was to assist the English. ' Surely,' says Murray, ' never had man more reason to believe than the Prince ; nor did ever man so basely betray as did Macleod.' Not awaiting replies from Sleat and Macleod, Charles sailed south of Muck and the strange serrated peaks of Eig and Rum, to Lochna-nuagh, in Arisaig, and (July 25 ?) landed at Borradale. Meanwhile Æneas Macdonald had sailed to the house of his brother, the laird of Kinlochmoidart, whom he brought back to meet Charles at Lochna-nuagh. To them came also young Clanranald, captain of the sept of Macdonalds which disputed the chieftaincy with the Macdonnells of Glengarry. The loyal lairds of Glenaladale and Dalilea (on Loch

Shiel) also arrived. With them was the anonymous chronicler (Macdonald of Morar), who wrote the 'Journal and Memoirs' in the 'Lockhart Papers.'

They found a kind of pavilion on the ship's deck, and 'a variety of wines and spirits.' Clanranald, alone, conversed for three hours with Charles, in the cabin. Later the Prince, 'a tall youth of most agreeable aspect,' came on deck. He was passed off as an English clergyman : spoke with the narrator about the merits and methods of the Highland dress, drank a glass of wine to the company, and went below. Not one man was in favour, at this moment, of the Prince's desperate resolve. Young Clanranald, however, was sent to Skye, to try Macleod and Sleat ; and Macleod, writing on August 3 to the Lord President, Forbes of Culloden, says he has 'been here with us, and has given us all possible assurances of his prudence !' Yet Clanranald's prudence vanished, and, later, the prudence even of Macleod and Sleat was all but overcome. It was probably on his return from Skye, with the news of Macleod's and Sleat's refusals (Murray declares that Macleod did not, even now, openly refuse), that Charles (as Home tells us) turned to young Ranald Macdonald, a brother of Kinlochmoidart. He saw the lad's eyes kindle, and his hand grasp his sword-hilt. 'Will *you* not assist me?' he exclaimed. 'I will ; though no other man in the Highlands should draw his sword,' cried the gallant lad, and the heather was on fire. The Prince learned to drink the King's health in Gaelic, *Deoch-laint-an Reogh,* and Macdonald of Morar was appointed his master in Celtic. The Clanranald loyalty had leaped up at Ranald's word, and when young Clanranald marched, Lochiel would not be left behind, After days of delay the die was cast, and there was no turning back when the noblest heart in Scotland, the heart of Lochiel, was won.

It is most unfortunate that the exact dates of events, in this dawn of the Rising, cannot be ascertained. Certainly the adhesion of Clanranald to the Cause appears to have preceded that of 'the Gentle Lochiel.' It was on August 3 that Macleod wrote his private letter of information to the Lord President, Forbes of Culloden. He announced, as has been said, Clanranald's promise to be 'prudent.' But on August 4 Charles appears already to have overcome the prudence of Clanranald. On that day he wrote from Loughaylort (Loch Aylort, near Borradale) to his father. 'I am joined here of Brave people, as I expected,' that is, probably, by Clanranald and his followers. 'As I have not yet set up the Standard I cannot tell the number, but that will be in a few days, as soon as the arms are distributed, at which wee are working with all speed.' He adds that his messenger to the Lowlands has not yet returned. He is prepared, in case of the worst, 'to dye at the head

H

of such brave people as I find here . . . and *that* I have promised to them, as you no, to be my resolution.' The French Court must 'take off the maske,' or 'have an Eternal sheme on them. . . and wee, whatever happens, will gain an immortal honour by doing what wee can do to deliver our country, in restoring our Master, or perish Sord in hand.'

Such were the promises that Charles was uttering, in all sincerity, and his words and looks, those of a fiery young leader throwing himself on the faith of his father's subjects, could not but win the hearts of the chivalrous Celts.　Even James, in Rome, while telling Sempil and the Earl Marischal that he would never have advised the step, added ' if it is a rash, I cannot but say it is a bold undertaking, and the courage and sentiments the Prince expresses on this occasion will always do him honour.'　(August 11.)　It must have been, apparently, after Clanranald's hand was forced by Charles and young Kinlochmoidart, that the Prince sent for Lochiel, who led the Cameron clan though his father was still alive.

Whig and Tory for once agree in admiration of Young Lochiel.　He had been winning his men from the old habits of caterans, and had been trying to introduce mills and other improvements in agriculture. As a Jacobite we find him in Murray's 'Memoirs,' always among the foremost ; and, when he heard the first hints that Charles would come alone, he declared that, if he did, no man of honour could draw back. Writing in old age, John Home, the author of '.Douglas', reports that Lochiel's brother, Cameron of Fassefern, a commercial Cameron (a burgess of Glasgow), warned the chief that, 'if this Prince once sets eyes upon you he will make you do whatever he pleases.' There is also a tradition that Lochiel hung back, till Charles bade him 'remain at home, and learn his Prince's fate from the newspapers.' But, though Scott seems to have credited this legend, Murray of Broughton represents Lochiel as coun-selling, not an abandonment of the enterprise, but secrecy and delay, till the chiefs could be consulted, and the clans mustered. Maxwell of Kirkconnell combines both versions; Lochiel advised first to return to France : then delay and secrecy. But Charles replied that secrecy was impossible, and that all depended on instant action ; on making men commit themselves, before they could consult cold reflection. He himself landed his slender stores, and 'burned his boats,' or, at least, dismissed his ship, the *Doutelle*. These were the arguments which Lochiel could not resist ; he lived for honour, and honour, he deemed, was inconsistent with deserting the desperate Cause.

A legend has crept into history to the effect that before Lochiel joined, he extorted (as did Cluny later) from Charles a written guarantee for the value of his estate.[1]   Such a document, in case of failure, would not have been worth a farthing.   Moreover the tale, accepted by Chambers, rests partly on the evidence of young Glengarry, who, several years later, when secretly acting as a paid spy in English service, corroborated the report in talk with Bishop Forbes.   When Charles finally left Scotland, he wrote a letter to Cluny, promising to do his best for the interests of that chief.   But security for his estate the Prince could not have offered.

Glengarry's evidence is dubious, he was jealous of Lochiel, was calumniating Cluny, as an embezzler of Charles's money, and in Lochiel we may undoubtedly admire the most stainless loyalty.

In his argument with Lochiel, Charles reasoned well ; his motto must henceforward be *de l'audace*. Old Glengarry probably gave a tacit assent : he was aged, and never was resolute.   After Culloden he was denounced to Government by several gentlemen of his clan for raising them, and keeping the money for their services in his private sporran.   He now tried to play Lovat's game, and make it appear that his younger son Æneas (the elder, Alastair, was in France) with his kinsmen, Barisdale and Lochgarry, had brought out the clan against his will.   Keppoch,

---

[1] Mr. Blaikie accepts this story (*Itinerary*, p. 5).   See, however, *Lyon in Mourning*, iii. 120, where Bishop Forbes says that he first heard the story as to Lochiel from Lady Strathallan.   Glengarry corroborated, and added the same tale about Cluny.

Stewart of Ardshiel, who led the Appin men, and
other gentlemen, followed Lochiel, and it was decided
to raise the Royal Standard at Glenfinnan, near the
upper end of the long stretch of fresh water named
Loch Shiel, which pours its clear and rapid stream
into the sea strait of Loch Moidart.

To Charles's eyes his own country must have
seemed strange enough. He had come to a land of
many isles, whose steep and serrated ridges rose
beyond winding sea-lochs that ran far into the
recesses of the mountains of the mainland. When
he arrived all the mountains were flushed with th
bloom of the heather, and the straths beside the
rivers and lochs were broken with patches of golden
grain. What he thought of scenes now beautiful
beyond all others to our eyes, though then deemed
'horrid,' we cannot know; doubtless he was not in
advance of his age in admiration of landscape.
Taking boat from Kinlochmoidart he probably
landed under the blackened shell of Clanranald's
Castle Tirrim, burned by the chief's own orders
when he left home in 1715. Long it had resisted
the galleys of the Campbells of Argyll : now it was,
as to-day it is, a frowning ruin, looking across the
sea-strait of Loch Moidart to Eilean Shona. Thence
a march of less than two miles up the Shiel would
bring Charles to his boat on the long narrow fresh-
water lake, Loch Shiel, which centuries ago had

barred the northward march of the Reformation. Thus advancing from the little grey house of Kinlochmoidart, where 'the Prince's avenue' hard by the old home may still be seen, Charles kept tryst at Glenfinnan beneath the clustered mountain peaks, on August 19. There his statue, on a tall column, raised by a Glenaladale of later days, still looks southward, still gazes towards the throne.

What did the English Government know of the events between the winning of Clanranald, about August 4, and the raising of the standard on August 19? On this head the information of Murray of Broughton is confirmed by letters of Craigie, the Lord Advocate. The Government, as we saw, had captured Maclean of Dowart, in June, and, guided by a note in his possession, had tried to lay hands on the Duke of Perth. The Duke escaped cleverly from Campbell of Inverawe (later the hero of the ghost story of Ticonderoga), who, by a rather disloyal stratagem, arrived as his guest at dinner, and then sought to seize him. The Duke fled northwards, and was trying to make his way to France, but came into the Cause on hearing, from Kinlochmoidart, of the Prince's arrival. At the same time, on a Saturday late in July, a message reached Murray of Broughton. He at once secured the safety of the printed Proclamations which he had in readiness, and joined Macdonald of Kinlochmoidart at the house of Buchanan of Arnprior, later hanged. Murray makes a great merit of not betraying the gentleman who aided him in these measures, and in getting French gold changed for English guineas. He now devised a very ingenious blind, which took in, or perplexed, the Government.

James Mor Macgregor, son of Rob Roy, was a spy in Government service, and had just been in Edinburgh with the Lord Advocate and Sir John Cope, commanding the forces in Scotland. James's business, then, was to track the fugitive Duke of Perth, but Murray finding James 'far from unsusceptable of flattery,' secured his aid in a clever combination. James Mor went to Edinburgh, to see the Lord Advocate, with the following news. He had heard at home that Charles was landed at Arisaig. He had then consulted the Duke of Perth's factor, who was better informed. Charles, he learned, was really lying incognito at St. Omer in Flanders : only young Glengarry and Æneas Macdonald had landed. James Mor himself promised, if permitted, that he would draw men from the garrisons of Fort William and Fort Augustus, and, with their aid, would seize old Glengarry and Lochiel. By thus weakening the garrisons on a false pretence, he hoped to take the forts. He gave his false news to the Lord Advocate and, thenceforward, while the Rising lasted, showed as much courage in the Jacobite cause as, later, he was to display treachery, for Rob Roy's son was a double spy, though a dauntless warrior.[1]

Murray himself now joined Charles at Kinloch-moidart (August 18), was presently appointed his secretary, and, while displaying great resource and energy, disgusted the jealous chiefs and lords of the party. They reckoned him, Kelly, Sullivan, and others among 'little people,' and 'favourites.'

James Mor's false news was accepted at first by Craigie, the Lord Advocate, and probably secured a few days of delay. Meanwhile the unlucky Sir John Cope had really been showing more energy and intelligence than most of the English party. His character has suffered because of his defeat, and under the handling of tradition, and satirical ballads. Yet the evidence given at his Trial, too much neglected by historians, but cited by Robert Watson, editor of the 'Memoirs of the Chevalier Johnstone' (1822), and, recently, by the late General Sir Robert Cadell (in his 'Sir John Cope') clears, in part, the character of the General. He was for long trammelled by the distant English Government of the vacillating Duke of Newcastle, and his pre-parations were postponed and thwarted. George II. and his son, the Duke of Cumberland, were abroad with the Army. Stair, Argyll, and Tweeddale

---

[1] He turned informer in 1754, but his revelations were almost wholly apocryphal. See *Pickle the Spy*, chap. x.

managed Scottish affairs, and Argyll was on bad
terms with Tweeddale, the Secretary of State. In
Edinburgh the managers were the Lord President,
Forbes of Culloden; the Lord Justice Clerk (Lord
Milton); Craigie, the Lord Advocate; and Grant of
Preston Grange, then the Solicitor-General.

These officials Cope was bound to consult, and
little good came of the system. Of troops he had
but 3,000 men, including Gardiner's and Hamilton's
dragoons; all the forces being scattered in small
detachments, while the horses of the dragoons were
out at grass. It was in July that Cope heard from
Forbes a report that Charles was about to land. He
wrote to Tweeddale for a supply of arms for Whig
clans, but received none till August. By July 9
Cope was calling in his scattered parties, and wished
to call in absent officers, but was chidden for needless
alarm. However, by August 1 Newcastle wrote to
Argyll, informing him that the King had authentic
news of the French resolution to invade.

This was premature intelligence. Charles, in fact,
when leaving France, had bidden the Earl Marischal
to bestir himself at the French Court, and demand
aid, and the Marischal was doing his best. He acted
reluctantly, as he absolutely disapproved of the
adventure. He was helped, or hindered, by Lord
Clancarty, an Irish peer of slovenly appearance, who
had lost an eye in a singular affray. Braddock, later

noted for his defeat and death in America, had thrown a bottle at Clancarty's head, in a tavern brawl, and had bereaved him of one eye. If we may trust the spy, Oliver Macallester, when the Earl and Clancarty approached the French minister, d'Argenson, at the camp in Flanders, d'Argenson offered Clancarty the not superfluous services of his perruquier. France could get no *signed* appeal from the English Jacobites: so old a suitor as the Earl Marischal was little regarded, the one-eyed Clancarty did not inspire confidence. This we learn from the memoirs of d'Argenson, the French minister. He was beset by foolish female Jacobites like Madame de Mézières, one of the sisters of General Oglethorpe, and by Irish adventurers who wanted to borrow money. The French ministers wished for better security, yet the opportunity, for France, was good. Newcastle assured Argyll that he had made little progress in getting together a strong Channel Squadron, and Cumberland had only now been asked to select reinforcements for England from the army abroad. Now too (August 1) Newcastle had intelligence of the Prince's departure for Scotland. For all these reasons Cope was bidden to call in his isolated detachments, and to take the horses of the dragoons up from grass. Yet more than a fortnight passed, and left Tweeddale, in London, still uncertain as to whether the Prince had landed or not! These facts prove that Charles had chosen his opportunity well, save for the one circumstance that harvest was at hand, and his Highlanders would assuredly desert to get in their oats,—as they did in great numbers.

Meanwhile Cope had not been idle. In July he rode to Aberdeen, whence he sent Guise's regiment of foot to garrison Fort George, Fort Augustus, and Fort William. He asked for artillery, and money ; of which he got little (he had but one trained artillery-man !), and he sounded Argyll as to arming his great clan. But the Duke would not act except by open permission from Government, which was not forth-coming. He was not, of course, the Argyll of Mal-plaquet and Sheriffmuir, as Mr. Ewald alleges. That nobleman had died in 1743 and was now succeeded by his brother, the Earl of Islay. The Whig clans, the Campbells, Grants, Munroes, Macleods (as far as they followed their chiefs), and Mackays, had obeyed the law of disarming : the Jacobite clans, on the other hand, had often retained and concealed their best muskets, targets, and claymores. The Whig clans were of little service to Government, for they were not fully trusted. By August 9, however, Forbes had accurate information of the Prince's arrival, and, after a conversation with Cope, he rode north to Culloden. He was a man of remarkable merit, and really watched over the chiefs as a father, foreseeing their ruin. Honest, learned, and kind, he was an excellent golfer, and the most hospitable of hosts. He did inestimable service by encouraging the Whigs, and by keeping Sleat and Macleod firm, while he practically paralysed his cunning neighbour, Lovat. He was less successful with Cluny Macpherson, then an officer in King George's service. Cluny, on August 19, warned Forbes that the advancing High-landers would burn and ruin his lands and cattle if his clan did not join them. The famous ' fiery cross,' now sent round, was really a ' symbol letter,' and meant that the huts would be burned, and the cattle houghed, of all who did not join the Standard.

This was the ancient Highland method, and very many of Charles's army were thus ' forced out,' as they pleaded at their trials, when all was ended. The majority, especially the Mackenzies, Rosses, and Atholl men, were most reluctant to fight, and many ' Volunteers ' were dragged from home and carried, bound hand and foot, to their regiments. So, at least, they alleged at their trials. Cluny, foreseeing these operations, urged Cope to march north, and Cope tried to secure the support of the Whig clans on his route. Atholl (James, the Whig Duke), younger brother of the Jacobite Tullibardine, ap-pointed his other brother, a natural soldier, Lord George Murray, as Sheriff depute, to aid Cope. But, as we shall see, both Cluny and Lord George were soon to join the Prince, whom, early in August, they were opposing. The Atholl Stewarts were, in truth, most reluctant to engage on either side, and their conduct, like that of the Grants, was to prove how vain were Cope's expectations of aid from clans whose chiefs were good Whigs. Meanwhile Cope's supplies of food and money were not ready till the very day of the raising of the Standard. Even before that great day in Glenfinnan, Macdonald of Tiendrish, with the MacUlrigs (a sept of Galloway Kennedys settled, at some unknown date, in Glengarry's country), had taken two companies of Royal Scots, near Spean Bridge, on their march from Perth to Fort William. Murray, who was then carrying letters from Charles, came across the tail of this skirmish as he approached the river Lochy, now so well known for its salmon fishing. Captain Scott, of the defeated party, was wounded, was kindly treated at Lochiel's house of Achnacarry, and was thence sent to the care of the surgeon of the English garrison at Fort William (August 16). His horse was presented by Tiendrish to the Prince.

The Raising of the Standard preceded, by two or three days, the setting forth of Cope from Crieff (August 22). It was the exile Tullibardine who raised the Standard, but as to what that Standard really was like, and as to its motto, if motto there was, evidence is discrepant and uncertain. Round the flag gathered six hundred men, under Clanranald and Keppoch ; and, later in the day, Lochiel brought in seven hundred Camerons, of whom he soon dismissed 150 for lack of arms. The celebrated Miss Jenny Cameron was present, and, for some unknown reason, the English believed that this lady, buxom but no longer young, was Charles's mistress, and accompanied him on his march. Miss Sophia Western, we know, was mistaken for Miss Jenny, at Upton, but the Highland lady was not really an Amazon. Her history is a mass of confusion, increased by a ' sculduddery' novel about her adventures, written by a Whig minister of low tastes. Her home was in Morvern, and lilies of her sowing still bloom at Acharn on Loch Ari Innes, near the beautiful Loch Aline : so tradition avers.

Charles addressed his little company in a speech which few of them were able to understand. They tossed their bonnets in the air, however, with great enthusiasm. He sent messengers bidding the Stewarts of Appin, with the Macdonnells of Glengarry and the Glencoe clan, to join him on his march ' to Fort Augustus.' He was at Kinlochiel on August 22, and there learned that Cope was also advancing on Fort Augustus, by way of Dalwhinnie. For want of transport Charles was obliged to bury twelve out of his twenty swivel guns. A Captain Swetenham, a prisoner, had been set free by Charles, had made his way to Cope, at Dalnacardoch, a little north of Blair

Atholl, and had informed him of the twenty swivels
in the Highland army. This report had some effect
on Cope's movements. It was at Kinlochiel that
Charles heard of the Government offer of 30,000*l.* for
his head. He replied in a proclamation denouncing
'a practice so unusual among Christian princes,' and,
'while abhorring and detesting it,' was compelled by
his followers to set a similar price on the head of the
Elector of Hanover. 'Should any fatal accident
happen from hence, let the blame be entirely at the
door of those who first set the infamous example.' He
was anxious to offer only 30*l.*, some say half a crown,
but was overruled. The reward really endangered
Charles, for it is said that fanatics and assassins were
not wanting, who endeavoured to earn the money.
On the other hand, Charles, though exposed, as his
father had been, to poison and the dagger, was
always most chivalrous in his refusal to countenance
such attempts by his own partisans, even when Lochgarry, after Culloden, proposed to lay an ambush
for the Duke of Cumberland. George Kelly also
denounced all such measures.

It was not till August 26 that Charles marched to
Invergarry Castle, the seat of Old Glengarry. Here
he was received by young Æneas Macdonnell, a lad
of nineteen, whose father, Old Glengarry, had actually
been visiting Cope at Crieff. Sir John Cope's force,
now on the march, consisted of only about 1,500 foot.

At Crieff he was met by the Duke of Atholl, by Old Glengarry—loyal and apologetic—and by Lord George Murray, sheriff depute. Lord George had been out in the affair of 1719, and had been pardoned. His conduct at this juncture was truly strange. Atholl himself could do nothing : his tenants had been alarmed by Cameron of Glennevis, with threats of fire and sword. Many of them were attached, more or less, to his exiled elder brother, Tullibardine, now with the Prince. Moreover, Cope could not or would not pay the Atholl men whom he wished to join him. Presently the Duke left Blair Atholl for the South, and Lord George Murray, who stayed behind, was soon to go over to the Prince's side. Little comfort did Cope get at Crieff. None of the looked-for Whig clans, such as the Breadalbane Campbells, came in ; and, if he could have acted on his own judgment, so he declared, Cope would have stopped in his march. Now to advance northward was more than rash, considering Cope's small force and total lack of trained artillerymen, unless the clans of the Whig chiefs joined his army. But join they would not. A soldier of genius and decision would probably have now fallen back on Stirling, and there let Forth 'bridle the wild Highlandman.' But Cope 'had only his orders,' and he obeyed them. If he had any discretionary power (which Sir Robert Cadell denies) he did not exert it. Naturally Lord George Murray did not supply the transport which he is said to have promised. The drivers carried off two hundred of Cope's horses on August 24. His Highlanders of the Black Watch, and of Lord Loudon's regiment, with some Atholl men, deserted. Swetenham, next day, described the twenty guns which would line the long pass of Corryarrack, between Garvamore and Fort Augustus. While Charles, on August 26th, was being joined by the Appin men, and, on the 27th, by the men of Glengarry and Glencoe, and Grants of Glen Moriston, Cope, with his wasting army, found himself at the high bleak scalp of the Dalwhinnie country. Charles, at Aberchalder, lay far nearer than he to the perilous pass of Corryarrack, over which, on Cope's side, Wade's road climbed in a series of seven zigzags. At Dalwhinnie Cope received a letter from Forbes dissuading him from marching by Corryarrack to Fort Augustus. On the 27th he called a council of war. They decided that the pass was impracticable ; they believed it, erroneously, to be already occupied, and swept by artillery. Their information was bad.

What Cope ought now to have done a civilian must not pretend to decide. His initial error lay in moving north, after his experience at Crieff. His general orders to move forward ought not, probably, to have constrained him in this juncture. His recent apologist, Sir Robert Cadell, defends Cope both

I

against the criticism of Murray of Broughton and
Sir Walter Scott, and against the contemporary
opinion of officers in London.   They, according
to Tweeddale, writing from London to Forbes
(September 10), held that Cope should have 'stayed
somewhere near Dalwhinnie.'   This was also Murray's
view : 'had he encamped upon the plain about two
miles south of Dalwhinnie, he would have difficulted
the Chevalier very much, for by this means it would
have been almost impossible to bring him' (Cope)
'to an action, which was what the Chevalier wished
for, except upon very advantageous terms, and he had
Atholl in his rear, from whence to draw provisions,
whereas the Chevalier had no bread for his people, nor
was it in his power to procure any.'   But Sir Robert
Cadell seems to have considered, unlike Murray,
that Cope could not have detained 'more numerous
and more agile enemies,' who had the sympathy
of the country people, and that he would soon have
been starved out.   Neither army, it seems, had food
for three days, and it does not appear how Cope could
have drawn supplies from Atholl, where the natives
were apt to exclaim 'A plague on both your houses !'

On the whole, in this pinch, perhaps Cope's
decision to march on Inverness was the best for himself that he could have made.   First, he could tell
himself that it was in accordance with his orders 'to
secure the chain of fortresses across the Highlands,'

though he did not do so, and though the invading clans were already south of the chain. Next, he could argue that friendly clans would join him at Inverness, though he might have guessed that the Macphersons and Grants would be as backward as the Atholl Stewarts and Breadalbane Campbells had proved to be at Crieff. Indeed by going to Inverness he permitted the Camerons to capture and cajole Cluny, who was taken prisoner, probably by a kind of military fiction, and who joined the Clans. The best that can be said for Cope is that all possible plans were dangerous, and that, at least, he preserved his little force intact, even if, for weeks, it could hardly be reckoned an army 'in being.' Moreover, the Prince's force would have beaten him wherever they met him. He moved on Inverness, leaving Cluny behind him, to yield to what he called 'the soothing close applications' of the Prince ; and he was disappointed in the Grants, who stayed at home to look after Castle Grant.

Charles, for his part, on August 28 sent forward Murray and Lochgarry to reconnoitre Corryarrack, which, in Cope's erroneous opinion, they had *already* occupied with artillery. Lochgarry and Murray found nobody but a few deserters. Cope had sent them on to make a show of advancing, and divert attention from his evasive march by Ruthven, towards Inverness. They had orders to wheel about later and move on the fortalice of Ruthven, but they preferred to join the Jacobites. Charles was disappointed; he had expected to fight Cope 'before taking off his brogues that night,' but he advanced to Garvamore, where his men rested and dined on newly slain cattle. It was proposed to follow Cope, but Charles deemed this impracticable, and an assault by a small party on Ruthven barrack was beaten off by a brave Irish sergeant, Molloy, who held the little post, and, as he said in a humorous letter, gave the assailants 'bloody noses.' On August 29 Cope reached Inverness, while on August 30 Charles was at Dalnacardoch, six miles from Blair Atholl. All the most rugged part of his march was now behind him, and a fertile land was in front. Killiecrankie was not occupied by the enemy, and before the Prince lay the wide Strath Tay, comfortable quarters at the castle of the Duke of Atholl, and abundance of provisions.

Cope's strategy had served the Prince to a wish, and though perhaps Cope had really no choice in the matter, his conduct was equally condemned by the military critics of either party. It may be urged, in his defence, that he probably expected the Prince to follow him north, and so to allow time for English reinforcements to reach the south of Scotland. Had the chiefs carried their point at Garvamore, Charles would have been obliged to follow the English General, but he and Tullibardine were rightly anxious to overrun Atholl, and occupy Edinburgh. It is Murray's opinion that, once arrived in Inverness, Cope ought to have remained in the North, when Charles would have been obliged to return and fight him. Thus whatever Cope did was wrong; such is the fortune of an unsuccessful general.

It was on August 31 that the Prince occupied Blair Atholl Castle, a place then of great strength but now denuded of its battlements. The Whig Duke, James, had retired, leaving his commissary, Mr. Bissatt, a strenuous Whig, and useful source of intelligence to the English. Murray describes the joy with which the tenantry received their rightful lord, Tullibardine, the Jacobite Duke William, an exile since 1715. 'Men, women, and children came running from their houses, kissing and caressing their master, whom they had not seen for thirty years before, an instance of the strongest affection, and which could not fail to move every generous mind with a mixture of grief and joy.' The affection did not carry the tenants far as volunteers: perhaps in no district were followers so backward, and deserters so numerous, though, when it came to fighting, the Atholl men were as good as the rest of the army. That army Bissatt described as 2,000 of 'the poorest naked creatures, ill armed.' He thought that the Prince 'hath not very much in him,' though 'good-natured.

Charles here saw two things which were novelties

to him, pineapples (a fact which somehow reached
Horace Walpole's ears) and a bowling-green. Bowls
had been sent to him at Rome, where bowling-greens,
however, did not exist. The honours of the house
were done by Lady Lude, wife of the Laird of Lude—
'a giglet,' says Bissatt. Most of the Atholl gentry,
such as Ballechin, stood for the White Rose. When
music was played, the Prince called for 'This is no
my ain house,' one of the best of the genuine contemporary Jacobite songs. Festivities were disturbed
by the rudeness of the Irish Sir John Macdonald,
one of the original 'Seven Men of Moidart.' He
insulted Keppoch, and was regarded as 'drunk or
mad, if not both,' an anticipation of Dickens.

At Blair many recruits of note came in. The
poet soldier, Colonel John Roy Stuart, arrived from
France, and was sent to negotiate with Lovat. That
bad man, a bully, a traitor from of old, vain, sentimental, a braggart, was at odds with the English
Government, who, in 1739, had deprived him of his
command of an Independent Company. When
Charles was at Invergarry, Lovat had, says Murray,
sent in Frazer of Gortuleg, to ask for two commissions previously granted by James to himself.
He asked for a warrant to take Forbes, 'dead or
alive,' but Murray says that he only gave a permit
'to apprehend Forbes's person, and keep him in
safe custody till further orders.' The Frazers, later,

did try a feeble attempt on Culloden House. George Kelly made out a commission for Lovat as Lieutenant General, and a letter to him from James was also forwarded. But Lovat continued to dally, and his correspondence with Forbes, in the 'Culloden Papers,' is a singular proof of his false and tortuous dealings. Cluny had also dallied : his wife, a daughter of Lovat, laid stress on his oath to the English King, taken by him as a captain of an Independent Company. But if Cluny hesitated between what appeared to him as contending duties, when once his mind was made up no chief was more loyal and much-enduring, none braver in battle, none more unlike the would-be Duke of Frazer, the calculating Lovat.

While King George was arriving in England (August 31), while James Mor was capturing the garrison of Inversnaid in the Macgregor country, and while Charles was at Blair, he was joined by Lord Nairne, one of his firmest friends, and by Mercer of Aldie, of a house distinguished in the wars of Jeanne d'Arc. Her page was a Mercer by the mother's side. On September 2 Charles slept at Lude, and took his part in Highland reels. On the 3rd he slept at Old Dunkeld House, and on the 4th dined at Nairne.

Here, when somebody spoke of the probable anxiety of James, in Rome, Charles said that he was yet more sorry for his brother. 'For the King has been inured to disappointments and distresses, and has learned to bear up easily under the misfortunes of life. But poor Harry! His young and tender years make him much to be pitied, for few brothers love as we do.' So writes Duncan Cameron, and here we find Charles as yet unembittered against his father and brother, though both James and Henry suspected that he was, to some extent, alienated. Almost as Charles spoke, at Nairne House, James was confiding (August 30) his anxieties to O'Brien in Paris. For years, he says, certain Englishmen of his Court, notably Strickland and Townley, had been trying to sow discord between Charles and Henry, on the ground of religion. 'The great vivacity of the Prince, his love of all kinds of diversions, and the slight taste for wine which he seemed to have at that time, made them erroneously believe that they had a hold over him, and he instantly became their hero.' This is the earliest hint at the vice which became Charles's ruin. Not to drink freely was then, in England and Scotland, the mark of a milksop: Henry could not be a toper, but, if strictly sober, Charles could not be deemed a hero. Unhappily he carried his popular vice far beyond approval. Henry, being quiet, and not of strong health, nor fond of amusement, was constantly criticised. Strickland's conduct, in sailing with Charles, 'would have been more than enough to have caused trouble between any father and son less attached than we are.' Even Dunbar (Murray, Charles's tutor) was now in James's disgrace, as implicated in these affairs. Meanwhile 'poor Harry' was leaving Rome for Avignon, in hopes of being allowed to join the French expedition, which kept hanging off and on, now promised, now delayed, till the day of Culloden.

While Charles was at Nairne's, Lochiel occupied Perth, and proclaimed the Prince, who entered the town in the evening, at the head of his forces. Five hundred pounds of public money were seized : it is said that, on entering Perth, Charles possessed but one louis d'or. Arms and ammunition were taken from Dundee and other towns. Many notable recruits came in.

First was Lord George Murray, whose motives are obscure. He had, a fortnight earlier, been the ally and informant of Cope. He seems, from the first, to have anticipated failure. Charles, his son, still at Eton, held a commission in Loudon's regiment, and was anxious to fight for King George. Perhaps a conscientious sense of duty to the exiled House moved Lord George : perhaps he was urged by the sight of his elder brother and old companion in arms, Tullibardine. Certainly he never wavered again in his loyalty to the Cause : certainly he played the parts of an adroit general, and daring soldier, sword in hand. But, if we may believe the undoubtedly honest Maxwell of Kirkconnell, Lord George was suspected from the very first by Murray of Broughton, who stood high in the confidence of the Prince. Why, it would be asked, had Lord George first taken office as sheriff on the English side, conferred with Cope, and then come over to Charles? Murray of Broughton, says Maxwell, 'assured the Prince that Lord George had joined on purpose to have an opportunity of delivering him up to the Government. It was hardly possible to guard against this imposture. The Prince had the highest opinion of his Secretary's integrity, and knew little of Lord George Murray. So the calumny had its full effect. Lord George soon came to know the suspicion the Prince had of him, and was affected as one may easily imagine. . . . The Prince was partly undeceived by Lord George's gallant behaviour at the battle' (Prestonpans), . . . 'but Lord George's haughty and overbearing manner prevented a thorough reconciliation, and seconded the malicious insinuations of his rival. . . . Lord George now and then broke into such violent sallies as the Prince could not digest, though the situation of his affairs forced him to bear with them.' The relations between Charles and Lord George were so important, that a digression concerning the evidence may here be permitted.

Maxwell's remarks are corroborated by an astonishing statement in the manuscript 'Memoirs' (*not* 'Journal') of Lord Elcho. This gentleman was the eldest son of Lord Wemyss, and was about the same age as the Prince, whom he had met in Rome.

He was educated at Winchester, not, he says, in the most edifying way, but rather 'with a taste for pleasurable vice,' in the Duke of Wharton's manner. Smollett was not a Winchester man, but, for what it is worth, his account of Peregrine Pickle at Winchester confirms Lord Elcho's opinion of the state of the school. His Lordship's maternal grandfather was the wealthy and infamous Colonel Charteris, one of the few men who have acquired a large fortune by sheer roguery and gambling. This reprobate left much of his wealth (with the condition of bearing the name of Charteris) to Elcho's younger brother. He, not caring to come into the Cause himself, 'for he had great possessions,' presented his elder brother with 1,500 guineas, at the beginning of the enterprise. Elcho joined Charles on the night before he occupied Edinburgh, and lent him this sum of money. It was never repaid, and Elcho, an exile after Culloden, and, despite all his suing for mercy, never pardoned by the English Government, passed a good deal of his time in vainly dunning James and Charles for this 1,500 guineas. James regarded it as no private debt, but money contributed to the Cause ; and very

possibly that was the view of young Charteris himself, when he gave Elcho the gold. The Duke of
Hamilton, if we are to believe Murray, had secretly
subscribed precisely the same sum. As for Charles,
he was perhaps never in a position to satisfy his
creditor, and, probably, would not have paid even if
he had been able. Forbes of Culloden was even
worse used by George II., never being recouped
by a solvent monarch for his great expenditure.
Elcho did not forgive his debtor, and, in old age, he
wrote, in French, 'Memoirs' in which he assiduously
blackens the memory of his Prince.[1]

From Mr. Ewald's 'Life of Prince Charles' the
following statement of Lord Elcho's is quoted.
'Charles' (on September 16) 'received Elcho most
cordially, and appointed him his first aide-de-camp,
at the same time bidding him not take Lord George
Murray into his confidence, as he knew that Lord
George had only joined him to betray him. . . . He
carried his suspicions against Lord George to such
an extent that he employed two Irish officers to
watch his conduct, and to assassinate him should he
ever attempt to betray him.' Elcho was writing in
anger, he was writing, too, long after the events, in

---

[1] These *Memoirs* have never been published; two or three MS.
extracts on the Forty Five exist, but the entire work, which is of
curious interest, remains unprinted, I have read it, but am not at
liberty to make citations. Mr. Ewald, however, was permitted to use
the MS. by the kindness of Mrs. Erskyne Wemyss of Wemyss Castle.

his old age.   An illusion of memory on Lord Elcho's
part might, conceivably, have suggested this extraordinary first confidence of Charles.   But, taken with
Maxwell's evidence, and with Henderson's, who, in
his 'History of the Rebellion' (1748), says that
Tullibardine himself 'signified his distrust' of Lord
George, when he came in, and knelt to him at Perth,
Lord Elcho's story demonstrates that Lord George
was very gravely distrusted.   Lord George himself,
as Maxwell declares, suspected that he was suspected.
A singular and hitherto unnoticed piece of evidence,
to be cited later, corroborates Lord Elcho's story of
Charles's confidences about Lord George.   Again,
when Charles had crossed the Border a strange
rumour ran through the army.   A Highlander was
said to have broken the stick of a wayfarer, in a
quarrel, and to have found wrapped round it a note
to Lord George from his brother, the Whig Duke of
Atholl, advising him, in case of a battle, to desert
with the Atholl regiment, and to betray Charles.
Now, as a matter of fact, the Duke's factor, Mr.
Bissatt, was wont to send secret intelligence rolled up
beneath the leather of the handle of a whip.[1]   This
point is dwelt upon, because Charles's relations with
Lord George greatly harmed both his Cause and
his character.   Lord George, later, insisted on retreat from Derby and from Stirling : Lord George

---

[1] Evidence from privately printed Atholl papers.

abandoned the attempt at a night surprise at Nairn, before Culloden. After that battle, surrounded as he was by Irish enemies of Lord George, and rebuked to the verge of insult by that officer himself, the Prince committed the fatal error of refusing to keep tryst with his army at Ruthven. He would then be reminded, by his Irish friends, of how a Scottish army, at Newcastle, had handed over his great grand-father, Charles I., to death. Later, in France, he treated Lord George, in disobedience to James's commands, with consummate insult. Taught by experience of his party's agents neither to trust nor to be trustworthy, Charles was destined to wreck himself on suspicions of a gentleman who had lost all by his gallant and able service of a forlorn Cause. The Chevalier Johnstone says that, had Charles slept all the way, Lord George might have settled him on the throne. While both were awake, and at strife, success was impossible. Had Lord George been asleep, Charles would probably have advanced from Derby.

In Murray of Broughton's own Memoirs there is little or no trace of his prejudice against Lord George. Perhaps a sneer may be detected when he describes the joy of the Atholl Jacobites on finding that ' for many years ' Lord George's ' behaviour had proceeded from policy, not from principle ; ' that, while appearing to be reconciled to the House of

Hanover, he was ready to fight for that of Stuart. But Murray's Memoirs do not encourage that suspicion of Lord George which wound its way even into the songs of the disappointed Jacobites.[1]

This affair of Lord George Murray is of essential importance, and must never be forgotten by those who would understand the failure of the enterprise, and the character of Charles himself. Manifestly Lord George either had not played fair with Cope and the English Government, or—he meant to play false by Charles. Suspicion was inevitably aroused by Lord George's own action, and then was fostered by Murray and by the Irish officers, such as Sullivan, whom Lord George detested.

Of Sullivan, the Quartermaster-General, whom the Scots regarded as Charles's evil genius, and who, according to Lord George, was only trained to look after the baggage, not much is known. He was certainly employed by Charles till 1759. According to 'The True Patriot' (1745) Sullivan had been educated for the Church, and was in priest's orders. He was tutor in the family of the Marquis de Maillebois, who 'perceived in him some symptoms of a genius better adapted to the sword than to the gown, and encouraged him to apply himself to the former rather than the latter profession.' He accom-

---

[1] In the Townley MSS. a song written in 1745 calls Lord George Murray 'brave.' A marginal note runs 'or rather Traitor.'

panied Maillebois to Corsica, where 'he gained a very
high military reputation, as well as much knowledge
in what is called the art of irregular warfare.' He
afterwards served two campaigns, one in Italy, and
the other on the Rhine ; 'in which latter campaign
a French general, giving a character of him, said that
he understood the irregular art of war better than
any man in Europe, nor was his knowledge in the
regular much inferior to that of the best General.'
This is an estimate of Sullivan very different from
that entertained by Lord George, who was not exempt
from jealousy.

Charles was apt to play practical jokes on Sullivan,
and, at Perth, dragged him out of bed. Yet there
were jealousies, and among these jealousies, whom
was Charles to trust ? No wonder it is that his air of
melancholy was remarked by observers, even in the
triumph of Holyrood. No marvel is it that his confidence in men broke down, as his own character
collapsed under distress and disappointment. In
fact, Lord George remained invincibly loyal to the
Cause, but, none the less, disbelief in his loyalty was
not a mere baseless freak of the mind of the Prince.

Another recruit of mark was the Duke of Perth,
who, as we saw, had narrowly escaped from the treacherous trap set for him in his own house by Campbell
of Inverawe. The Duke was grandson of James,
fourth Earl of Perth, who followed James II. into

exile, and from him received his ducal title. He was
the brother of that Lord John Drummond, in French
service, who had quarrelled with Sir Hector Maclean
of Dowart, just before the chief returned to Scotland
in June and was arrested. Perth was a very honourable and loyal man, an ardent adherent of the Stuarts,
brave, liberal, kindly, but not gifted with much genius
for politics or war. Having been brought up in
France, he spoke English ill, and, says Murray, had
' an overfondness to speak broad Scots.' He was
prolix, ' rather overtedious in his discourses but of
undaunted courage ; the most exemplary, humanely,
and universally beloved.' Later Lord George became not unnaturally jealous of the Duke's position
as virtually his superior officer (at one time they
commanded on alternate days), but Perth honourably
withdrew from the coveted eminence. With Perth
came in the Oliphants of Gask, father and son, whose
lands for many centuries had been held on the tenure
of a yearly gift of White Roses. Both gentlemen set
one of those examples of courage in war, and patience
in poverty and exile, which give the real element of
noble romance to the enterprise of the Prince. But
Lowland lairds could no longer raise their Presbyterian tenants for either Cause. On the Whig side
Lord Home brought in but a few servants, in place
of the army whom his ancestors had led to Flodden.
It is matter of family tradition that Charles, march-

K

ing through Gask's country, saw the heavy harvest
hanging uncut, and asked the reason. Being told
that, as his men would not follow him, Gask had
inhibited them from cutting their corn, Charles drew
his sword, topped a few ears, and declared that the
prohibition was now removed. It was a graceful
act, and we may hope that tradition here speaks
sooth. But a long and interesting letter of Charles
to James, dated 'Perth, September 10,' and published
by Mr. Ewald and others, is not genuine, being a mere
manuscript pamphlet, perhaps by Kelly or Sheridan.

Lord Strathallan also came in, the fourth Viscount,
destined to fall gloriously at Culloden ; and Lord
Ogilvie, who finally escaped, and obtained a French
regiment. Less noted, though notable, was Johnstone, son of an Edinburgh tradesman of good family ;
his sister had married the son of Lord Rollo, as, in
his 'Memoirs,' he often lets us know. The Misses
Rollo introduced him to Perth, and to Lord George,
for whom he acted as aide-de-camp. His 'Memoirs,'
written in French, were partly translated, and edited,
in 1822, by that extraordinary adventurer, Robert
Watson, who added Whiggish notes. A dissatisfied
man, Johnstone wrote with spleen, and often he
merely romances, but he had literary talents, as he
proved in his accounts both of the Forty Five, and of
the Canadian campaign of Wolfe. He himself was,
in that war, the aide-de-camp of the brave Montcalm.

While Lord George drilled his men, at Perth, in such style as to improve without confusing their natural mode of warfare, while he saw to the commissariat, providing 'pokes' or bags, in which each soldier could carry bannocks, O'Sullivan was made Quartermaster-General, and the 'drunk, or mad, or both' Sir John Macdonald trained such cavalry as the Lowland lairds could equip. A few Glengyle Macgregors came in, and a hundred or two men of Robertson of Struan's, the old Jacobite poet, 'In verse Apollo, and a Mars in war,' whose ancestor arrested the murderers of James I. of Scotland. The friend of Fénelon, the pious, mystical, and kind old Lord Pitsligo, a veteran of 1715, announced his intention of joining, as soon as Cope left the north.

Thus, at Perth, the Prince, who visited Scone where so many of his ancestors had been crowned, began to find himself indeed at home, and encircled by chiefs of ancient names, whose forefathers for many centuries had been the trusted servants of his House. Not only the Celtic Fergus MacIvors, but the Lowland Bradwardines were now ranged beneath his standard. Of the Celts, a few were to betray him, or try to do so, men like James Mor, Barisdale, the truculent tyrant of Knoydart, Æneas Macdonald who, when a prisoner, gave information, and others better forgotten, though, in some cases, not forgotten by Highland memories. But, of all the Lowlanders,

only one man failed in the hour of trial : the fluent
and energetic coward, Murray of Broughton.   It is
not from Murray's own work, but from his so-called
'Genuine' but really apocryphal 'Memoirs,' that we
hear of Charles's personal charm, his wearing of the
Highland dress, his plunging foremost into fords
(vouched for by the 'Caledonian Mercury'), and
generally of all that Charles probably did to win the
hearts of the Clans.   From September 4 to 10 Charles
was employed at Perth.   But he was obliged to hurry
onwards.   Lovat had warned Lochiel of the danger
involved in leaving Cope 'hanging at your tail with
3,000 men,' really some 1,600, counting 200 doubtful
recruits from the Munroes, who soon went home
again.

On September 4 Cope set out for Aberdeen,
whither he had ordered transports to be sent.   On
September 11 he reached Aberdeen, and Charles
reached Dunblane.   It was a race for Edinburgh, but,
as Cope returned by sea from Aberdeen, Charles
won easily.   He had again resisted the proposal to
march north against Cope.   He might have been
met on the Spey, or decoyed to Inverness, and probably many of his men would have returned to their
crofts.   On the 13th (if the Jacobite newspaper, the
'Caledonian Mercury,' may be credited) he plunged
first into the Forth, at the Fords of Frew, unharmed
by the iron crows' feet or calthrops, which the enemy

had thrown into the river. Gardiner's dragoons now fell back on Linlithgow. Charles himself expressed his amazement at the desertion of this important ford. Gardiner had but 350 dragoons, and was in the worst of health. He is described by Dr. Carlyle as weak, ill-educated, and a fanatic, fond of boasting of his own conversion. While waiting at a tryst with a married woman, in his youth, he read a book of religion, and, with or without a marvellous vision, became an altered man. His biographer, Doddridge, reports the vision, Carlyle says that the Colonel told the story without it.

Probably Gardiner might have harassed the Highlanders on the march, but, in fact, he wore out both the strength and spirits of his men by a series of sudden retreats, which culminated in mere flight and rout. Himself the bravest of men, his conduct certainly demoralised his little force.

About this time a mysterious event of evil omen occurred. A Mr. Buchanan, of Arnprior, had been dimly connected with Jacobite affairs, and was useful as treasurer in a subterranean sort of way. To his house, Leny, near Callander, on his way to join the Prince, came Stewart of Glenbuckie. Next morning Glenbuckie was found dead in bed, a pistol in his hand, and it was said that he and his host had disputed about the Majorship in Perth's regiment. His men carried home the dead body of their chief, and

did not return. Arnprior was later hanged, on slender
evidence, at Carlisle. He took no overt part in the
Rising, with which he was undoubtedly connected.
In the manuscript Journal of Professor Mackie (kindly
lent to me by Mr. D. Stewart), Arnprior is described
as 'an execrable villain, who had committed many
notorious crimes.' Probably the death of Glenbuckie
was regarded as a murder, though it may have been
suicide or merely accidental. Arnprior, before his
death, made a solemn denial of the deed.

The Highland army, moving south, camped near
the old House of Touch, the home of the ancient and
loyal House of Seton, now Seton-Stuart. Here the
sheets in which the Prince slept are piously preserved.
Next day Charles marched past Stirling, fired on by
the guns of the castle, and dined with Sir Hugh
Paterson at Bannockburn. He was close to the
scene of his ancestor's crowning victory over England,
but he may have been more interested in the dark
eyes of Sir Hugh's niece, Clementina Walkinshaw,
though it is probable that they did not meet at
Bannockburn House till the spring of 1746. From
Bannockburn House, the Prince went after dinner to
Lord Kilmarnock's house of Callander. Here he
met Lord Kilmarnock, who had been dining at the
mess of the dragoon officers at Linlithgow. Charles
thus learned that the dragoons were still at that
ancient palace of his ancestors, the birthplace of Mary

Stuart. According to Murray, Charles himself led a detachment to surprise Gardiner's force, but got information that they had retired to the Kirkliston burn, nearer Edinburgh. Lord George Murray, however, says that it was *he* who led 1,000 men through the night : he does not mention the Prince. Linlithgow was occupied on the morning of Sunday, September 15 : Charles in vain invited the magistrates to let public worship go on as usual : the minister declined to preach. The Glencoe Macdonalds here insisted that they, and no others, should guard Newliston, the house of Lord Stair, grandson of the author of the massacre of Glencoe. The chief declared that he would withdraw the clan if his request was not granted. He was of a chivalrous temper, but what an army was that in which clans could always carry a point by threatening to desert ! Charles later, in natural indignation, told his officers that, of all the force, he alone could not use this argument.

In the afternoon the army marched to a place near the twelfth milestone from Edinburgh: not that Scottish roads were graced with milestones in 1745. Next day Gardiner's men again retreated to Colt's Bridge, and Charles advanced to Corstorphine, within three miles of Edinburgh town, and so to Gray's Mill, whence he sent a summons to surrender the city.

Meanwhile, what was going on in Edinburgh ?

Alas! the state of that capital could best be represented by the methods of comic opera. The mob was Jacobite, merely because that attitude was 'against the Government.' The ladies, too, were, as a rule, Jacobite from sentiment, and because the Prince was a handsome young man; and Jacobite were the Episcopalians, the victims of some sixty years of Presbyterian persecution. Many of the Advocates and of the other gentry were, at least, in sympathy with the Cause, partly from ancestral tradition; mainly because they still detested the Union, as the ruin of Scottish independence. Yet several of the young men, such as Home, the author of 'Douglas,' and Carlyle ('Jupiter Carlyle'), were enthusiastic and daring Whigs. They were leaders of the young 'liberal,' card-playing Presbyterian clergy. Home, in old age, wrote his History, Carlyle penned his amusing Memoirs, both are good authorities for the events of the time. On one point the new Liberal clergy and the 'Wild' or 'High-flying' Calvinists of the older school were agreed: they were irreconcilably hostile to the White Rose.

Meanwhile the Castle, with its guns, and a garrison of 600 men under the aged and invalid General Guest, was safe enough. Hamilton's dragoons, at Leith, might join Gardiner's heroes of a dozen flights, and might combine with a volunteer force. They might thus make a stand outside the town, which, with its ricketty old Flodden wall, in part occupied by houses commanded by higher houses outside, was assuredly not defensible. On that point Murray's evidence leaves no doubt, and the 'offensive defensive,' an attack by Volunteers and dragoons on the Highland army at Gray's Mill, was the only practicable form of resistance. It seems highly improbable, at least, that the Highlanders could have been held at bay from behind the walls till Cope arrived, and the consequences of a capture by storm were too terrible to be risked. Therefore the jury which, later, tried and acquitted Provost Stuart (just as Cope was tried and acquitted), probably gave a just verdict. Murray demonstrates the impossibility that a perfectly raw and unofficered rabble of Volunteers should have held walls weak and of wide extent, and accessible to the besiegers from the old collegiate church of the Trinity, built by Mary of Gueldres about 1462, and now destroyed in the interests of a railway station.

But why were the hardy and eager Whigs of town and country left untrained, and untaught in arms? The answer is that, precisely as distrust ruined the adventure of Prince Charles, so distrust and official 'red tape' did their best to ruin the cause of King George. For a month Lord Milton had been imploring Tweeddale to sanction the raising and arming of regiments, paid or unpaid. Letters took from three to six days on the road between Edinburgh and

clashed their swords; but the mothers, wives, aunts, sisters, and cousins of the Volunteers fell weeping on their necks. Fathers and uncles proffered arguments (with entire justice) against the desperate resolution of their dear ones, and finally the dragoons rode forward alone to victory and honourable graves. The Volunteers did not follow. In fact the Minister himself, Dr. Wishart, Principal of the Town's College, with 'several other clergymen' (it is a pity that the Church should meddle with these matters), had arrived on the scene, and 'conjured the Volunteers, by whatever they held most sacred,' to stay at home. Drummond tried to make Stuart responsible for the acceptance, or refusal, of the counsels of the Kirk. Stuart said he was glad to hear that the men did not mean to go out, and bade the Town Guard and the 'Edinburgh Regiment' join the dragoons. Home's friends, resolute fellows, 'went to a tavern, where they unbosomed themselves.' Dr. Carlyle adds a few details as to the unbosoming and the general behaviour of the Volunteers. While they stood in the Lawn Market, 'in one house on the south of the street there was a row of windows, full of ladies, who appeared to enjoy our march to danger with much levity and mirth. Some of our warm Volunteers observed them, and threatened to fire into the windows if they were not instantly let down, which was immediately complied with.' Such was the valour of this absurd company.

As they marched 'down the sanctified bends of the Bow,' a young militant minister, the Rev. Mr. Kinloch, said to Hew Ballantine, 'Mr. Hew, Mr. Hew, does not this remind you of a passage in Livy, when the Gens Fabia marched out of Rome to prevent the Gauls entering the city? . . . You must recollect the end, Mr. Hew, *Omnes ad unum periere*—" they perished to a man." ' The listeners laughed, and Ballantine bid Kinloch sneak away if he was afraid.

The 'unbosoming' mentioned by Home took place among twelve or thirteen of the boldest, over supper, at Luckie Turnbull's tavern, adjacent to the Tron Kirk. After 'a warm altercation' they decided to get recruits next day, if possible, and, if not, to restore their arms to the Castle and then offer their services to Cope. Scott learned from one of these devoted men, probably old Dr. Carlyle, particulars of their expedition through East Lothian. They drank success to the Protestant cause at every alehouse of reputation. Two were surrounded and captured, over their oysters and sherry (a horrid mixture), by a Jacobite writer's apprentice. A less humorous but more probable account of this incident is, however, given on better evidence. The narrator of the more amusing anecdote, with a friend, finished the Madeira at his father's house, and was called by the maid, just in time to see Elcho, Sir Henry Threipland, and two or three other gentlemen with their grooms, 'the whole cavalry of the Highland army,' chasing Cope's routed regulars off the field of Prestonpans. Home, however, as we shall see, carried good information to Cope, before the battle.

It is needless to report, in detail, all the confused scufflings of the contending authorities at Edinburgh on Monday, September 16. Outside the town, Gardiner's dragoons were in a mournful state of fatigue, their legs so swollen that they could not wear boots, while Hamilton's fresher body needed food. Brigadier Fowke was ready to advance if a supply of boiled beef (which was sent) recruited the spirits of his men, but Guest ordered the dragoons to fall back, so as to be ready to join Cope on his arrival by sea. About 10, a Mr. Alves, a writer to the Signet, informed Stuart that he, while riding into Edinburgh, had met the Duke of Perth, who sent a message to this effect : If the townsmen would keep their arms and grant peaceful admission, they would be civilly dealt with, if not, they must look for 'military execution.' Perth had asked the Prince if this was not his will, and the Prince seemed to assent. The Provost said that the message was 'extraordinary,' and it was one of the chief charges against him at his trial, that he did not at once commit Alves. By his version he consulted the Town Council and then the Lord Advocate, but, in any case, Alves had spread his tale before he was arrested. The Lord

Advocate gave a different version at Stuart's trial. He himself was making out a warrant to commit Alves, when the Lord Justice Clerk sent for and rebuked the Provost, and Alves was then put into custody. Sir Robert Cadell argues that Stuart should also have been arrested. It is enough to say that Stuart was unanimously acquitted of all charges by a substantial jury.

Out in the country, Fowke received Guest's order to withdraw the cavalry, but sent a party to reconnoitre. Gardiner feared that 'His Majesty would lose two regiments of dragoons.' His reconnoitring patrol had been met by a few horsemen of the Prince, who galloped up and let off their pistols, the advanced men of Fowke retired, a retreat was ordered, and it degenerated into the famous 'Canter of Colt Bridge. Most of the City Guard, 'notorious pimps,' according to Henderson, who was present, retired with speed, while the dragoons were visible from the town as they galloped off in disorder along the ground which is now occupied by George Street. They made for Musselburgh in a demoralised condition. Instantly the town was full of clamour and mob. The multitude, meeting Stuart, implored him to surrender. He reproved them, and met the magistrates at the Goldsmiths' Hall. They sent for the Justice Clerk Lord Milton, but he had retired to Brunstane 'to put some papers out of the way.' Returning he encoun-

tered an excited crowd, who bawled that the Highlanders were entering by the West Port, whereon he
went back to his country house.

The Lord Advocate and the Solicitor-General
were sent for : they too had decamped. Stuart adjourned his meeting to the New Church Aisle, which
was flooded by contending orators, most of them
crying for surrender. At this moment a 'man in
black clothes' met Donald Mackay, a caddie, in the
Luckenbooths, and handed him a letter for the
Provost, saying 'Here is threepence for your pains,
and next time I see you, I'll give you a shilling.'
Donald did see the man in black clothes later, 'and
craved from him his shilling that he had promised
him, but did not get it.' The caddie, in fact, was the
pursuivant by whom the Prince summoned the Provost
to capitulate. The Prince ordered the Provost to
take measures to protect the peace of the city : to
keep out the Usurper's troops, to hold the arms for
his service ; disobedience he would punish as a
heinous offence, and inhabitants found in arms would
not be treated as prisoners of war. They were in
little danger, for the Volunteers had restored their
muskets to the Castle.

When the meeting in the Church found that the
letter brought by Donald Mackay was signed 'Charles
P. R.,' the Provost refused to read it, and retired to
the Goldsmiths' Hall. Here the debate broke out

L

afresh, and Mr. Patrick Haldane, a solicitor, declined
to give an opinion as to the legality of reading such an
epistle. ' Good God,' cried Stuart, ' I am deserted by
my arms and assessors !' Somebody, unnamed, said
that he saw no harm in reading the letter, whereon
it was read aloud by William Henderson, Writer.
After the reading, three Bailies and the Convener
were sent out to wait on Charles. This was about
eight o'clock at night. But instantly came news that
Cope's ships would land his troops at Dunbar, and
march to the relief of the town next day. The Lord
Advocate, from Musselburgh, six miles off, had sent
a zealous Mr. Grosset with this intelligence. Bailie
Mansfield was therefore hurried off to overtake and
bring back the deputation which had gone to see
the Prince. A squabble went on between Guest, in
the Castle, and the Provost, in the Goldsmiths' Hall,
as to whether Guest should return the dangerous
arms of the Volunteers without the Provost's *written*
order. But as Mansfield returned without having
overtaken the deputation, it became clear that the
three Bailies and the Convener might be sacrificed to a
Celtic vengeance if they remained in Charles's camp
while the town resisted him. The City Guard was
presently found to be disguised in drink! The
envoys returned with a mere repetition of Charles's
orders, and a demand for an answer by two on
Tuesday morning. The meeting deliberated till that

hour, and then sent a new deputation to Charles in a
cab. They asked for delay, and induced Lord George
to second them in their application. He was rebuffed,
and ex-Provost Coutts, one of the envoys, declared,
at Stuart's trial, that he heard Charles exclaim, ' My
Lord Elcho, Lord George has not spirit to put this
order into execution ; you must go and do it for him.'
Lord Elcho, therefore, came forth and said, ' Get you
gone.' Lord George followed the envoys out, and
whispered, ' I know your pinch ; you want to have
the consent of your principal inhabitants. Make
haste to town ; you'll have an hour or two to
obtain it.'

Here we have the most undesigned confirmation
of Elcho's story about Charles's distrust of Lord
George. Elcho had only joined that night ; Lord
George had practically acted as General ever since
he came in at Perth. Yet Charles addressed to
his latest recruit a remark highly insulting to Lord
George. It is plain that he then expected his
General to betray him on every occasion. Meanwhile
Lord George was taking pity on the poor envoys,
whose necks were at stake unless they had warrant
for their inevitable surrender from the principal people
in Edinburgh. In later years it was Elcho, not Lord
George, who left Memoirs reviling the Prince.

On the return of the envoys, it was decided to call
the principal inhabitants out of their beds, but it was

too late. The cab, or coach, which had brought back the second deputation, was being driven home to the stable in the Canongate. The Nether Bow Port was opened for its exit; the porter was gripped by Lochiel, and in marched Lochiel, Sullivan, and the Camerons! As soon as the first deputation left Charles's camp, the Prince had ordered Lochiel to move on the town, Murray of Broughton acting as guide. They went round by Merchistoun Castle, heard the patrols call the rounds in Edinburgh Castle, saw the unguarded guns on the city wall, and halted outside the gate of the Nether Bow. Day dawned, and Murray had just proposed to withdraw to St. Leonard's crags : when the gate opened, out came the empty coach, on its way to its stable in the Canongate, and in walked the gentle Lochiel. The Camerons marched to the Cross ; Sullivan posted his guards at the gates ; the people brought provisions for the Highlanders, but, acting on Lochiel's orders, they all declined to take their ' morning,' a dram of whiskey. A citizen, on an early stroll, found a Highlander sitting on a gun. ' You do not belong to yesterday's guard ? ' he said. ' Oh no, she be relieved,' said the Celt. Thus lightly, and luckily, and in the nick of time, did Charles win the capital of his ancestors.

While the burgesses of Edinburgh had been rehearsing ' The Mistakes of a Night ' on a large stage,

with a full company, His Majesty's forces, outside
the beleaguered city, had not been less busy. When
they fled from Coltsbridge, Fowke had intended
them to bivouac at Musselburgh, about six miles east
of Edinburgh, where a resolute force might have held
the passage over the river Esk. But quarters were
not suitable, and Gardiner offered hospitality near his
own house, adjacent to Prestonpans. A dragoon
happened to fall, with a clatter, into a shallow coal
pit, and his comrades stampeded in terror. About
this time, young Carlyle came up, having walked
from Edinburgh. He reported that there was not a
Highlander on the road, yet the dragoons fled towards
Dunbar, strewing the road with pistols, swords, and
other accoutrements. Next morning they joined
Cope's men, who, unable to make the Port of Leith,
by reason of the wind, were landing at Dunbar. They
may have reached Dunbar by ten in the morning of
the 17th, when Charles, avoiding the Castle guns by
marching on the village and lake of Duddingston, on
the east side of Arthur's Seat, came to Holyrood by
the Duke's Walk. He had come home at last, to
'that unhappy palace of his race,' where Riccio was
slain, and where the ruined Chapel and desecrated
graves of Kings spoke of his grandfather's fall.
Home describes the Prince, 'tall and handsome, of a
fair complexion : he had a light-coloured periwig with
his own hair combed over the front : he wore the

Highland dress, that is a tartan short coat without the plaid, a blue bonnet on his head, and on his breast the star of the Order of St. Andrew.' Henderson, who was present, says that Perth rode on his right, Elcho on his left. 'He seemed very thoughtful,' as well he might, thus brought, as by miracle, to the central scene of the tragedy of his race. 'He was a slender young man, about five feet, ten inches high ; of a ruddy complexion, high-nosed, large rolling brown eyes, long visage ; his chin was pointed, and mouth small in proportion to his features ; his hair was red' (a Whig inaccuracy ; it was of a rich brown verging on gold towards the tips), 'but at that time he wore a pale peruke ; he was in Highland dress, with a blue sash wrought with gold coming over his shoulder, red velvet breeches, a green velvet bonnet with a gold lace round it, and a white cockade which was the cross of St. Andrew.' Even the Whigs, says Home, 'acknowledged that he was a goodly person,' but 'languid and melancholy,' rather like a man of fashion than a hero and conqueror. Henderson noted that, for full five minutes, he kept his left eye on Elcho, probably musing on the character of his new adherent.

Having allowed himself to be seen by the curious crowd, he mounted, and rode with singular grace to Holyrood. At this moment, says tradition, a ball from the Castle lit on a turret of Queen Mary's rooms, and brought down a clatter of stones and slates. Be

this as it may, Charles walked to the apartments of
the Duke of Hamilton, where Hepburn of Keith,
with drawn and uplifted sword, ushered him to his
rooms. (So says Home, but Dr. Carlyle declares
that Hepburn's son denied the fact, apparently on
the *a priori* ground that his father was too modest a
man to put himself forward. Mr. Hepburn escaped
unharmed after the end of the Rising, and seems
to have been concerned in the projects of 1752.)
Charles now bowed to the multitude from the open
windows, and then retired to arrange the details of
his father's proclamation. At midday the Heralds
and Pursuivants, surrounded by the Camerons, were
at the Cross, the trumpets blew, and the Declaration
of James VIII. was read, with an appendix signed at
Paris by Charles, on May 16 ; the ladies waved their
handkerchiefs from the windows, and the people
cheered. The beautiful wife of Murray of Broughton,
Margaret Fergusson of Cailloch in Nithsdale, sat on
horseback, with a drawn sword in her hand, distri-
buting white cockades. This lady's later fortunes are
obscure. She was living with her disgraced lord in
1749, after which she is lost to history. There is no
evidence for the legend that she was, at any time, the
mistress of the Prince, and documents do not contain
a trace of proof of the story that she followed Charles
into exile. She had her little hour of highhearted
triumph ; when, fair of face, and flushed with hope

fulfilled, she sat, the centre of the day's rejoicings. Rare are the moments when romance blossoms into reality, when dreams come true, and of these moments one was hers.[1]

On September 18 the Highland army lay in camp near Duddingston; the MacLachlans came in, some 150 men, and Nairne brought 250 from Atholl. Scott knew an old chief, perhaps Stewart of Invernahyle, who had ' billeted 300 men in the old Assembly Rooms.' Probably the Prince's sergeants enlisted a few score of the Edinburgh mob, but details are wanting. Cope's men, at Dunbar, were not all disembarked till the 18th. Home now came to Cope with intelligence. He had watched the Prince's army while food was being distributed to them, he had counted them 'man by man,' and thought they were not 2,000 in all. Probably, with the Atholl and Argyll men (MacLachlans), they were not more than 2,500. Only about 1,500 had both swords and muskets of all sorts. About 100 had only scythes fastened on poles. It is extraordinary that Sir Robert Cadell should prefer to Home's leisurely calculation of the numbers, man by man, Cope's theory, written from Aberdeen, that the Highland force contained ' at most not above 4,000

---

[1] For Mrs. Murray, see Mr. Buchan's novel, *A Lost Lady of Old Years*. She certainly left her husband at an unknown date after 1749, and he had a second family by another lady.

men,' or Gardiner's guess at the same number. Mr. Patullo, the Muster Master of the army, in later years gave Home the numbers at Prestonpans as 2,500, inclusive of the 400 from Atholl and Argyll. Whence, indeed, could the 5,500 of Sir Robert Cadell's hypothesis have been drawn? Watson, editing Johnstone, mocks Cope's statement, at his trial, that 'the rebels were about 5,500 in the field,' though Colonel Whitefoord got this myth from the Jacobite officers. The Clans engaged were Macdonalds of all septs, Camerons, Atholl men, Stewarts of Appin, Macgregors, Perth's regiment, MacLachlans, Nairne's band, and a few Lowland gentry and servants. The sum of 2,500 is quite the highest possible estimate. Cope's force was probably no stronger. His Highlanders of Loudon's regiment, including Alan Breck Stewart,[1] who came in after Prestonpans, were not to be reckoned upon. 'He had about 600 horse,' says Sir Robert Cadell, 'and 1400 foot,' six small galloper guns, six intoxicated sailor gunners, and six small mortars. Johnstone reckons his men at 4,000, besides 'several Volunteers' of 'fanatic zeal,' but probably he had really little over 2,000 men, while of these the cavalry were totally demoralised.

Gardiner, whom Carlyle joined, was 'dejected,' His men, he said, 'had not yet recovered from their

---

[1] See Mr. R. L. Stevenson's *Kidnapped*, for Alan Breck. He was really a tall man, though Mr. Stevenson makes him of low stature.

panic, and I'll tell you in confidence that I have not above ten men in my regiment who I am certain will follow me. But we must give them battle now, and God's will be done.' According to a manuscript diary of the period, Gardiner made precisely the same remarks to Lord Loudon, on the night before the battle. Any man who knew this, and knew what Keppoch said, on the other side, that the chiefs would be among the enemy, and that their men would be where *they* were, could have prophesied the issue of the battle.

On the 19th Charles learned that Cope's army, reckoned at 2,700 men, says Murray, was marching on Haddington. The Prince joined the camp at Duddingston, and gave orders to meet the enemy next day, providing coaches and chaises for ambulance. At Perth the Prince had decided that the Clans (practically Macdonalds and Camerons) should draw lots for places, according to Murray. The Macdonalds drew the left, the Camerons, with the Stewarts, drew the right. The Macdonalds had been in Bruce's reserve, at Bannockburn ; he had thrown them in to support Edward Bruce, on his right, hence their claim to the post of honour. Yet they had fought on the left at Killiecrankie. When the Camerons, in the drawing of lots, won the right, the Glengarry Macdonnells at once objected. Lochiel waived his claim, like the gallant gentleman that he was, and the Macdonalds held the place of honour at Prestonpans, under Perth, Lochgarry, Barisdale, and young Æneas Macdonnell, second son of Glengarry. Lord George, Lochiel, and Ardshiel led the left, while Nairne commanded the Atholl reserve : which was not held in high repute, according to Lord George.

They moved off from Duddingston, and Charles, drawing his sword, said, 'Gentlemen, I have flung away the scabbard : with God's assistance I don't doubt of making you a free and happy people. Mr. Cope shall not escape us, as he did in the Highlands.' So says the 'Caledonian Mercury,' the gazette of the victory. Charles's address is sometimes put into his mouth just before the battle, but the newspaper is likely to be right. Cope's march from Haddington, to meet the Prince, and his choice of ground, were much criticised. Thus Carlyle, who was present, thought that he should have advanced by the high road, 'keeping the post road through Tranent Moor, which was high ground, and commanded the country south for several miles,' whereas Cope took the low road by the sea. But Sir Robert Cadell answers that the ground on the high road was then broken up with coal pits, hollow roads, and walls. Again, Scott, with Murray, thought that Cope should have fought on the open moor of Gledsmuir, a situation, as at Culloden, unfavourable to the Highlanders. Sir Robert replies that this was Cope's intention, but that he was informed of the want of water, while the moor 'was broken up by clumps of strong furze, which would have impeded the movements of his cavalry,' and 'was so extensive that he would have been certainly outflanked by an enemy whom he knew to be of more than double his own numbers.' The numbers, in fact, were almost exactly equal. Murray, again, criticises Cope's actual chosen ground as cramped by enclosures, marshes, and Grange park wall (round the home of the husband of the hapless Lady Grange), but Johnstone, a much better judge, admits that the Highland leaders, on arriving at the heights of Fawhill, whence they looked down on Cope's position, found that 'it was chosen with a great deal of skill. The more we examined it, the more we were convinced of the impossibility of attacking it: and we were all thrown into consternation, and quite at a loss what course to take. . . . The camp of the enemy was fortified by nature, and in the happiest position for so small an army.'

On his right Cope had park walls, in front a morass, with a deep ditch, ten or twelve feet wide, a drain for the boggy ground. On his left was another morass, and behind him the sea, while he occupied a vast bare stubble field. The Highland army manœuvred so that Cope changed his front, his right leaning on the ditch and enclosure, his left on the sea. 'What was to be done?' asks Ker of Graden (a Border man, and one of Charles's best and bravest officers). Mounted on a white pony, Ker carefully reconnoitred all the approaches, under fire, pulling down the loose stone dikes that his horse might walk through. He took a gentleman prisoner. Murray himself admits that Charles saw that it was impossible to attack. He therefore, says Murray, posted 500 Atholl men in the churchyard of Tranent, lest Cope should break through by that way to Edinburgh. These later rejoined the army and, from other accounts, seem to have been Camerons, posted by Sullivan, whose orders, unknown to Charles, Lord George countermanded, as Cope was shelling the detachment, and Lochiel thought their situation disheartening. There is some confusion here between Atholl men and Camerons. On this matter arose a dispute between Sullivan and Lord George.

There were vague manœuvres on the Highland side in the course of which Cope removed his baggage to Cockenzie House where, at last, it was guarded by his eighty Highlanders. From the top of his father's church steeple Carlyle viewed the movements, and brought in news to Cope. He later saw Gardiner, who remarked that the Highlanders had drawn to the edge of the morass, which, impassable as it seemed, alone now severed them from the English army. Cope's camp fires were blazing : on the Highland side the men, Prince and all, lay on the ground, or, at best, on pease straw, in darkness and silence. The

Prince, during his march, had passed the house of Mr. Anderson of Windygoul, had kissed Miss Anderson, who brought him wine, and had divided the red cloth within his claymore hilt, as relics, among the young ladies. These fragments of cloth were later treasured by Mr. Robert Chambers. Now an attack, from the east, had been decided on for the dawn, and at the council young Anderson of Whitburgh, cousin of the happy lady whom the Prince kissed, had been present. He seems to have been too modest to speak, but, during the night, he told Hepburn of Keith that he knew well the morass between the armies, having often shot snipe there; and that there was a dry pathway through it, which would make the detour from the east unnecessary. Keith sent Anderson to Lord George, whom he was obliged to waken, and Lord George, after examining the path, aroused Charles, who approved of the scheme.

As a consequence the army, about three or four in the morning, marched by this path, which, according to Ker of Graden, was wet to the knee. The Macdonalds, of course, formed the right wing, when they had crossed; Perth's command, on the left, was nearest to the sea. The Atholl men, with other details, about 700 in all, formed the reserve, under Nairne and the Prince, whom the chiefs, very naturally, would not allow to lead the charge in person. Johnstone, no friend of Charles, chanced to be by his side, and raised him when he slipped on his knees in leaping the twelve-foot ditch which has been mentioned. Johnstone remarks that, when the Highlanders had once formed up, and when the foremost line, some 1,500 men, had delivered its charge, he and Charles were but fifty paces behind, yet found no enemy left on the field. Cope's army had been swept out of military existence ' in less than five minutes.' If we understand this to mean a quarter of an hour, the pace was still astonishing. Carlyle reckons ten or fifteen minutes between the first shot and the rout.

What exactly occurred before the second line joined the first? As in most historical battles, it is not easy to be certain as to details ; and historians are apt to select and combine into a flowing narrative what they find most picturesque, or best supported, in contending accounts. Thus Mr. Ewald makes the English infantry stand fast, give a regular and well sustained fire, meet claymore with bayonet, and so on. There was no such resistance. Of authentic witnesses there are three classes : the narratives of contemporary Whig writers, like Carlyle, Home, and Henderson ; second, the versions of Jacobites engaged, such as Ker of Graden, Lord George Murray, Murray of Broughton, Johnstone, and Macdonald of Morar in the ' Lockhart Papers.' Lastly, we have the evidence of Whig officers at Cope's trial. Now Sir Robert

Cadell, who was both an officer of experience himself, and a man absolutely well acquainted with the ground, discredits much that appears in the usual descriptions, relying mainly on the evidence at Cope's trial, and on Home.   But the witnesses there were naturally favourable to Cope, a brave and honest though unsuccessful leader.   Their reports are all vitiated by the theory that the Highlanders, ' 5,000 men,' outnumbered them by two to one.   Any one who knows the clans engaged, and their normal strength, perceives that this is impossible.   Again, why discredit Macdonald of Morar, who avers that Charles said to him, in Gaelic, as they crossed the marsh, '*gres ort, gres ort*, make haste, make haste ? '   To be sure this officer makes Charles give his orders to Lord George and Perth, after crossing the marsh, and if we follow Johnstone's records this seems unlikely.   At the trial, again, as Sir Robert Cadell insists, nothing was said as to Gardiner's fighting on, after receiving a bullet, rallying some of the foot, and then falling under swords and Lochaber axes.   That Gardiner acted thus, and thus died, is Dr. Doddridge's story, received from Foster, an English soldier, and we would fain believe that a devout and gallant man, near his end from natural causes, perished by a death so worthy of a warrior.   Murray of Broughton was not, like Dr. Doddridge, a pious biographer of a Christian hero, and he says that Gardiner ' seemed determined not

to survive the odium that might have been thrown
on him by the shameful behaviour of his regiment,
and by his obstinacy occasioned his own fall.' The
Colonel fell ' by some of Lochiel's regiment,' that is,
by sword or axe, for the Camerons threw away their
muskets before going in with the claymore. Murray
can hardly, perhaps, have borrowed from Dr. Doddridge, and the English actually hanged one John
Macnaughton, a watchmaker, for the alleged offence
of cutting down the Colonel. No English officer,
probably, was present at the moment, and therefore
none could attest Gardiner's brave conduct at the
last.

On the other hand, the legend that Cope slept
comfortably at Cockenzie, and so was wakened by
his own drums, as in the song, is entirely refuted by
the evidence. He was on the watch all night, and
himself ordered the evolution by which his troops,
warned of the approach of the enemy by his dragoon
patrols, wheeled round to face the attack. It was so
far a surprise that the dim light made the Highlanders,
who crouched behind their targets as they came on,
look like a hedge, and Cope, with Whitefoord, attests
the incredible speed of the charge. There was no
time to send the guns to the right to check Perth's
approach ; and only Whitney's squadron of dragoons
was in front of, with Gardiner's behind, the guns.
But there was also a gap in the Highland line, Perth

M

having moved too near the sea. The Camerons and
Macgregors were the first to deliver a 'popping' fire,
which alarmed the dragoons. The artillerymen fled,
and Colonel Whitefoord, with his own hand, fired five
guns, which, for a moment, shook the Camerons, but
they were on Whitefoord in an instant. He would
have been cut down by the miller of Sir Walter's
friend, Stewart of Invernahyle, but the chief saved
him—and furnished an incident to 'Waverley.' Over
the guns swept the Camerons, a prey to Whitney's
dragoons, on their flank, if they would have charged,
but they wavered; while, of Gardiner's only eleven
men (he trusted not ten) came on with their doomed
leader. He fell, and the regiment fled, followed by
all the English cavalry. It is probable that he really
did try to rally some foot soldiers, after his first
wound, and was then hacked to pieces by claymore
and Lochaber axe. The Macgregors, of the Prince's
left, now came to the charge with their scythes, and
the right wing went into action. James Mòr fell,
with five bullets in his body, says Johnstone, but
'being altogether whimsical and singular,' he cried,
'My lads, I am not dead; by God I shall see if any
of you does not do his duty.' The English infantry
now broke from their right, Lascelles's orders being
ill given or not understood, whence their confusion.
The line only gave 'an infamous puff, and no platoon,'
says Lord Dunmore. The officers and Cope could

not re-form them, or even make them load again. They ran, ' like rabets,' as the Prince wrote to James about the cavalry, and heads and arms were lopped off by the claymores in pursuit. ' Not a single bayonet was blood-stained.'

Such was the battle of Prestonpans : a few shots from cannon ; a tempest of plaids, as the Highlanders tossed them down, and ran on, half naked, in their smocks : a scattered fire from their ranks, one weak volley from the English infantry ; no clash of steel, but a wild yell from the Celts, and then a pursuit and slaughter.

' The strength of the enemy's camp now became their destruction,' says Johnstone. Very many fugitives fell, sliced from behind as they climbed the park wall on the west of Loretto cricket field, almost all the rest of the infantry were taken prisoners. Cope had collected the dragoons, but could not rally them for a charge. It was here, apparently, that Mr. David Threipland, son of Threipland of Fingask, was slain. Like Balmawhapple, in ' Waverley,' he was pursuing alone, or with two servants only, and was cut down. Scott, as a child, sat on his grave, which was dug where he fell ; ' the grass long grew rank and green,' distinguishing it from the rest of the field. Some dragoons are said to have fled to the Castle followed by Colquhoun Grant. Through Edinburgh High Street they scampered, and Grant struck his

dirk into the closed gate. This anecdote is tradi-
tional. Most of the dragoons reached Cornhill and
Coldstream, and got into Berwick next day. Skir-
ving's famed satirical ballad says :

> Now, Johnnie, troth, ye was na blate,
> To come with the news of your ain defeat,
> And leave your men in sic a strait,
> Sae early in the morning.

But Sir Robert Cadell shows that Fowke, Lascelles,
and another officer reached Berwick before Sir John,
on the night of the battle, while Cope arrived next
day. Practically without artillery, deserted by his
cavalry, his foot soldiers were terrified by the speed
of the Highland rush, and all was over. Only Sir
Peter Halket, of Pitfirrane, kept his company together,
fired from a ditch, and got terms from his assailants.
Such was the battle of Prestonpans. After he
marched north from Crieff, Cope never had the
shadow of a chance. He was defended at the
moment, and his courage and activity were applauded,
by an officer who wrote in the 'Evening Post' of
December 12. This witness throws the entire blame
on the dragoons, who communicated their panic to
the foot. 'The affair was, without dispute, an infamous one, and yet I cannot, with justice, attack the
conduct of any one officer who was present.'

As to Charles's own conduct, Henderson narrates
that he breakfasted, on a slice of cold beef, among

the cries of the wounded (where else could he breakfast?) and remarked with glee, 'My Highlanders
have lost their plaids.' The sight of a hairy hurri-
cane of Celts in their smocks no doubt awoke his
mirth. The slaughter, according to Maxwell, was soon
stopped 'by the Prince and the gentlemen of his army,
who all exerted themselves on this occasion, and got
more honour by their humanity than even by their
bravery.' 'Charles,' says Home, 'remained on the
field of battle till midday, giving orders for the relief
of the wounded of both armies, and preserving, from
temper or judgment, every appearance of moderation.'
He slept at the beautiful old house of Pinkie, after
sending for surgeons from Edinburgh. The contrast
of Cumberland's brutality after Culloden was notable.
Carlyle, exerting himself to get up the surgical
instruments, was kindly received by Lochiel 'who
was polished and gentle.' Elcho, who met him,
asked the way to a tavern 'with an air of savage
ferocity that disgusted and alarmed.' The English
Government never pardoned Elcho, who, according
to Horace Walpole, had a bad character for cruelty.
The Duke of Perth, who also met Carlyle, showed
'victorious clemency.' Captain Brydone protected
the manse of Carlyle's father, and, in rising from
family prayers, accidentally knocked a plate from the
table with his sheathed broadsword : Mrs. Carlyle
picked up the unbroken plate, and hoped that the

omen was good for the Whig cause.   The Macdonald
journalist gives examples of the humanity of the
Highlanders, the privates running to Seton to fetch
ale and other liquors for the wounded.   One man
carried in a severely wounded soldier, 'and left him
a sixpence at parting.'   The Highlanders of Cope,
placed over the baggage and money-chest, surrendered,
and probably Alan Breck Stewart was not alone in
mounting the white cockade.   Johnstone was given,
by the Prince, the charge of the captured officers, in
whose faces Carlyle observed the misery of a dis-
creditable defeat.   Later they were commanded by
Cumberland to break parole : an order honourably
disobeyed by Sir Peter Halket, who said, ' His Grace
commands my commission, but not my honour ;'
and not relished by the intrepid Whitefoord.

Reports were late in reaching James at Rome,
for there were scant opportunities for messengers, and
Charles, also, was long without letters from James.
When James did write, his epistles were mainly
about Strickland, whom he dreaded as dangerous to
Charles's religious principles.   Mr. Ewald prints, from
a copy in the State Papers, a long letter written by the
Prince on the night of the fray (September 21).[1]   As
Lord Mahon remarks, it is apocryphal.   No doubt it
is a manuscript pamphlet of the day.   What Charles

---

[1] Mr. Ewald thought that this was unpublished, but Chambers gave
it in 1827.

did write, on October 7, is quoted by Lord Mahon, but the following preserves the Prince's orthography :

Edinburgh, 7th Oct. 1745, O. S.

Tis impossible for me to give you a distinct gurnal of my procydings becose of my being so much hurried with business, which allows me no time ; but notwithstanding I cannot let slip this occasion of giving a Short accoun of ye Batle of Gledsmuire, fought on ye 21 of September, which was one of ye Most Surprising action that ever was ; we gained a complete Victory over General Cope who commanded 3000 fut and to Regiments of ye Best Dragoons in ye island, he being advantajiosly posted with also Baterys of Cannon, and Morters, wee having neither hors or Artillery with us, and being to attack them in their position, and oblijed to pas before their noses in a defile and Bog. Only our first line had occasion to engaje, for actually in five minutes ye field was clired of ye Enemy, all ye fut killed wounded or taken prisoner, and of ye horse only to hundred escaped like rabets, one by one, on our side wee only losed a hundred men between killed and wounded, and ye Army afterwards had a fine plunder.

From this moment Charles only wrote once or twice to James : or, if he ever wrote between December 1745 and his return to France, the letters do not seem to have been preserved, a great loss to history.

The Prince's laconic despatch may probably be trusted for the Highland losses. The numbers of escaped dragoons appear to be under-estimated, but a contemporary report, in Sir William Fraser's

'Sutherland Book,' makes Barisdale and his swift
Celts cut off and capture a body of horse, for
which the chief was dubbed a Knight banneret on
the field of battle. James's own letters were full of
fears for Charles, and far from sanguine about
French assistance. Charles later sent over Kelly:
Marischal was 'cold,' says the Duke of York, who
was incognito in France. In truth, though Henry
had hopes of a command in a French expedition,
France dallied as usual. And thus, despite his
victory, Carlyle, watching the Prince at Holyrood
gate, 'beheld his countenance thoughtful and melancholy. . . . The Court at the Abbey was dull and
sombre, the Prince was melancholy; he seemed to
have no confidence in anybody, not even in the
ladies, who were much his friends; far less had he
the spirit to venture to the High Church of Edinburgh and take the Sacrament, as his great uncle,
Charles II., had done the Covenant, which would
have secured him the low country commons, as he
already had the Highlanders by attachment.' The
Reverend Dr. Alexander Carlyle, Minister of In-
veresk, speaks thus cavalierly about an interested
change of creed! Such liberality became a leading
'Moderate' and bosom friend of David Hume. But
Charles, though later he proved less scrupulous, was
not yet ready to break his father's heart, by bartering
a creed for a chance of a crown: a 'spirited' act in

Dr. Carlyle's opinion. The Highlanders, after Prestonpans, made a triumphal entry into Edinburgh. They had an awkward habit of firing off their pieces at random, which later led to a great misfortune. On this occasion a bullet grazed Miss Nairne, of a Jacobite family, who was looking on from a balcony. Sir Walter Scott knew this lady, and reports that, when she recovered consciousness after the wound, she said, 'Thank God, the accident happened to me, whose principles are known. Had it befallen a Whig, they would have said it was done on purpose.'

As to the character of the Court at Holyrood, which Carlyle calls so gloomy, and which Scott, in 'Waverley,' paints so brilliantly, accounts differ. Maxwell says that, at Holyrood, he never danced. Henderson avers that the Prince disobliged the ladies by declining to give even one ball. Plenty of balls awaited him, he said, and he would give a dance on his return in safety. But Home, who was not in Edinburgh at this time, extracts a short passage from the Memoirs of a Jacobite officer, unnamed, as to Charles's proceedings day by day. The Prince held a levee of officers and partisans till the Council met; after the Council broke up he dined in public with his chiefs. After dinner he rode out with his Guards, to the Camp, where he sometimes slept under canvas. 'In the evening he returned to Holyrood House, and received the ladies who came to his drawing room ; he then supped in public, and generally there was music at supper and a ball afterwards.' Thither would come the fair Jacobite toasts, of whose names and qualities Mr. Blaikie has discovered a curious list in manuscript. Doubtless, with so many young Highland gentlemen present, there were 'dancing and derray,' white roses, and tartan sashes. But the ladies did not often convert their Lowland lovers, who came, says Maxwell, 'either out of curiosity or affection, or the desire of seeing the Prince . . . a vast affluence of well-dressed people.'

Fancy can populate with these lairds and ladies that long empty gallery, where the Dutch pictures of centuries of fabled kings now look down, once a year, on the mirth of ministers, and the hospitality of the Commissioner. To that brief junketing have dwindled the gaieties of the dusty and darkling palace, where Riccio died, where Mary wept, where Charles brooded over wild rumours, high hopes, and dark misgivings. 'Everybody,' says Maxwell, 'was mightily taken with the Prince's figure and general behaviour. There was but one voice about these.' His 'great gilt French box' contained costumes many and rich enough, silks, velvets, and lace, while in a man named Morrison he possessed an accomplished coiffeur. His dark eyes, girlish complexion, now becoming embrowned by the sun, with his flowing bright hair and red lips, may have won many a heart. But 'Charles was chaste, William (Cumberland) was brave,' said a Whig newspaper. The same cruel charge of being chaste had been brought against the Prince's father in 1715. 'These are my beauties,' the Prince exclaimed, pointing to a bearded Highland sentinel, when he was blamed for neglecting the ladies. He was infinitely attractive to women, who did not attract him. There are no scandals about Charles at Holyrood. He had no leisure for the dalliances of the old gay Jameses, his ancestors : his mind was set on other things. Sombre indeed were the laurels, and heavy the heart of the victorious Prince.

CHAPTER III

FROM PRESTONPANS TO CULLODEN

Ah, my Prince, it were well
  Had'st thou to the gods been dear,
To have fallen when Keppoch fell,
  With the war pipe loud in thine ear,

To have died with never a stain
  On the fair White Rose of renown,
Striking thy stroke, if in vain,
  For thy Father, thy Faith, and thy Crown.

IMMEDIATELY after Prestonpans, according to Henderson, ' it was dreaded by the friends of the Government, that the Adventurer would have marched directly into England, pell mell with Cope,' and so upset the Hanoverian line. England was almost destitute of troops, and the expedition, at a first glance, seemed feasible to Charles. With less excuse it has seemed feasible to several historians of his adventure. ' He not only proposed it, but for some hours considered seriously of it,' says Murray. But the feat was impossible. The Highland army was already weakened by many desertions : the clansmen carrying home their spoils, the famous watches that 'died' when not wound up, the chocolate erroneously regarded as 'Cope's salve,' and the rest of their booty. England could easily have recovered Edinburgh, by her command of the sea, and have landed her recalled regiments, with Dutch, Hessian, and Swiss contingents, at Newcastle. An invasion of England with some 2,500 men would have been insane.

Charles, therefore, tried to regulate and confirm his position in every way : for example by issuing Proclamations ; sending to France for aid in officers, arms, and men ; despatching Kinlochmoidart and Macleod of Muiravonside to Macleod at Dunvegan, and to Sleat ; with Barisdale to stir up Lovat and the rest of the North.

The results of these efforts must presently be narrated ; meanwhile, in England, George II., when spoken to about the Rising, would exclaim 'Pooh, don't talk to me about such stuff ! ' 'His Majesty inclines to the views of Lord Granville and his faction, who persist in persuading the King that it is an affair of no consequence, and, for the Duke of Newcastle, he is glad when the rebels make any progress, in order to confute Lord Granville's assertions.' So writes Horace Walpole on September 20. New-castle, meanwhile, was grumbling at the King's want of confidence in himself and his abler brother, Henry Pelham. Horace Walpole felt trust in the navy, in the nobles who were raising regiments, and in the public spirit of Yorkshire, whose Archbishops had often rolled back the tide of Northern war. The Archbishop, Dr. Herring, was as bold and forward as his martial predecessors ; like them he wore military costume. But the regiments of the nobles soon became a scandal for jobbery and extortion, and were satirised in a ballad by Hanbury Williams. The day before Horace Walpole wrote to Mann, Henry Fox, in a letter to the satirical Williams, re-peated a saying of Marshal Wade's, ' England is for the first comer, and if you can tell whether the 6,000 Dutch, and the ten battalions of English, or 5,000 French or Spaniards will be here first, you know our fate.' And Fox believed that 5,000 French, if landed, would have conquered the country without a battle. As may be read in ' Tom Jones,' the populace cared little for either House. Contemporary evidence of this incurious calm occurs in a poem on ' Cards and Politics : '

> ' *The North*' (begins the Knight) '*is all in dumps*
> *At this new march*—What, is it Hearts are Trumps ? '
> The dame replies, ' *I hear their plans are laid*
> *To enter Lancashire.*—You led a spade ? '

The poet later speaks for himself:

Down with your cards,—methought I cried, for shame,
Is this a season for your trifling game?
When hell-born treason sounds the loud alarm,
And Britain calls for every heart and arm:
One choice alone is left in reason's eye,
To live with Freedom, or with Fame to die.

While squires were at whist, while Charles was
issuing Proclamations (written, according to Murray's
Evidence as informer, by Sheridan and Sir James
Stewart); in London the Earl of Marchmont, with
other Scottish peers, was endeavouring to get leave
to serve his country. They wished to be allowed to
raise and arm companies, but George II., who disliked
to see English peers thus display the remnant of old
feudal power, still more distrusted the Scottish lords.

Little has been said, hitherto, on the political
aspect of the dynastic struggle, because Jacobitism
was so much a matter, not of politics, but of sentiment. We can see into the hearts of the ordinary
English Jacobites, because Fielding has unveiled
for us that of Squire Western. The father of the
delicious Sophia, in the first place, hated Lords and
courtiers whose elegancies were a reproach to a
Master of Harriers, a rude, roaring, hard-drinking
oaf. This dislike of the Court was very general, and
the Court was, in fact, a centre of political and moral
corruption. Ugly German mistresses, a graceless

and stingy King, and a crew of jobbers in places
and pensions, could not be popular. No sentiment
was blended with loyalty to 'rats of Hanover,' mere
foreigners, in love with their native Herrenhausen.
Again, the squires felt the burdens on land, the
weight of the National Debt, contracted since the
Stuarts were expelled. Repudiation, 'Down with
Consols!' was their cry. A Dutch caricature of
'Perkin's Triumph' shows Charles surrounded by
priests and itching Highland scarecrows ; Protestants
are being burned in St. James's ; the Prince drives
his coach over the body of a holder of Consols.
The Squires were not afraid of being martyred for
their religion, but they did detest the National Debt,
the Court, and Taxation. In one Proclamation,
Charles asked the essential question, which few if
any friends of any revolution have been able to
answer in the affirmative, 'Has the nation,' since
James II. was driven out, 'been the more happy and
flourishing for it?'

Scotland, certainly, had been less flourishing, for
the good effects of the Union, in commerce and
comfort, had scarcely begun to develop themselves.
Mr. Graham, in his 'Social Life in Scotland,' minutely
describes a country so poverty-stricken and squalid,
that it proves degeneration since the time of
James IV. (say 1510), when the Spanish ambassador,
Ayala, attests a much more prosperous social condi-

tion than that of 1745. In fact Scotland had lost her old connection with France, without, as yet, gaining much by her new connection with England. Agriculture was inconceivably ignorant, wasteful, and famine-stricken. Of coin the country had little; rents were still mainly paid in kind. Roads were bad, or non-existent. Education was starved. Churches and schools lay open to the rain. The greater nobles had resorted to London, where they were disregarded. Burning with shame and anger, they bitterly felt their impotence. The Court despised them; they might not raise their tenants to fight for their Faith; the one point which severed them from their ancient line of native kings. They were, and felt that they were, used as inhabitants of a subject province, puppets of Tweeddale, or of Argyll, whom they regarded with intense jealousy. The Prince was at one with them here. 'The King cannot possibly ratify the pretended Union of the two nations,' said Charles in his Proclamation. Whig Scottish Earls, like Marchmont, born of the old True Blue Covenanting House of Home of Polwarth, felt the degradation of their estate under the Union as much as did Gask or Strathallan. They would not go over to the White Rose, but they were impatient of the White Horse. Protestantism and Property, not devotion to George II., kept them on the winning side.

N

The Diary of Lord Marchmont, at this time in London, shows 'the staggering state of Scots Statesmen' during the crisis. On September 10 Marchmont met Stair and the Duke of Montrose, to consult on the posture of affairs at Edinburgh. Neither was anxious to offer to raise a regiment for George II.: for fear lest the offer should be mocked. In fact, probably neither could have done such a thing, if permitted. On the news of Prestonpans that veteran traitor, Bolingbroke, told Marchmont 'that people should endeavour to keep themselves cool, and that, unless there was a third part for the Constitution, there was nothing worth fighting for!' Stair treated Marchmont's and Montrose's patriotic enthusiasm with cold neglect. Both were furious at being reckoned subordinate to Argyll, and thought that Tweeddale, for personal reasons, had neglected the safety of the country. 'At Court we' (the Scottish Peers) 'were treated as little better than slaves.' Thus the Duke of Bedford, soliciting their votes, put all his notes in one envelope, and directed it to them, in a batch, at a tavern! The Duke of Queensbury was also chilled by Tweeddale, who said 'that now' (after Prestonpans) 'the thing must be decided by the King's army.' In brief, the loyal Scottish Lords were distrusted, and felt most bitterly the loss of the power and favour which their ancestors enjoyed before the Union. They also, as good Whigs, longed for a declaration by George 'for liberty and *Free* Parliaments.' Now these very privileges, and repeal of the degrading Union, were what Charles was offering in public Proclamations.

That Scotland was degraded by the Union, and her Peers laughed at; that Parliament was a thing bought and sold by hucksters like Walpole, this was Charles's contention, and Whigs like Marchmont felt its truth as much as Jacobites like Alderman Heathcote, with whom Marchmont was then actually in correspondence. Montrose angrily declared that his ancestor, the great Marquis, 'had lost his estate at the head of a party; he would not lose his at the tail of one.' They were all as jealous of the Duke of Argyll, as afraid of the Highlanders. Even Argyll himself complained of not being allowed to arm, whereas the Camerons had never given up their arms, and he, therefore, was obliged to pay a large percentage of his rents, as blackmail, to Highland cattle-stealers. The English Government, in short, preferred to employ Hessian, Swiss, Dutch, and Danish troops, rather than loyal Scots, raised by Scottish Lords.

All this did not destroy the hereditary Whiggery of Marchmont, but, when Whigs felt as he did, that Scotland was a mere neglected province, a realm for Argyll, we can understand what Jacobites and Highlanders were feeling. Nothing but the question of

religion prevented Charles from having all Scotland
at his back. But that difficulty was insuperable.
His protests and promises were uttered in vain. As
he declared, his father was represented, especially in
sermons, as 'a bloody tyrant, breathing out nothing
but destruction to all those who will not immediately
embrace an odious religion.' He offered 'the most
ample security' for religious freedom. It was useless.
Even Scottish Whigs thought themselves injured,
neglected, nay enslaved and impoverished by the
House of Hanover. But anything, slavery, insult,
the National Debt, was better than a Papist on the
throne. The reigning House was nowhere loved: it
had not one amiable quality except personal courage.
But it was better than an invasion of popish Macdonalds, French, and Spaniards. Indeed the very
aid without which the English Jacobites would not
stir, the aid of France, would have damned their
Cause in England, even if it had secured their
momentary triumph. George might bring in mercenaries from Holland and Hesse. The nation did not
love such foreign assistance, but it could not cry,
with Squire Western, 'Huzza for old England!
Twenty thousand honest Frenchmen are landed in
Kent!'

There was no danger from French or Spaniards,
despite the promises of the Duc de Bouillon and of
the Spanish ambassador to Versailles, if they really

town could have stood ' a siege of two or three days,'
and Cope *might* come up in time.   But Stuart had to
reckon with the other chances, and with that of a
sack of the town, if Maclaurin proved wrong, or if
Cope was late, or was defeated when he did come.
No sane man would have risked all on the idea that
the Professor might happen to be right in his expectations.

The Provost had named his opponent, Drummond,
first, among his Volunteer captains, a sign of good
faith.   Cannon, from warships at Leith, were mounted
on the town walls, and 400 Volunteers were armed,
and taught to know one end of the musket from the
other.   On the 15th the valiant Drummond professed
his readiness to lead 250 Volunteers to the field, if
chaperoned by fifty of the Town Guard, a body of men
of no very definite political opinions and of loose
moral character.   The young College men, such as
Carlyle and Home, cheered ; but a want of enthusiasm
was visible among the burgesses.   Guest granted the
use of the fifty Town's Guardsmen, but Stuart had not
been even apprised of the proposal.   He was astonished, as it was his affair, but he granted ninety of
his civic guard.   Guest sent to Leith for Hamilton's
dragoons to join this imbecile crowd : the Volunteers
were summoned by the ' jowing' of the Fire Bell, and
then the general public ' scaled' precipitately out of
all the Kirks.   The Volunteers cheered ; the dragoons

wrote the letters to Charles with which they are credited. The Duc de Bouillon, on August 10, assured the Prince that Louis XV. had declared that 'everything you could possibly have occasion for was ready.' Campo Florido, for Spain, promised equal assistance. The English copies of these letters, in the Culloden Papers, are not, perhaps, exactly convincing. Yet the letters may well be authentic. Their authors declare that France and Spain are only waiting for news of Charles's safe arrival in Scotland. Now, on August 30, James wrote to Ormond that 'the French King and his ministers seem inclined to assist and support the Prince, but they will do nothing till they know of his arrival and reception in Scotland . . .'

It seems probable that Louis XV., with his easy good nature, had made to the Duc de Bouillon these promises which Charles used to encourage his party, and to win Sleat and Macleod. An enthusiastic manifesto was even drawn up by Voltaire. But, while Louis XV. smiled, and promised 'mountains and marvels,' he had to reckon with his ministers. We have shown how cavalierly one minister, D'Argenson, treated the Earl Marischal, and Clancarty of the slovenly perruque. Another minister, Maurepas, was not more enthusiastic. James had written to Louis on August 5, to Maurepas on August 11, asking for aid, and assuring Louis of his own intention to abdicate in favour of the Prince.[1] Maurepas added a note, perhaps meant for D'Argenson. 'Do you think that the King should, or should not answer this poor King James? A word of consolation, I think, would be worthy of His Majesty's kind heart.' A word of consolation! It is far from the spirit which De Bouillon attributes to Louis. On August 20 Marischal put in a Memoir to the French Court, making the most of the *verbal* promises of the English Jacobites to Clancarty.

The Duke of York left Rome for Avignon, whence he wrote to the French Court, urging them to make haste. They declined to reply in writing : they would do nothing openly till success was probable.

On arriving in Paris the poor young man was ill received. De Luynes describes the tortuous back stairs by which, shy and confused, he was admitted to a secret interview with Louis. He found the Earl Marischal's endeavours 'as cold as himself,' while Clancarty was as much warmer as he was less trustworthy. But the real spirit of the French Ministry shows undisguised in their instructions to the Marquis d'Éguilles, who was to be sent over to Charles. The Instructions, printed by Pichot, are of

---

The letter is in the appendix to Murray of Broughton, but had already been published by Amédée Pichot.

September 24.[1] The King, D'Éguilles is to know, will not refuse assistance, if he can be certain that he will be useful. D'Eguilles is merely to ascertain exactly the situation of the Prince. If the account is satisfactory, Louis will assist more or less openly, for, so far, the attempt is merely rash, though heroic. D'Eguilles is accredited to Charles, but this must be known to none but the Prince, and his most intimate companion. He must act as if he were merely a curious volunteer. He must not be the dupe of Jacobite enthusiasm, of which intense distrust is expressed. D'Eguilles was more generous than his orders. What occurred on his arrival in Scotland, about October 14, will be described later.

Meanwhile, Murray of Broughton seems to be wrong in dating the mission of Charles's envoy to France, Parson Kelly, on September 26. Kelly, with Sir James Stewart, as we shall see, must have set out much later. The plan of a large French expedition was only being discussed in the middle of October: later, too late, Richelieu took the command, but all vanished before Christmas. France was a broken reed. The Court liked to have a Pretender, to annoy Eng-

---

[1] See also *Un Protégé de Bachaumont*, by M. Paul Cottin (Paris, 1887), and an article by M. G. Lefèvre-Portalis, in the *Annales* of the École Libre des Sciences Politiques (1887). We have also the *Mémoires* of the Marquis d'Éguilles, in *Archives Littéraires de l'Europe*, i. 78–101. For these sources I am indebted to the present Marquis d'Éguilles.

land with pinpricks, but had neither the resolution, the money, the ships, nor even the desire, to restore the House of Stuart. Thus the 6,000 Dutch, and the 2,000 Swiss, and the ten English battalions, reached England late, yet in plenty of time. To the English Jacobites Charles vainly appealed, his messenger, Hickson, a vintner at Perth, later an informer, was taken ; and, even had he escaped, the English were afraid of their 'shaddo,' as Charles had already observed. They 'would drink for him, and swear for him, and wench for him, they were not a praying and a fighting people,' to use a Puritan phrase of an earlier date. Charles, in his intercepted letter of September 24, told the English Jacobites that they would be 'inexcusable before God and man' if they deserted him. But they went on hunting and drinking healths, when Beaufort should have raised the West, when Cheshire and Wales should have risen, and Sir John Hinde-Cotton, M.P., should have called out the sentimentalists of the City.

Meanwhile (September 25), Newcastle was corresponding with the Mayor of Newcastle-on-Tyne. He was sending down General Huske, a useful officer, and disembarking two Dutch regiments, to add to the force about to march north. Wade, who had plenty of artillery, if not a very stout heart for the business, for he was senile, and despised by his officers, was to command at Newcastle. Two regiments were coming from Dublin to Chester, and the Dutch and English battalions were already in the Thames. The Mayor of Newcastle, on September 26, sent the grateful news to Forbes of Culloden, and added that 700 Dutch had already landed at Berwick. The English reinforcements, to concentrate under Wade at Newcastle, were far in advance of Charles's fresh levies from the North.

But, before returning to Charles's vigorous efforts, we may repeat an absurd myth about the 700 Dutch at Berwick, which is found in a letter in French. It is in the Stuart Papers, and dated *Du Camp du Prince Royal d'Écosse*, 15 *Octobre*, 1745. The gist of this odd intelligence is that a strong force of Orkney men, accompanied by several hundreds of ferocious dogs, has joined the Prince, Perth has made a secret expedition with 5,000 men, and, by help of the dogs alone, has devoured 500 Dutch at Berwick! The doomed foes, in a word, were 'surrounded by a multitude of hounds of extraordinary size.' Many Hollanders fled at the mere sound of their bark, their bite was worse. They caused terrible slaughter, till the bagpipes sounded the recall. Two hundred prisoners, and sixteen dying officers were taken to Perth's camp. 'On our side we have only lost one Orcadian, four dogs killed, and ten wounded.' This must be the jest of a French officer, and internal evidence casts suspicion on Nick Wogan, brother of Sir Charles. After losing an arm at Fontenoy this gallant and irrepressible humourist joined Charles in Scotland. The jest is either a skit upon, or the original source of what 'they affirmed in the newspapers of London, that we had dogs in our army trained to fight,' and so won at Prestonpans. Johnstone mentions this English belief.

To return to Charles : on the very day of Preston-pans he desired the ministers to continue public worship as usual. But only Mr. MacVicar, of the West Kirk, safe under the guns of the Castle, obeyed ; and prayed that 'to the young man who came seeking an earthly crown, Heaven would send a heavenly one.' For several Sundays Edinburgh was deprived of Presbyterian sermons. On the 23rd, Charles, with good taste, forbade all public rejoicings for his victory, and again appealed to the clergy to officiate as usual, ' since we are resolved to inflict no penalty that can possibly look like persecution.' He next invited the timid volunteers, who had fled, to return in safety. They had only to report themselves to Murray of Broughton, and promise, henceforwards, to be peaceable subjects. Carlyle appears to have promised, and he saw the Prince at Holyrood, as has been said. Other proclamations did not much reassure the Banks, nor prevent marauders from donning Highland dress, and extorting money in the country. One rogue came to Selkirk, pretending to be the Prince himself ; he was laid by the heels. The burgh of

sutors, however, furnished shoes for the Highlanders.
The real Highlanders themselves occasionally asked
for money, and to the question 'how much?' replied
'a penny,' according to the 'Scots Magazine' of September 1745. Excise, customs, and rents on forfeited
estates were collected, and Glasgow was mulcted in
5,500*l.* Smuggled goods impounded in the Custom
House were seized, and sold for what they would
fetch.

Meanwhile, the Castle had kept quiet, but it opened
fire on the evening of the 25th, and damaged some
houses. On the 29th Charles forbade coming and
going to the Castle. Lord George says that he was
opposed to a blockade, and only meant to set guards
against a sally. Sullivan, of course, placed a guard
very ill, and they were taken. If this was a blockade,
Guest resented it by informing the Provost that he
would fire on the Highland blockading parties.
Murray maintains that a real blockade was inconsistent with Charles's plans : he merely meant to keep in
spies and keep out fresh butter and eggs. In answer
to remonstrances from endangered citizens, Charles
said that the Castle might as well ask him to quit
the town as to remove the guards, the Camerons
under Lochiel. Their position was really perilous
under artillery fire, but Lochiel and Lord George
were with them, and encouraged them. There was
a respite of six days, to await orders from London,

then the Castle fired, and wounded a sentinel and a girl. Other townsfolk were hit: sorties were made, and the English soldiers robbed the deserted houses. On the 5th Charles announced that, for the sake of humanity, and to save innocent lives, he would take off the blockade on the Castle, and would not, as he had threatened, make reprisals on the property of the Castle officers.

Maxwell of Kirkconnell, unlike Carlyle, insists, as we saw, on the gaiety and 'splendour,' at this time, of Charles's Court. The Prince won golden opinions by 'several instances of good nature and humanity.' Charles, it seems, was urged to send to London a cartel as to exchange of prisoners, threatening, if it was not accepted, to give no quarter. This cartel was very necessary, as many people were waiting 'to see what side the hangman would take.' Charles, however, declared that 'it was below him to make empty threats, . . . he would never in cold blood take away lives which, in the heat of action, he had saved at the peril of his own!' With this conduct people contrasted Tweeddale's authentic orders to the Castle, not to spare the town, and especially to cut off the water supply.

On September 24 Charles had sent Macleod of Muiravonside to work on Sleat and Macleod. He was to encourage them by news of Prestonpans, and to say that the Prince 'had most undoubted assur-

ances of assistance from France and Spain,' a reference to the letters of De Bouillon and Campo Florido,
to which Charles explicitly alludes. It is probable
that Sleat was nearly won. Macleod of Brea, in
Rasay, a Jacobite island, told Bishop Forbes that,
late in September, Rasay, Sleat, Macleod, and Kingsburgh met at a tavern at Sconsary, in Skye. A
Glenelg man brought news from Prestonpans.
Macdonald told Rasay that he would raise 900 men
for Charles : Rasay was to bring in 100. The whole
plan was arranged over the bottle. But next day
the wine was out, and a letter from Forbes of
Culloden to Sleat came in. ' He was now quite
upon the grave and thoughtful, . . . and dropt the
declared resolution of his own mind.' The case
against Macleod, ' the wicked Laird,' as he is
traditionally styled, is blacker even than the evidence
against Sleat. Macleod certainly visited Lovat early
in October, and made large promises. On October 9
Frazer of Foyers wrote to Tullibardine ; the letter
was printed by Home. He had met Macleod at
Lovat's, and learned that Sleat's Skye Macdonalds,
Macleod's men, the Mackenzies under Lord Cromarty
(who, in public, was ' sitting on the fence '), the
Mackintoshes and the Frazers were to gather and go,
' on Tuesday next.' ' All the certainty I have of
this is, that I have been present when the Laird of
Macleod was dispatched, Saturday last, by express

to Skye, and is engaged in honour to be Tuesday next at Corryarrack, with his name' (his Clan), ' where the Frazers will join them.'

This entirely corroborates Murray. ' Nothing was to be had from Macleod but oaths and curses that so soon as he went to Skye ' (that is, from Lovat's house of Beaufort, or Castle Downie) 'he would raise his men and march South, at the same time that he had no sooner made his solemn promises, and consulted of how he was to march, and where to meet the other clans, than he went directly to Mr. Forbes of Culloden, and told him what had passed.' Throughout, Macleod was a vacillator and a boaster, or an *agent provocateur* and spy ; or possibly both. A letter of Lovat's to Lochiel, read at Lovat's trial, repeats the same fact. At Castle Downie Macleod had sworn to bring in his Clan.

We blame Charles's habit of suspicion, but, once more we ask, how could he trust the perjured men with whom he too often had to do ? The Highland people were loyal as steel, but certain of the chiefs were even as Barisdale, Macleod, Lovat, and Glengarry. It is fair, however, to remark that, trick for trick, Murray of Broughton was a match for the Celts. One of his envoys to Macleod, Macdonald of Kinlochmoidart, was captured at Lismahago, thanks to a zealous minister, and in his possession were found directions from Murray, writing for Charles, dated October 27. He was to give out, if Sleat and Macleod would not rise, that they had risen, and were on the march. This was to encourage the Mackenzies, Clan Chattan, and the other tribes. The lie had travelled as far south as Perthshire by October 23. Such was the school of double treachery to which Charles was accustomed : from early and long experience of betrayal he learned the fatal lesson of universal distrust.

To Lovat, Charles sent the huge, truculent, Coll Macdonnell of Barisdale : an egregious and cruel ruffian and blackmailer, finally discovered and punished by both parties. In his recess of Knoydart he had long plundered the country, and had invented a kind of engine of torture, called 'Barisdale.' Immediately, after October 7, Lovat's letters to Forbes begin to change in tone. First he merely complains of 'villainous lying reports,' about his immaculate character. Then (October 11) after Loudon had joined Forbes, and was collecting forces for the defence of the North, Lovat begins to deluge Forbes with tales of Charles's good fortunes. Thus 10,000 French are landed in England. Beaufort, Sir Watkin Williams Wynne, and Morgan of Tradagan, are up in the West, 6,000 strong. Campbell of Auchinbreck has joined with 1,200 men, and Pitsligo is leading the cavalry of the Lowland east coast, which chanced to be true. Clan Chattan is gathering, and

' I find it morally impossible to stop my own people.'
Forbes (October 19) replied that this meant Lovat's
ruin.   Lovat was sending out his son, the Master, an
undergraduate of St. Andrews, under the pretence
that he could not stop the fiery youth.   Culloden
was attacked by the Frazers, on the night of October 16, in compliance with Lovat's permission from
Charles.   The Frazers only robbed the gardener, and
stole cows :   Lovat apologised, and Forbes passed
the matter over lightly.   Lovat dallied, and, on
December 1, Forbes wrote an affectionate letter to
the Master, who had already marched with many of
the clan.   Lovat disavowed him, of course, but his
guilt was conspicuous.   He might have acted like
Macleod, with safety : like Lochiel, with honour : as
it was he weakened the Jacobite cause by delay, and
most deservedly lost his own head in the end.
Murray of Broughton claims credit for veiling his
dealings with Lovat, when he gave evidence.

Barisdale failed to raise men in August, but
Pitsligo the Venerable came to Edinburgh with his
handful of horse, and with a reputation for virtue
which was sorely needed.   Elcho had a troop of
mounted Guards in red and blue.   Kenmure was to
have another troop, but he and Nithsdale were not
' on and awa.'   They remembered 1715, and, after
coming to greet Charles, went soberly back and
skulked after the fashion of Traquair.   Arthur

Elphinstone (later, by his brother's death, Lord
Balmerino) was unlucky enough to receive the command intended for Kenmure; Mackinnon brought
120 men from Skye: Cluny arrived with Clan
Vourich: Tullibardine collected his deserters from
Atholl. Gordon of Glenbucket joined the Cause,
and Lord Lewis Gordon did his best to raise the
retainers of his brother, the Duke.

The unhappy Kilmarnock also came in, though
originally a Whig. He 'had four earldoms in him,'
as Horace Walpole says, representing, as he did,
the House of Boyd. They had intermarried with
the Royal House, in the minority of James III., but
fell under the House of Hamilton. Kilmarnock had
lost a pension which Sir Robert Walpole had been
wont to pay him, and Horace says that he was often
hard pressed for a dinner. The gloomy prophecies
of Gardiner, with whom he had dined when Charles
was at Linlithgow, had given him hopes of recovering his fortunes by the Prince's success. Marchmont
described him to George II. as 'a man of desperate
fortune.' He was not without a 'Warning.' 'About
a year before the Rebellion broke out, his Lady's
Maid, inspecting some linen in an upper room, was
suddenly presented with the View of a Bloody Head,
which, by the Door opening of its own accord, entered
the room, bounded on the floor, and appeared to be
his Lordship's; on its approach towards her, she

O

lifted up her foot to kick it off, when she became powerless, and was obliged to cry out ; on its second appearance she had again to repeat her efforts and her cry ; the shrieks were heard by his Lordship, who with his lady went up to the room, and had the story from the Gentlewoman's own mouth, which at that time he too much ridiculed,' says Henderson, the schoolmaster historian. A similar tale is told of Argyll, just before he lost his head at the Restoration.

Among other less picturesque additions to the Prince's party, D'Éguilles arrived, as we have seen, on October 14. He had landed, after some dangers, at Montrose. He brought arms and money, and Charles (October 15) thanked Louis, and conjured him to send more substantial assistance. D'Éguilles wrote that Charles's joy was inexpressible. He said, ' I leave for England in eight days, England will be ours in two months. If assistance does not come, or comes too late, I cannot resist the English, Dutch, Hessians, and Swiss.' He then asked D'Éguilles if he might expect an immediate landing. The envoy hesitated, and advised him not to march south without hearing again from France. Charles, however, replied that he could not delay. D'Éguilles reckoned Charles's force at 10,000 men, with seven guns and four mortars. His letters to his Government prove that he did his best to procure speedy and sufficient assistance. I

add the epigrammatic description, by M. Lefèvre
Portalis, of the Prince's army :

Mélange de paresse fataliste et d'action furieuse, de
résignation passive et d'audace illimitée, les qualités et les
défauts d'un peuple de cette souche en font nécessairement,
de toutes les nations, la plus guerrière et la moins militaire
à la fois. Tel était l'état moral de l'armée du dernier
Stuart.

On October 28 Charles wrote to France asking
that his brother and Ormond might come with the
expedition. On October 10 the Earl Marischal wrote
in sad terms to James. He had ever told truth to
the French, considering their interests as well as those
of the Cause. 'A vigorous resolution' was needed,
but the Ministers, among themselves, confess to their
dread of a long war. Yet, at Fontainebleau, on
October 24, O'Brien and D'Argenson signed a Treaty
of Alliance between France and the House of Stuart,
the ratification to be exchanged in two months.
Louis engaged to aid Charles 'as far as is practicable.'
He is to send a corps from his Irish regiments. The
contracting parties are to work 'in union and concert
for the restoration of Peace.' This provision, at the
Peace of Aix-la-Chapelle, Louis found not to be
'practicable.' It is plain that the Treaty bound
Louis to very little, and that at his own discretion.
However, the treaty neutralised the 6,000 Dutch.

On October 26 (15th Old Style) Charles wrote to James the following letter :

Charles from Edinburgh.

October 15.

Sir.—I have at last had the Comfort of receiving Letters from you, the latest of which is of ye 7th of September N.S. I am Confounded and penetrated with so much goodness and tenderness yr Majesty expresses to me in all your Letters. It is a grife to me that my keeping Strickland has given you one Moment's Concern, but shall send him away in all hest. I hope yr Majesty is persuaded that this fault or any others I may have committed, is not want of ye Respect and Submission which you will always find in me. I remark your Letters to ye K. of F. in which you do me more honour than I deserve. I wish to God I may find my Brother landed in England by the time I enter : and which will be in about ten days, having with me near 8,000 men and 300 Hors at lest with which as matters stand I shal have one desive Stroke fort, but iff ye French land perhaps none. I cannot enlarge on this subject as on many others for want of time, because of such a multiplicity of things, which hourly occor for ye service of ye affair. Adam (Louis XV) has sent me a Gentleman (d'Eguilles) (who brought me ye Letters) to stay with me for to give notice of anything I may want, which as he says will be don immediately. Accordingly I am sending off immediately three or fore Expresses all to the same purpose, so that sum may arrive. What is sed is very short, pressing to have succor with all heste by a landing in England, for that as matters stand I must either Conquer or perish in a little while.

As to Strickland, he really followed Charles, as Master of the Household, to Carlisle, where he fell ill and died, after the Prince's retreat. James suspected him of causing ill-will between Charles and the Duke of York. There does appear to have been a belief, on the Duke's side, that, politically, Charles had even now a grudge against him : in writing to James from France he often speaks of this, but we find no traces of it on Charles's side. The Prince's letter shows that he was aware of his absolute dependence on a French landing. With habitual audacity he tried to force the French Court into action by a victory in England. Wade's men, meanwhile, were in Newcastle. Charles appointed Glengyle as Governor of Doune Castle, near Stirling : and Strathallan, with Gask, as Governor of Perth, where late recruits from the North were concentrated. Other such arrangements were made : Tullibardine brought in 600 Atholl men, a gunner from France, named Grant, arrived, with others, and driblets of clansmen came in, while French ships brought stores, arms, and money. Lady Mackintosh, in contrast to her Whig husband, was raising such men of Clan Chattan as would rise at her command. From Moy her ladyship wrote to Tullibardine on October 16. Her spelling is more original than that of the Prince himself.

My Lord Douke,—The Bearer of this is a Very Pretay Fellew, Brother of Mcenzie of Killcoway. He has a Compannay Resed for the Prince's Service, but was handered by Lord Siforth to keray them of, which meks me geve this trobal to beg of your Grace to geve hem en ordar for resing his men, and thene he can wouse a littel forse.   My God preaserf Your Grace, and all that will searve ther Prince and contray, which is the ernast woush of

> Your Grace most
>
> Affnett and Obd Sarvant,
>
> A. McIntosh.

From Stonehaven, Colvile announced not only French ships with hundreds of cartloads of supplies, but news that the French expedition was ready at Dunkirk, Lord Marischal heading 6,000 men. This intelligence, with the French supplies, which were brought round by way of Alloa, encouraged the Prince, and, on October 30, a Council at Holyrood discussed the march into England. The Council was habitually divided. Probably Johnstone is right in saying that many wished Charles to make Scotland alone his Kingdom : the hated Union would not survive that decision. Others must have misdoubted the perils to be run by his little force. On the other hand, Wade would soon enter Scotland, backed by all the power of England and her mercenaries, unless the English Jacobites were brought to the Standard.

It was decided to invade, but by what route ? Charles was for the bolder course. *Tu contra auden-tior ito*. He would attack Wade, not yet prepared, at Newcastle. The Dutch would be paralysed by the Capitulation of Tournay, which forbade them to encounter the allies of France. A victory at New-castle would encourage the Jacobites of the North and of the City. Moreover, an advance by the West, from Carlisle, would leave Wade on the Prince's flank and rear. Lord George and the majority pointed out the difficulty of a retreat from Newcastle, with the wintry Tweed to cross, while the route by Wooler would be impossible for the artillery. At Carlisle they would be joined by Lancashire, notably Jacobite, as were Cheshire and Wales. If thus aided, they might march on Wade at Newcastle. A retreat, if necessary, might be made into the Highlands by Menteith. After long debate, the Council was adjourned to next day. Charles, on reflection, said that he now shared the opinion of the majority, which 'seemed to give great contentment.' Either Charles or Lord George then suggested a march of one column to Kelso, which would deceive Wade, draw him north, and make it impossible for him to reach Carlisle before the Highlanders.[1] The other column, with artillery and baggage, would apparently follow the same course, but would diverge by Selkirk, and up to Moffat, and so to Carlisle. Most of the Clans, the Prince, Lord George, and Perth went by Kelso : Tullibardine, Cluny, Elcho, Balmerino,

[1] D'Éguilles says that he suggested this strategy, and that the Prince was very anxious to fight Wade at once.

and Pitsligo (in the Prince's carriage, for he was very kind to the good old man) travelled by Selkirk. The whole force may have mustered 7,000 or 8,000 men.

It must be observed that, on the following march to Derby, Charles displayed important personal qualities. 'His body was made for war,' says Lord Elcho, and he did not spare it : usually sleeping in his boots. He marched at the head of the Clans. 'People thought it was only for a mile or two, to encourage the soldiers at the beginning, and were surprized to see him continue all day, but it was the same every day after during the whole expedition : in dirty lanes and deep snow he took his chance with the common men, and would seldom be prevailed upon to get on horseback and cross a river. It's not to be imagined how much this manner of bringing himself down to a level with the men, and his affable behaviour to the meanest of them, endeared him to the army. He came to Lauder . . . when hearing that some of the Highlanders lagged behind, with a view, as was thought, of deserting, he got on horseback next morning, before it was light, went two or three miles back, and brought most of the stragglers up with him.' So writes Maxwell of Kirkconnel, who was with the army, and is a thoroughly trustworthy witness.

On the night of October 31 Charles slept at

Pinkie House. Dalkeith, Lauder, and Kelso were
the next stages ; from Kelso, Ker of Graden scouted
across Tweed, under Flodden Edge, towards Wooler.
On the 6th, Charles reached Jedburgh. One good
recruit he lost: Mr. Davidson, father of Scott's
Dandie Dinmont, rode into Jedburgh too late, the
army had gone, and he went back to Charlieshope :
so Professor Ritchie of St. Andrews relates, on the
authority of his father, the minister of Jedburgh.
For the rest, the strength of the Border yeomanry, so
ready to rise when Napoleon threatened invasion,
remained neutral. On November 8 Charles crossed
the Esk into England, and slept at Reddings. On
the 9th he was joined by Tullibardine's column, and
lay at Moorhouse, two miles from Carlisle, that old
strength of William Rufus, which, in its day, had defied Bruce. On November 10 a heavy fog fell: when it
rose, Cluny's men with the Atholl regiment, Perth, and
O'Sullivan, reconnoitred: a four-gun battery opened
fire, and the Citadel guns played on Charles's division.
No harm was done : but the deputy Mayor, Pattison,
declined to surrender. He had a small force of
Invalids, with the Militia of Cumberland and Westmorland. Trenches were begun, opposite the Penrith
gate, but Charles went ten miles east, to Brampton,
in case Wade approached, and there the Highland
force lay, from the 11th to the 13th, when Lord
George, with half the army, returned to resume the

by Lord George, 'which completed the dryness that had almost from the beginning subsisted between them.' Elcho sided with Lord George, in almost universal opinion the better general. Maxwell says that Perth had the first place in the affair of Carlisle, where he showed enthusiastic energy, but, as a Catholic, he was thought likely to give offence in England. Maxwell himself, apparently, sounded the Duke, who at once insisted on giving up his command. 'A plain narrative of the Duke of Perth's behaviour on this delicate occasion is the best encomium that can be made of it.' Both Lord George and the Prince were heady, obstinate, and impatient of contradiction. Their quarrel remained unabated, till Lord George, after Culloden, wrote to Charles a letter from Ruthven, which was, practically a defiance.

While the chiefs of Charles's army were thus at odds among themselves, the surrender of Carlisle was decidedly premature. The town was not the rambling city of suburbs which it is to-day. The old red sandstone walls girdled a compact mass of buildings, crowned by the Cathedral, and flanked by the citadel. The four-pounders of the Highland army (especially at the distance, then reckoned vast, of 300 yards) would have had little more effect than fives-balls. The surrounding country had been scoured for ladders, which Colonel

Durand had stored in the citadel. Probably the Militia might have served to man the walls, till Wade could come up, but the town surrendered because the Militia, with touching unanimity, declined to fight. The deputy Mayor, Pattison, became the laughing-stock of both parties, but, in fact, he had no chance to resist. Such Militia men as did not declare for surrender had already deserted by dropping from the walls. Durand, Pattison, and the officers in vain adjured them to pluck up heart.[1] Before the actual capitulation, in form, at Brampton, Durand spiked the light guns on the walls, which Charles thought unsportsmanlike, ' an impudent and audacious infringement of the capitulation,' says Murray. Wade had marched by the 17th as far as Hexham : but he was old, the roads were heavy with snow, and he trudged back to Newcastle.

Charles stayed in a house in English Street, now marked by an inscription, till November 20. He met with no support from Cumberland. Only two Volunteers came in. The Prince dined at Warwick Hall, on the Eden, and was welcomed by Mrs. Warwick, a daughter of Howard of Corby Castle. In Corby a set of portraits of the exiled

---

[1] The Court Martial on Durand, his Journal and Letters, with the letters of Dr. Waugh, are given in full in Mr. Mounsey's *Carlisle in 1746* (1846). Mr. Ewald also published the documents from the *State Papers*, being, apparently, unaware that they were already in print.

Stuarts exists, as others do from the Esk to the Exe, in Jacobite houses from which not a man nor a guinea was sent to help the Cause.

As far as treasuring miniatures went, hundreds of English county families were extremely loyal. But they had learned their lesson of timidity, under Forster, in 1715. In Cumberland the common people were ignorant. In Charles's rooms, a rustling was heard, and a little girl of six was found hidden under the bed. The mother screamed to the gentleman to spare the child, the only survivor out of seven. 'She had been assured from creditable sources,' says Murray, 'that the Highlanders were a savage sort of people and ate all the young children.' A variant of this tale makes the adventure occur in the lodgings of Lochiel. At Rose Castle, an old servant implored Macdonald of Tiendrish not to enter, as his lady had just given birth to a child. Tiendrish took off his white cockade, gave it as a token of protection, and, with his men, in reverend silence, witnessed the christening of the baby. The child, later Lady Clerk, wrote an account of what she had learned of the occurrences, in 'Blackwood's Magazine' for 1817. It is curious that in a district where Charles's information taught him to expect no aid, except perhaps from Hyltons and Haggerstons, the people preserve a Jacobite country-dance in his honour. Though stories of Highland freebooting were rife, discipline was strictly enforced. Lochiel had shot a thieving Cameron, near Stirling, and a Munro was executed at Edinburgh. 'It is forbid, above all things, to shoot sheep, hens, &c., or break open the country people's houses, or cause any disturbance :' so writes Captain James Stewart, of Ogilvy's, in his Day Book. Perth and Tullibardine, approaching Moffat, had complained of 'cruel plunder,' and a man of Perth's regiment was court-martialed. Yet desertions were so common that, when Charles left Carlisle for Penrith, on November 21, he probably did not lead more than 4,500 men.[1]

According to Murray, Charles was joined at Carlisle by one of his emissaries, who brought the most distinct promises from Lovat and Macleod. The Prince was moving on Lancashire, where he had the best hopes of support. Behind him, in Scotland, the Judges, gentry, and other refugees, had returned from Berwick to Edinburgh on November 13, and the Castle men had maltreated the wounded, and pillaged houses where the officers had lodged. There were other official rejoicings and speech-makings. Handasyde, from Berwick, brought in Price's and Ligonier's Foot, with the heroes of a hundred flights, the dragoons of Gardiner and

[1] Interesting traditions of Charles's stay at Brampton are published by Mr. Whitehead, in 'Transactions of the Cumberland and Westmorland Association,' 1886-1887.

Hamilton. 'An invitation was sent them, we hear, by some of the eminent citizens,' says the 'Scots Magazine.' Edinburgh, Glasgow, and Stirling raised Volunteers, and about 300 Seceders appeared in arms, under some 'Gifted Gilfillan.' The opinions of the strict Cameronians, as far as we may trust 'The Active Testimony of True Presbyterians' (1749), were hostile to 'Charles, Pretended Prince of Wales.' But even more odious to True Presbyterians was 'The Idolatrous Occupant of the Throne.' George II. was allied with 'two of the most Idolatrous and Bloody Limbs of Antichrist, the cursed Jezebel of Austria, and the little fierce Tiger of Savoy.' Of all poor Charles's offences, the worst was 'his foolish Pity and Leniency, in sparing these profane blasphemous Red Coats . . . when by putting them to death, this poor land might have been eased of the heavy burden of these Vermin of Hell, Charles's prisoners. So speak the Persecuted Remnant, who had learned nothing and forgotten nothing since Claverhouse broke their resistance to all power that was not 'from on High.'

While Edinburgh returned to her calm, protected by the brave dragoons, the town of Perth had a brush with the men of Gask and Strathallan. At Perth Strathallan had a considerable force from the North, though the Reverend John Maclachlan probably over-estimated it at 5,000. Charles sent back Maclachlan of Castle Lachlan to bring up Strathallan's force, Frazers, Mackintoshes, Mackenzies, and so on, but, says the Reverend writer, 'Lord Strathallan refused to comply with the Prince's orders, though the men were willing.' From France Lord John Drummond brought his own regiment of Royal Scots, and fifty men from each of the six Irish regiments in French service, to Montrose, Stonehaven, and Peterhead. But two of Drummond's transports were captured ; in one of them was young Glengarry, later unhappily notorious. Walpole tells us that Young Glengarry was mistaken, in London, for the Duke of York. The Dutch troops being neutralised, under the capitulation of Tournay : George II. secured in their place 6,000 Hessians, for at this time the French preparations at Dunkirk caused some alarm to England, and gave some hopes to the Prince. But nobody in England or Scotland need have hoped or feared, so far as France was concerned.

On December 15, when Charles was in Carlisle, when a French force should have been moving, if it was to move at all, the Duke of York wrote to Louis XV. from Bagneux. 'Every day of delay discourages our friends, and may cause their entire desertion.' The French ministers were still refusing 'Bardolph's security,' that of Clancarty. Henry had written to ask another English envoy to come over and attest the devotion of the English Jacobites

P

He was a wealthy man, but we know not who he was, perhaps Barrymore, and he never came. Henry announced the arrival of two emissaries (George Kelly, and Carnegie, or perhaps Sir James Stewart), who were arrested in Holland, and driven to George's old resource of burning his papers. Charles, through them, asked for Lord John Drummond, who was sent, as we have observed, indeed his orders are of October 25. But Charles especially desired the embarcation of the force at Dunkirk, without which all was useless. Even had Charles advanced, presently, from Derby, it is extremely improbable that the French force would have reached English shores.

It is true that, at the end of November, a Jesuit, named Gordon, brought encouraging but erroneous news to France. He averred that Charles had received assurances from 'more than a hundred nobles in various parts of England,' and considerable sums of money. This Gordon was later taken, and proved to have been the bearer of money ; as to the 'assurances' they must, at most, have been verbal. He estimated the Prince's army at 12,000 men, at least double the real numbers, but even he admitted that the English Jacobites would not rise till the French landed. But the Duke of York, on November 26, wrote to Charles a letter which must have fallen into English hands, probably with a captured ship. Mr. Ewald prints it from the 'State Papers.'

Henry declares that the French ministers visit him *sans façon*, and that d'Argenson sent to Charles a message to the effect that Louis was 'absolutely resolved,' and that the French expedition would be ready about December 20, New Style. At that very date the officers were leaving for Christmas in Paris. But if such news reached Charles, he might well insist on persevering in his advance.

Otherwise the Prince had a sorry prospect before him in England. Wade, not much to be dreaded, was behind him on his left. Ligonier, marching from the South, on Lancashire, is credited with 8,250 foot, and 2,200 horse, and thirty guns. What were 4,500 men against so much larger and better provided a force?

Halting a day at Penrith, probably to give Wade a chance of coming up and being beaten, Charles next marched to Kendal. In the gorge of Shap Fell his Highlanders must have deemed themselves at home: here were such precipices and such a stream as they knew in Lochaber and Glencoe. Charles is said to have wearied on the march, and supported himself on the shoulder of a stalwart mountaineer. The anecdote of the blacksmith who knocked nails into his shoes, and to whom Charles said 'You are the first of your trade that ever shod the son of a King,' occurs in the 'Scots Magazine' of the day. Strict orders were given that everything

taken by the troops was to be paid for : when stay-
ing in gentlemen's houses Charles was wont to leave
five guineas as presents for the servants. His expenses at Penrith, for food, lights, and so on, amounted
to about forty shillings. The accounts, kept by
Mr. Gibb, are extant, and the Prince's behaviour is
in contrast with the rapacious looting of Cumberland and Hawley. The bills for wine, brandy, and
ale are not large, considering the numbers of thirsty
officers who supped with the Prince. Lancaster was
reached on November 25, on the 26th Lord George,
to abolish the 'freit' or superstition against bad luck
at Preston, marched the army over the Ribble.
Here, at Preston, a council was held, says Johnstone,
and the Prince gave hopes of recruits at Manchester.
He examined the scene of the fight behind barricades
at Preston, in 1715, and was not unnaturally surprised at that unfortunate surrender. At Preston
came in Morgan and Vaughan, from Wales, 'with
a few common men.' It is difficult to be certain,
but probably Morgan had hopes to hold out of a
rising in Wales, under Sir Watkin Wynne, and the
Cycle Club. But though Wynne and the rest were
certainly beginning to stir, they moved too late, and
the retreat from Derby paralysed them. Morgan, a
lawyer and a poetical enthusiast, was later hanged
for treason.

At Preston a townsman asked what was the

Prince's religion? 'That is still to seek,' answered
Elcho. On the 28th the army reached Wigan.
Here Johnstone tells us how Dickson, a sergeant of
his who had enlisted from the prisoners at Prestonpans, asked leave to hurry on, and recruit at
Manchester. Not getting leave he took it, marched
ahead with a drummer and his mistress, terrorised
the Whigs in the mob, was rescued by the Jacobites
of the town, and enrolled 180 recruits. Thus Manchester 'was taken by a sergeant, a drummer, and a
girl.' The anecdote is authenticated by contemporary
letters in the 'State Papers.' Some 250 or 300 men
were raised, and the unhappy little band was entrusted to Mr. Townley, of an old Lancashire Jacobite
family. At Manchester there were acclamations,
bonfires, and illuminations; 'the Prince had met
nothing like this since his reception at Edinburgh,'
says Maxwell. He adds, however, that a retreat
was already talked of, as there was neither a rising
in England nor a landing from France.

On leaving Manchester the Prince repaired a
broken bridge, publicly announcing that Wade might
find it convenient. He forded the Mersey, near
Stockton, where a few of the Cheshire gentry met
him. The reports he had received (probably from
the sanguine Sempil) prepared him to find many
adherents in Lancashire, 'sous la conduite des
Lords Derby, Barrymore, Petre, Chesterfield, Moly-

neux, et de MM. Shutleworth, Curzon, Fenwick,
Muster, Lister.' In Cheshire were to be expected
'Warrington, Molyneux, Sir Robert Grosvenor,
with 22,000*l.* a year, Sir John Wren, Cholmondeley,
Warburton, and the Leighs.' In the secret drawer
of an old bureau at Lord Leigh's house, Stoneleigh,
in Warwickshire, a miniature and a little relic of the
Prince were lately found. Nothing overt was done in
Cheshire, however, except that old Mrs. Skyring, who,
as a child, is said to have seen Charles II. land at
Dover, came in and greeted her Prince. Yearly she
had sent half her income to James, only concealing
her name. She had now sold her plate and jewels,
she gave the money to Charles, kissing his hand,
and saying, 'Lord, now lettest thou thy servant depart
in peace.' Her prayer was heard, she died of the
news of the retreat from Derby: the last of the old
loyal line of the Cavaliers.

At Macclesfield (December 1) a council of war
was held. John Hay of Restalrig (in Home's Appendix) writes : ' It was unanimously agreed to make
some forced marches, so as to get between the Duke's
army' (at Newcastle-under-Lyme, Stafford, and Lichfield) 'and London, and then march on as fast as
they could to London. One of the keenest for that
measure was Lord George Murray.' Lord George
himself says : ' We resolved to march for Derby, and,
to cover our intentions, I offered to go with a column

of the army to Congleton, which was the straight road
to Litchfield, so that the enemy would have reason
to think we intended to come on them, which would
make them gather in a body, and readily advance on
that road, so that we could get before them to Derby.
This was agreed to. A little before we got to Congleton, the Duke of Kingston and his horse retired to
Newcastle-under-Lyme, where Mr. Weir, with one or
two others, were taken. . . . This Weir was principal spy,' in France, in 1744, as well as at home,
adds Murray of Broughton. Charles refused to let
the spy be shot, and Weir's evidence was later fatal
to many of his adherents.

The Prince insisted that Weir 'was not found in
his army in disguise,' says Maxwell, whether 'guided
by his opinion or his inclination ; I suspect the latter,
because it was his constant practice to spare his
enemies when they were in his power.' Long afterwards, when, in 1754, the Earl Marischal accused
Charles of a treacherous act, the unfortunate Prince
replied, almost in Maxwell's words, that he could
not injure his worst enemy, if in his power. And
indeed he possessed, as he proved in the case of
Weir, this noble attribute of clemency.

The English troops having retired to Stone, Lord
George marched through Leek to Ashbourne, and was
joined by the Prince at Derby, on December 4.
Charles had found the roads lined by applauding

crowds, wearing the White Cockade, yet a Whig observer remarked his melancholy.

Next day was held that fatal council which decided on retreat. Hay of Restalrig avers that no council was held, that Lord George only went and came, in a tangle of intrigues. But Charles, in Rome, thirty years later, replied, to the queries of Home, that a council was held, and that all the members, except himself, 'were of opinion that retreat was absolutely necessary; and that Monsieur le Comte' (Charles) 'endeavoured to persuade some of them to join with him, but could not prevail on one single person.' This is decisive. D'Éguilles writes that he saw no overwhelming danger in an advance, but probably he was not of the council. In his Mémoire to Louis XV. he speaks of a division of opinion *dont je dois taire les causes.*

Lord Macleod, who was in Scotland, and Johnstone, who was not of the council, maintain that the retreat was caused by letters from Lord John Drummond, who exaggerated his numbers, and advised retreat and a junction with them. In reality, Lord John brought but 800 men, at most, and guns without ammunition. Charles must, however, have heard from Lord John, before reaching Derby. Indeed Lord Macleod says that Lord John disobeyed Charles's order to march south, though his instructions, from France, placed him absolutely at the

Prince's commands. Yet, according to Macleod, Louis had commanded him first to reduce the castles in Scotland. The orders, in the 'Stuart Papers,' do not bear out this assertion. In fact, as Ker of Graden shows, the command to Lord John to march south must have been given by Charles *after* the retreat was decided upon.

The story about the necessity of joining Lord John was clearly a tale told to soothe the army, who were in the highest spirits, and were taking the sacrament, and sharpening their swords, 'in crowds, before the shops of the cutlers,' says Johnstone.

The wisdom of the retreat has been much disputed. That the Duke of Newcastle was in a fright, and spent a day in pondering over which side he should choose, may be true, but neither his terror, nor the run on the Bank in London, on that 'Black Friday,' proves that the Highlanders had a chance of entering the capital. 'If they please to cut us off from the main army they may,' wrote the Duke of Richmond from Lichfield to Sir Everard Fawkener, on the morning of December 5. 'And also, if they please to give us the slip, and march to London, I fear they may, before even this avant-garde can come up with them ; and, if we should, his Royal Highness' (Cumberland) 'knows best what can be expected from such an inconsiderable corps as ours.' In truth, the English generals overestimated, by three times, the little army of 4,500 Jacobites : hence their undeniable anxiety, of which the Prince and Lord George were unaware. As to France, 'the French ministers were now in the very crisis of decision as to their projected expedition,' says Lord Mahon. But, even had Charles reached London, it is improbable that France could have sent her troops across the Channel. A better hope was in Wales, but Barry, who had been sent to Charles from Lord Barrymore and Sir Watkin, with promises, arrived in Derby two days after the retreat. So Charles, years afterwards, informed James. Probably the strongest chance lay in disaffection among the English troops, if once Charles had given the Duke of Cumberland the slip. The terror in London is attested by Fielding, and might have reached the disorderly camp at Finchley. We see that all might have been well, but what Lord George saw was that he would be surrounded by three armies—Wade's, the Duke's, and the Finchley force—of 30,000 men. Not one of his army would escape, in case of defeat, and the Prince, if he fled, must be taken. 'His Royal Highness had no regard to his own danger, but pressed with all the force of argument to go forward.' 'Rather than go back,' he cried, ' I would be twenty feet underground,' according to Captain Daniel, a Lancashire volunteer, whose manuscript is cited by Lord Mahon. Lord George adds, contrary to Charles's statement (made

much later), that the Duke of Perth was won over by
Charles's persuasions. The Prince at last suggested
marching on Wales, 'but every other officer declared
for a retreat, which some thought would be scarcely
practicable.' Lord George supposed the camp at
Finchley to have been formed, but, on December 4,
Cumberland was only suggesting the assembling of
the infantry there : while, on December 6, Newcastle
was pressing Cumberland to return to London.

It is vain to argue about what might have been.
Lord George, imperfectly informed, was compelled to
look at the situation in the light of what he knew.
Charles beheld it in the spirit of romance. *De
l'audace, et toujours de l'audace*, had been his motto,
and it had served him well. Advance might mean
a glorious death : retreat emphatically meant irre-
trievable ruin. Lives might be saved, lands would
assuredly be lost, the crown would be for ever
unattainable. It is clear that Charles did not set his
own life at a pin's fee : thinking that

> One crowded hour of glorious life
> Is worth an age without a name !

Here sympathy cannot fail Charles. On *his*
head alone was a price set, and he alone, among the
leaders, was ready 'to win or lose it all.' In this
hour he lived up to the ideal in which he had been
instructed, and chose the better, the heroic part. All

was vain, and the Council left him a sullen and embittered man. No young and generous heart has
ever read of the retreat from Derby without a pang.
The iron entered into the soul of Charles. A greater
man, no doubt, would not now have lost temper : he
would have been as active on the retreat as on the
advance. This he owed to his followers. But
Charles was not a Bruce. He was bitterly disappointed : more, he had been disobeyed. Those
deep and salt waters of pain, anger, resentment,
began to flood the heart which they were later to
overflow, drowning, at last, love, kindness, trust,
compassion, deeper than plummet could sound.

The Prince had entered Derby on the night of
December 4, the retreat was resolved on next day,
and the secret was kept, as far as possible, till the
morning of the 6th, when the troops marched. In
his 'History of the Present Rebellion' (1746)
Marchant, a mere compiler, gives a curious 'Letter
from a Gentleman at Derby.' He had six officers
and forty privates quartered upon him. 'Most of
the men,' says this alarmed citizen, 'looked like so
many fiends turned out of Hell, and under their
plaids nothing but various sorts of butchering weapons
were to be seen.' However, far from being car-
nivorous, they were content with bread and cheese
and ale, and fresh straw, on which they slept in the
hall and the laundry. These apartments, not un-

naturally, began to smell disagreeably, so many men, so long unwashed, being their tenants. Next day they waxed bolder, and, before leaving, 'eat up near a side of beef, eight joints of mutton, three couple of fowls, four cheeses, with abundance of white and brown bread, and,' we learn with regret, 'would have drams continually, as well as strong ale, beer, tea, etc. But really what did afford me some matter for an unavoidable laugh (tho' my family in this miserable situation) was to see these desperadoes, from the officers to the common men, first pull off their bonnets, and then lift up their eyes in a most solemn manner, and mutter something to themselves by way of saying Grace . . . as if they had been so many pure primitive Christians.' The red-coated 'vermin of Hell,' in Scotland, did not astonish their hosts in this way. The poetical Celtic speech seemed to this gentleman of Derby to be like that of 'a herd of Hottentots, wild monkies in a desert, or vagrant gipsies.'

There is usually some fact at the foundation of a fable, and Hay's tale of a day of *brigue*, as he calls it, at Derby, is clearly based on his recollection of circumstances described by Lord George Murray. Old Sir John Macdonald discovered the secret of the retreat, and 'What,' says he to Keppoch, 'a Macdonald turn his back!' And, to Lochiel, 'For shame, a Cameron run away from

the enemy ! Go forward, and I'll lead you !' This
gentleman was old, and had dined heartily, for he
was much subject to his bottle. Others grumbled at
the resolution in which they had acquiesced in
the morning ; such were Sheridan and Murray of
Broughton. Old Tullibardine 'seemed much for
going forwards,' and in the evening the chiefs and
officers told Charles that forwards they would go,
after all, if Charles's secret advisers would 'sign
their opinion.' But they did not do that, and the
army marched northwards on the 6th, between nine
and ten o'clock. Johnstone tells us of the disappointment of the army, when they found, what
they had not at first observed, that they were on the
backward route. Nothing was heard, 'but expressions of rage and lamentation. If we had been
beaten the regret could not have been greater.'
Macdonald of Sleat says that Charles was 'the best
officer in his army.' He certainly was most in
sympathy with the spirit of his men.

The army, in retreat, saved time by occupying
its old quarters. Lord George was with the rear,
Charles, his vivacity lost, rose late, and rode to the
van. At Manchester the mob was now hostile, and
a fine was raised from the town. At Preston they
halted for a day, and Perth set out for Scotland, but
was turned back by the hostility of the country, for
beacons were blazing on every hill. The country

yokels had false news of a defeat of the Highlanders, hence their daring.

At Lancaster Lord George says that the Prince thought of fighting, and bade him select a good position, but Charles changed his mind.

Lord George's narrative is throughout written in the tone of an injured man. He says that, at Lancaster, he with Sullivan, and, by his request, Lochiel, chose a good position, and captured two or three of Oglethorpe's Rangers, a green-clad body of mounted Volunteers, detached from the force of Wade, who retired on Hexham and Newcastle. From them it was learned that the Rangers were at Garston, eight miles back, while a large force of dragoons were at Preston. Lord George gave the Prince his information, adding that he had chosen a position to his desire, but the Prince now replied that he would march next day. Lord George believed that Charles only spoke of fighting for the purpose of hearing himself contradicted by his General. But Ker, who had reconnoitred the ford, says that the party guarding it would necessarily be too remote from the main body, and for that reason it was thought proper to march. Ker was usually with Lord George, who praises his skill and courage, and Ker's evidence may be accepted.

At Kendal they were rejoined by Perth, and Lord George Murray found Sullivan supping with the

Prince. ' He had got some mountain Malaga, which he seemed very fond of, and gave me a glass or two of it.' But he was dilatory in writing out his orders, and next morning there was confusion. Cumberland was following with all his cavalry, and 1,000 mounted infantry, horsed by the local gentry. Charles and the van reached Penrith, where he seems to have been reviewing his men on the 18th. The pursuit had been delayed a day by messages from Newcastle. He had news from Vernon of French intentions, and desired Cumberland to return to London, after sending reinforcements to Wade, while Ligonier was also ordered to the South. The alarm died out, and Cumberland was requested to continue his pursuit.

In spite of this delay, he was only prevented from overtaking the Prince's long straggling line by a gallant resistance offered by Lord George at Clifton, close to Lord Lowther's house, and two or three miles from Penrith. The affair was fought at night, *sub luce maligna*, the moon being in her second quarter, and the details are disputed. The evidence, however, of Lord George, Ker, and Macpherson of Strathmashie, all of whom were engaged, carries most weight. In the morning of the 17th Charles, from the van, sent to bid Lord George leave ' not the least thing, not so much as a cannon ball behind.' In a mile or two, Lord George was delayed by a derelict gun and a quantity of ammunition. He paid his Highlanders sixpence apiece to carry the cannon-balls up the hill.   On the morning of the 18th Lord George had similar troubles of transport, and, observing small bodies of horses hanging about, he sent news to Charles, who thought they were mere militia.   Chancellor Ferguson, in a valuable tract on these affairs, shows that the hovering horse were Chasseurs from General Bland's force.   They fled when the Glengarry men cast their plaids for a charge.   From Clifton Lord George sent the artillery to Penrith, and then scouted about Lowther, Lord Lonsdale's park and house.   The park gates were shut, but, on some Highlanders climbing the walls, a footman rushed out of the house.

He was a servant of Cumberland's, and had been sent on, says Ker, to notify that his master would sleep at Lowther.   Being taken, he said that the Duke was close at hand with 4,000 dragoons.   By this time Pitsligo's horse had been sent back by Charles ; most of them, however, retreated again, to Lord George's indignation.   According to Thomas Savage, a Quaker, whose house was near by, Pitsligo's men tried to lay an ambush : young Savage gave information, and Pitsligo's horse fled under fire : Lord George sent the footman and another prisoner to Charles, with a message that he would hold Clifton in the meanwhile. Between him and the open moor, which he had just passed, and where Cumberland's 4,000 dragoons now were, was the village of Clifton, with lanes, the park wall, and, apparently, three fields, separated from each other by strong hedges. On returning to the village from his visit to Lowther House (which was a place he knew well) Lord George found himself reinforced by Perth, Cluny's men, and Ardshiel's Appin Stewarts. He had also the Glengarry regiment and 200 men of John Roy Stewart's, 1,000 in all of the pick of the army.

The enemy was now visible, within gunshot, in several divisions and squadrons. Perth rode to Penrith, to bring back the whole Highland force, and it seems that Lord George thought he had a chance to give Cumberland a severe defeat. As it happened, Perth must have been crossed by Roy Stewart, with a message that Lord George was to retreat, and Charles himself was presently moving north to Carlisle. When Roy Stewart came in, Lord George acted on his own responsibility, and held his post in spite of Charles's orders. He had already deceived the enemy, before Charles's command came, by sending colours to various points which he did not really occupy, and retiring them behind cover. After an hour, Cumberland dismounted some 500 dragoons, on Lord George's estimate, and sent them from the moor to line the ditch of the nearest of the three hedged fields, behind which the Highlanders lay. The ingenious Quaker, Mr. Savage, had signalled the

Highlanders' position to the English by waving his
hat. The highway intersected those fields, of which
the Glengarry men occupied the right, and Ardshiel's,
with Cluny, the left. Roy Stewart's 200 held the
road itself: Glengarry's clan, with Lochgarry, were
nearest the moor, and flanked the advancing dragoons.
Lochgarry could not estimate their numbers, 'we
only heard the noise of their boots, and could plainly
discern their yellow belts.'

The dismounted dragoons were from Bland's,
Ker's, and Cobham's regiments. The Stewarts and
Macphersons advanced, firing, while Ker, says Lord
George, 'was riding through the fields at the time
of fire, as if it had been a review.' At the lowest
field they received a volley from the dragoons
in the ditch. Old Gordon of Glenbucket's target
was peppered, and Cluny shouted, 'What the dewil is
this?' Lord George replied that they must charge
sword in hand, cried 'Claymore!' and led the Highlanders. They were under fire as they cut their way
with dirks through hedges, severe on 'our light-tailed
lads,' and then rushed with the sword on the dragoons
in the lowest ditch. Says Strathmashie, 'the poor
swords suffered much, as there were no less than
fourteen broke on the dragoons skull caps . . . ,
before it seems the better way was found of going
their business,' doubtless with the point. About fifty
swords were taken from dead dragoons; the survivors

fled to the moor, enfiladed by the fire of the Glengarry men.   A few Highlanders who, despite Lord George's orders, pursued on the open moor were taken. Lord George, after waiting for half an hour, withdrew towards Penrith (Oglethorpe [1] was court-martialed and acquitted for failing to cut him off on Broughton Moor) : he found Charles just mounting to retreat. His Steward had there purchased three bottles of cherry brandy.   Lord George's Atholl men had returned to his aid, and were but half a mile from Clifton.

Where both sides claim a success, Lord George has the triumph.   He did what he wanted to do : checked the English, prevented their attack on the Prince at Penrith, and brought off his men, after routing part of the opposed force, and inflicting losses.   It was never his intention to remain all night at Clifton.   Home follows Lord George's account, which is corroborated by Ker, a good witness, Strathmashie, Lochgarry (who was wounded) and Cluny himself.   Johnstone's version coincides, but he places Lochiel where Cluny really was.   But, as Strathmashie writes, the English ' have their own way of telling stories, and even let them be doing with——'

---

[1] This gentleman, by Whig theory, was the Prince's uncle, James being, really, a young Oglethorpe ! The General was brother of Madame de Mézières, and, in 1752, she probably sheltered the Prince in the General's house at Godalming.

a phrase which Bishop Forbes leaves blank in ' The Lyon in Mourning.' 'Our men drove them out of Clifton, in an hour's time, with very small loss,' said Cumberland, adding that he dared not pursue, on account of the darkness. He owned to four officers wounded, and forty men killed or wounded : and admitted that the Highland charge broke Bland's dragoons. ' The (Scottish) dogs were obliged to run, and cried lamentably for mercy,' says one English letter, adding that 122 Highlanders were killed or drowned in ' the River Lowder ! '

Cumberland's men never again pressed so hard on the rear of the retreating clansmen. It is clear that the affair of Clifton rather discouraged the pursuers, and as Ker of Graden's account corroborates those of Lord George and Strathmashie we may hold that the Highlanders, by the lucky accident of taking Cumberland's footman, and getting his information, escaped a great peril. A large body of dragoons was on the moor, the advanced and dismounted dragoons were routed in the road, lanes, and ditch, the reserve had no heart to advance : and Lord George had done all that man might do.[1] Lord George marched right on to Carlisle ; having gone ' two days without resting from Kendal to Penrith,

---

[1] Some curious old maps of Clifton are given in Chancellor Fergusson's tract, ' The Retreat of the Highlanders through Westmorland in 1745.'

which is long twenty miles, and, without halt, sixteen more on to Carlisle, all without any sleep, and very little provision, yet we brought all the artillery safe, and lost very few men at the attack at Clifton,' says Lochgarry, whose report to Young Glengarry is printed by Mr. Blaikie. As for the useful footman, Charles courteously restored him to his cousin, the Duke. He made war like a gentleman.

On the dawn of December 20 Charles marched out of Carlisle, most unfortunately leaving a garrison of 300 men. Says Johnstone, ' he promised to return to their assistance in the course of a few days, though this seemed morally impossible. . . . ' Ker explains that Charles expected to meet Lord John Drummond's force 'well advanced towards the borders.' Lord George, in indignation, offered to stay in Carlisle with the Atholl men, 'though I knew my fate.' Who gave the fatal advice he did not know : doubtless he suspected Sullivan. Johnstone mentions a foolish theory that Townley's Manchester men were sacrificed to Charles's grudge against the English. Even his Editor, Watson, who ' has obtained a knowledge of Charles's public and private life through channels hitherto unknown ' (the ' Stuart Papers,' which fell into the hand of this adventurer), does not believe the Prince ' guilty of so infamous an act.' Watson adds that the Papers (of which he had the first reading) prove that Charles was ' first invited and then abandoned to his fate by a great part of the English aristocracy. . . . There is evidence of it in their own handwriting.'[1]

As to the foolish charge against Charles, reported by Johnstone, Watson reckons the English left in Carlisle at 114, the Scots at 274, which disposes of the absurdity. I think that Charles, who had set his heart on leaving not a cannon-ball behind, placed the garrison to guard his guns, all but three of which he could not carry across the Esk. Doubtless he was sanguine enough to expect to return, with the 3,000 men of Lord John Drummond and Strathallan. The mistake admits of a certain excuse. If Carlisle had been untenable, then Charles ought not to have trusted to the chance of relieving it with Lord John's and Strathallan's reinforcements. But Townley's adjutant, Syddal, left in writing a statement that 'it was the opinion of every one in the garrison who had been in foreign service, that the place was tenable for many days.' If so, Charles's hope was excusable.

Cumberland invested Carlisle on December 22. On December 28 cannon arrived from Whitehaven. On

---

[1] Of this evidence I have not found a single trace in the 'Stuart Papers.' It is true that in the wanderings, and half-begun editings or dealings with these MSS. (as by Lockhart, and by Watson himself, who, perhaps, abstracted compromising pieces for purposes of 'blackmail'), letters may have been withdrawn. But all evidence insists that the English would only deal by verbal messages, and never would set pen to paper.

the 30th the white flag was displayed. Cumberland avers that he offered no terms, except that the garrison should be reserved for 'the King's pleasure,' —which was to hang nine officers out of eighteen, including Townley. The Scots talked of breach of the capitulation, but Maxwell, who says that Townley desired to fight it out, does not countenance this complaint. Cumberland presently went to London, the French still causing alarm, and the Highlanders were not pursued into Scotland. Before following them, we may consider the aspect and the chances of the Rising at this juncture, when England learned, with heartfelt relief, that the brave Duke had driven the rebels from her soil. England lifted up her heart in hymns and songs :

> George is Magnanimous,
> Subjects unanimous ;
>   Peace to us bring :
> His fame is glorious,
> *Reign meritorious*,
>   God save the King !

Another minstrel chants to the tune of *Lillibullero :*

> O Brother Sawney, hear you the news ?
> Twang'em, we'll bang'em, and
>   Hang 'em up all.
> An army's just coming without any shoes ;
> Twang 'em, we'll bang 'em, and
>   Hang 'em up all !

Meanwhile all Grub Street rushed into Protestant tracts like ' A Protestant King and the Bible.' A Poem by J. Price, B.D., contrasted the religion of the 'Idolatrous Occupant of the Throne' (as the Cameronians called the devout George) with the creed of the bloodthirsty Pretender in Rome. 'The Poetical Works of the Young Chevalier,' I have not been able to procure. Sixteen new 'Antipapistical Works' were advertised in one month. 'Liberty and Property' is the title of one of these treatises and was also the motto on the flag of the Jacobite Manchester Regiment. Sixteen Whig Sermons were published in December, and thousands of them must have been preached. By these tokens, as well as by mob attempts at violence during his retreat, and subscriptions of money for the ' redcoated vermin of Hell,' Charles might have learned that his father's subjects did not desire the Liberty which he offered, and preferred to enjoy their Property under the pious rule of the German dynasty. No Prince was ever more plainly informed that he was not wanted. Yet Charles kept his flag flying, and the Rising became what Horace Walpole deemed a feeble thing, 'a rebellion on the defensive.' It argues well for the tenacity of the Celts, that there were not even more desertions from the army than actually occurred.

The hopes of French aid ought to have been extinguished. Government had taken up fifty mer-

chant vessels as cruisers: Vernon, Boscawen, and
Smith held the seas, each with a squadron: the
Dover privateers put themselves under jolly Vernon's
orders. Two privateers seized three French transports out of eight, convoyed by a man-of-war ; drove
seventeen smaller vessels on shore, sank two, captured
three, and blew one up. Vernon informed the
Mayor of Dover that ' a young person whom they call
the Prince' (the Duke of York) was at Dunkirk with
the French force, and he bade the seaboard towns
prepare to defend themselves (December 20). On
the 25th a great array of men-of-war went cruising
with Vernon. Martin, Smith, Boscawen, Stewart
(with the *Royal George*, 100 guns), Mostyn, and
Byng were in the Downs, at the Nore, at Plymouth,
on the Scottish coast, and, generally, where they
were likely to prove prejudicial to the designs of ' the
young person called the Prince.' Soon afterwards
Knowles and Gregory reconnoitred Calais, Boulogne,
and Dunkirk, finding, in each case, that the French
invasion had dwindled beneath the dignity of a
bugbear.

In the North late in November, Captain Hill, of
the *Hazard*, had been troubling Montrose, where
French ships often landed men and supplies. But,
on November 24, Erskine, of Ogilvy's, captured the
Hazard. On December 3 Lord Loudon, who had
been collecting forces in alliance with Forbes of

Culloden, relieved Fort Augustus, threatened by the Frazers, under the Master of Lovat. On the 11th Loudon carried Old Lovat in custody to Inverness : he escaped on the 20th and the Frazers marched south to join the Prince. Macleod, Munro of Culcairn, and Grant of Grant went forth to relieve Aberdeen. But fortune frowned on ' the false fairy flag of Macleod,' and Lord Lewis Gordon drove him across Spey (his men would not face a charge) with loss of a number of prisoners and a few killed and wounded. Lord John Drummond's scanty reinforcements had drifted, part to Lord Lewis Gordon, part to Lord Strathallan at Perth. About December 23 Lord Lewis marched to Perth, where the Jacobites now had some 4,000 men, on a high computation. They were Mackintoshes, Frazers, Mackenzies (under Lord Cromarty and his son, Lord Macleod, who had long hung undecided), Farquharsons, Gordons, Lowlanders, and Irish and Scots in French service. They were all at feud owing to the refusal of Strathallan (or, as Lord Macleod says, of Lord John Drummond) to obey orders, and join Charles on the Border. By this refusal was the Carlisle garrison lost. They did now obey the orders of the Prince, sent from Dumfries (December 21) to join him at Glasgow.

Such was the posture of affairs north of the Border. Edinburgh, though reinforced, was trembling ; Glasgow, and Edinburgh also, were raising Volunteers. We left Charles marching out of Carlisle on December 20. On the bank of the flooded Esk, seven miles from Carlisle, Lord George arranged the future movements. He with six battalions was to march on Ecclefechan, next on Moffat, next, after a day's halt, to make a feint on the road to Edinburgh, turn off to Douglas, and so to Hamilton and Glasgow. Charles, with the horse, and most of the clans, was to go to Annan, next day to Dumfries, and rest a day, then to Drumlanrig, Lead Hills, Douglas, and Glasgow. The Highlanders, shoulder to shoulder, forded Esk in red spate, a hundred men abreast. 'The water was big, and took most of the men breast high.' Lord George was in his philabeg. 'Some ladies had passed the water on horseback, just before us; but had they looked back they could have seen nothing, the water was so big. The pipes began to play so soon as we had passed, and the men all danced reels, which in a moment dried them, for they held the tails of their short coats in their hands in passing the river, so when their thighs were dry, all was right.'

Lord Mahon states that Charles, who forded lower on horseback, rescued, 'with great intrepidity and presence of mind,' a soldier who was being carried away by the stream; 'at the same time calling out *Cobhear, Cobhear*, that is, Help, Help, and supporting him until he could receive assistance.' This

anecdote may be from the manuscript of Captain
Daniel, a Lancashire recruit, but Lord Mahon gives
no authority, nor have I been able to see Captain
Daniel's account, which is cited occasionally by
Robert Chambers.   Elcho with his horse entered
Dumfries before the Prince, and found the bonfires
blazing for a rumoured defeat of the Highlanders.
As the Dumfries people had looted some baggage
waggons when the army was marching south, the
town was rather heavily fined.   The robbers of the
baggage were Seceders, probably Cameronians, who
had been out under a flag with an inscription about
Kirk and Covenants.   Charles stayed in what is now
the Commercial Hotel, boasting a fine old panelled
room, with an old portrait of the Prince on horseback.
On the 23rd the Prince slept at Douglas Castle,
whence the Highlanders carried off the sword,
later recovered, of the good Lord James, Bruce's
famous comrade.   The terrors of Edinburgh now
made it necessary to recall thither four regiments
that had been sent to Stirling in November, with the
Glasgow Militia, who were safer at a distance from
their city.   Glasgow, where the two Highland columns
met, was then a pretty little open town, with her
ancient Cathedral, her College courts and gardens,
her houses with tall crowstepped gables, situated on
a clear and beautiful river.   Already, however, the
place was wealthy, having flourished much on tobacco

and sugar since the days of Bailie Nicol Jarvie.
Charles lay at Shawfield House, belonging then to
Mr. Glassford, and now covered by the Trongate.

At Glasgow Charles heard of the fall of Carlisle ;
he had already sent for the forces under Lord John
Drummond and Lord Strathallan at Perth. His
army had entered the town in such condition as may
be guessed : ragged, shoeless, long of beard, and raw
of limb. Perhaps to make an opposite impression,
Charles dressed in Glasgow with unusual care and
splendour. He might hope, at least, to convert the
ladies of this hostile town. 'Our very ladies,' writes
Provost Cochrane, 'had not the curiosity to go near
him, and declined going to a ball held by his chiefs.
Very few were at the windows when he made his
appearance, and such as were declared him not
handsome. This no doubt fretted.'

After refitting the army at the expense of the city,
Charles held a review. Among the spectators was a
young runaway from Queen's College, Oxford, later
a Volunteer in the Glasgow corps. His manuscript
letters, to one of the Gilpin family, show a high spirit.
He ridiculed the Highlanders, laughed at the fears
and imbecile generalship of his countrymen, and told
how, as he stood near the Prince, he was tempted to
seize a musket and shoot him. One or two such
attempts are said to have been made, and forgiven
by the clemency of Charles. Captain Daniel de-

scribes his aspect, ' no object could be more charming, no personage more captivating, no deportment more agreeable than his.' Long afterwards a Glasgow citizen recorded his impression of Charles's ' princely aspect, its interest much heightened by the dejection which appeared in his pale fair countenance, and downcast eye.' Whig observers almost invariably note his air of profound melancholy : at this moment he may just have heard of the fate of his garrison at Carlisle. His exactions in Glasgow did not increase the popularity of his cause. Had he marched at once on Edinburgh, he could probably have refilled his coffers there, such was the terror that prevailed. But troops under Huske, Cholmondeley, and, later, Hawley, were reinforcing Edinburgh, from New Year's Day onwards : the whole force amounting to three regiments of dragoons, fourteen battalions of foot, and Volunteers.

On January 3 Charles set out for Stirling : with sanguine trust in his French engineers and artillery he hoped to capture Stirling Castle. His French guns were with difficulty brought round from Perth, by Alloa, and the Ford of Frew, Lord George securing the use of a vessel, and the Camerons protecting the movement.

From January 4 to 16 Charles was at Sir Hugh Paterson's house of Bannockburn. Here he suffered from fever and cold : his nurse was the black-eyed

Clementina Walkinshaw, niece of Sir Hugh, and one of the many daughters of Walkinshaw of Baronfield, of an old Jacobite family. We must suppose that the lady's charms do not receive justice in her portrait.[1]

Tradition declares that she vowed fidelity to Charles, even in desperate fortunes : whether she actually became his mistress at this time is uncertain. The Marquis D'Éguilles says that he was not *coquet* or *galant*, which made the fair sex admire him all the more. A letter of Clementina's in 1760 is ambiguous as to her precise relations with Charles, at this time, but rather suggests that she loved unwisely. Several years passed before he asked her to join him in his obscure exile, and this return to so old a love is one of the most curious, as it was one of the most unfortunate and ill-judged, steps in his career. At Bannockburn he had (as Murray of Broughton later revealed to the English Government) a short and secret visit from Sir James Douglas, with promise of English aid in money.

On February 8 the town of Stirling surrendered : not so General Blakeney, who retired to the Castle, on the precipitous rock. The stony soil made it hard to dig trenches : the Highlanders lost men,

---

[1] There is a brilliant sketch of Clementina's personal aspect, sharp and dark, with large bright black eyes, and a clever though necessarily fanciful drawing of her character, in Mr. McAulay's novel, *Poor Sons of a Day*.

their guns were dismounted, their French engineer
is said to have been a model of vanity and imbecility,
and he *was*, if the site of his low and unprotected
battery, under the Castle guns, is correctly pointed
out. Though now joined by all his forces, the
Prince's army was probably reckoned rightly, by
Patullo, at only 9,000 men. Meanwhile Hawley was
setting out from Edinburgh to relieve Stirling.
Hawley is described by Horace Walpole (January 3,
1746) as ' a military magistrate of some fierceness. . . .
He will not sow the seeds of future disloyalty by too
easily pardoning the present.' Later Horace writes :
' He will give a mortal blow to the pride of the Scotch
nobility,' who were mostly on his own side. But
England, at this time, in her winning way, insisted
on regarding all Scots as ' rebels,' actual or potential.
Hawley was called ' The Lord Chief Justice, frequent
and sudden executions are his passion. . . . He is
very brave and able ; with no small bias to the
brutal.' In addition to his courage and brutality,
Hawley had, as he later confessed, an unwarrantably
low opinion of his adversaries. This he excused as
the natural result of misleading information.

Meanwhile things were going ill in the camp of
the Prince. Since Derby he had not summoned a
Council : the last held was too unpalatable. On
January 6 Lord George presented him with a
memorial, demanding a Council, and the appointment

of a standing Committee of chiefs and officers. 'What a catastrophe might have followed,' it was asked, 'had not a Council determined the retreat from Derby?' A Council would not have lost a day at Lancaster, nor left a garrison in Carlisle. Charles was reminded that his men were Volunteers. He replied that there could be no army where there is no general, or, what is the same thing, no obedience or deference paid to him. He expected from gentlemen Volunteers 'more zeal, more resolution, and more good manners, than in those that fight merely for pay. He alone had a price on his head, and alone could not threaten at every other word to throw down his arms and make his peace with the Government.' He took advice every day, especially the advice of Lord George. As to Carlisle, 'was there a possibility of carrying off the cannon and baggage, or was there time to destroy them? And would not the doing it have been a greater dishonour to our arms?' Had not Lord George offered to stay with the Atholl Brigade? These last were very weak arguments. 'My authority may be taken from me by violence, but I shall never resign it like an Ideot.'

While the leaders were on these ill terms, the men were deserting, and Tullibardine had to go to Atholl to look for, and force out, many of the Atholl regiment. Hawley's army, with which he was to encounter Charles's waning and distracted force, is commonly estimated at about 8,000, including some 1,300 cavalry, in part Hamilton's and Gardiner's, now Ligonier's dragoons. These had not yet recovered their moral tone. Hawley himself, after Falkirk, tells Cumberland that he outnumbered the foe by 2,000. To reconnoitre, Lord George took five battalions, and Elcho's and Pitsligo's horse, as far as Linlithgow, on the 13th. He came into touch with the English dragoons, who retired ; nor, when Lord George went back by the bridge, did they offer to cross. Two gentlemen in the Highland horse discovered the whole of Hawley's army coming on, and Lord George withdrew.

On the 17th, all his Northern reinforcements being now collected, Charles left 1,200 men to watch Stirling Castle, and, on Lord George's proposal, set out to gain the hill of Falkirk. His movements were cleverly disguised by a feint. The weather was threatening, and Lord George, unlike Sullivan, wished to fight at once, and avoid a night in the open. The Carron had to be crossed, but did not delay the Highlanders. The Macdonalds held the right wing, the Camerons the left, being outflanked by three English battalions. Here there was 'no superior officer,' says Lord George, which led, in his opinion, to a great loss of advantages. A hill separated the armies, and Hawley (who had been lunching with Lady Kilmarnock) was rather hurried in his dispositions. His infantry was in two lines, the dragoons were on his left, the Glasgow and Lothian Volunteers behind them, *en potence*, ' to make a show.' Home was with them and describes their conduct. The Campbells, some 800, were on the right of the regulars. Maxwell reckons the whole at 10,000 to 12,000 men. Hawley, according to Ker of Graden, began marching his forces up the hill, and Home censures his conduct in sending his dragoons in front, on unknown and broken ground, to charge a whole army. Ligonier exclaimed that 'it was the most extraordinary order ever given.' The hills rose and fell in different heights, so that ' neither of the parties could see from their right to their left.' This fact, combined with falling night, and showers of heavy rain in the faces of the English, makes the details of the encounter very confused.

It would be easy, by selecting the most picturesque statements, to give a thrilling account of the fight. We should hear of a glorious charge of dragoons in face of fire, of horse and men mingled in the broken yet resolute Highland ranks : of fallen warriors dirking horses, and finally sweeping through the struggling cavalry on to and over the English infantry, while two or three brave English regiments keep their order, repel the Highlanders, and gloriously remain masters of the field. But these details are the romance of Johnstone, and of the

' London Gazette,' though not wholly unfounded on facts.

In an unconscious repetition of a remark of Thucydides, Lord George says : ' It is not an easy task to describe a battle. Springs and motions escape the eye, and most officers are taken up with what is immediately near themselves ; so that it is next to impossible for one to observe the whole.' He reckons the Highland position excellent, they charged downhill, the wind and rain in their enemies' faces, while a morass protected their right from being outflanked by cavalry. The dragoons, therefore, followed by the English infantry, trotted up to within pistol shot of the Macdonalds, who fired, broke them, and pursued, losing, as they went, their own formation and getting hopelessly out of hand. The pipers had thrown their pipes to their boys, and were charging with their claymores, so could not sound the recall.   The left, Camerons, Appin Stuarts, and Macphersons, also routed the dragoons, and went, sword in hand, among the infantry.   Now the Highland left was outflanked by three English regiments of foot, posted on the further side of a ravine.   With these the second Highland line should have dealt, but their best men ran forward mixed with their front line : the rest went back to their hill-top, and, probably, out of sight.   Indeed they seem to have abandoned the field.

Ker of Graden now hurried the Irish, and the Prince's Guards, to the brow of the hill, whereon the three steady English regiments (who could know nothing of what had occurred on their own left) withdrew in perfect order. This is Ker's own account. In the mist and confusion, Macdonald of Tiendrish saw these English regiments, took them for Highlanders, went up to them, and asked why they did not charge. He was taken prisoner, and, later, was hanged. Lord George, who could not stop the Macdonalds, also fell in with the three English regiments, and one of dragoons (part of Cobham's), but had not collected forces enough to attack them. Lord George proposed following the rout into the town of Falkirk, 'concluding with Count Mercy's expression at Parma, that he would either lye in the town or in Paradise. His Royal Highness came up at that very time, and approved much of the resolution of attacking the town, and was himself advised to stay in some house in the face of the hill, till Lord George sent him word of the success.' Charles, therefore, with Sheridan and Sullivan, sat over the fire in a cottage on the hill. The pursuit was not close, and Hawley had time to try to burn his wet tents. But few prisoners were taken, the enemy flying to Linlithgow, while a contemporary diary declares that some dragoons raced as far as Musselburgh !

Meanwhile, the Highlanders, all distraught and unled, were pillaging the camp, instead of cutting off the enemy from Linlithgow. His private correspondence, and published report, show that Lord George, even in victory, drew gloomy conclusions as to the probable fortunes of such an army as his if pitted in fair field against regulars. Lord George blames the absence of officers who, he says, were with Charles in the reserve. On the other hand, Macdonald of Morar 'must acknowledge that the Irish officers were of great use to us in going through the different posts, and assisting in the several dispositions that were made.' As usual, Lord George censures Sullivan, 'whom the Prince chiefly trusted with the disposition,' and who should have brought up men from the second line, or 'corps de reserve, to have extended the first line—nothing was more easy ; but that gentleman had no knowledge in these affairs, nor was he ever seen to do anything in the time of action.' It is curious that Sheridan (in a letter quoted by Mr. Ewald), the Macdonald narrator, Morar, and Johstone, who much disliked the Prince, all, with Home, represent Charles as doing what Lord George says was left undone, 'extending to the left,' and encouraging his forces. D'Éguilles confirms these statements in his Correspondence.

Home timed the first shot at ten minutes to four, on a dark evening of January. Spectators beheld the English army 'enter the misty and storm-covered moor at the top of the hill; then saw the dull atmosphere thickened by a fast-rolling smoke, and heard the peeling sound of the discharge; immediately after they beheld the discomfited troops burst wildly from the cloud in which they had been involved, and rush in far-spread disorder over the hill.' So Chambers quotes local tradition. This was 'the *break* of the battle,' and from the Highlanders, lost in pursuit and plunder, Lord George, and Charles, if we follow many narrators, could but tardily collect 600 men.

The confusion was natural enough, considering the ground, the storm, and the darkness. If the Highlanders lost an opportunity, so did Hawley, who, it is easy to say, might have made use of Huske's unbroken regiments.

Hawley, writing to Cumberland from Linlithgow, that night, says, 'My heart is broke.'

Hawley himself obviously did much to secure his own defeat, and he did nothing to repair it. His disaster horrified every one at Court, except sturdy King George,—and Sir John Cope, who felt a little consoled, as was natural. The losses on both sides were not very considerable, but many officers fell on the English side, including the brave Sir Robert Munro, and several of Wolfe's regiment, which seems to have failed to distinguish itself. Home reports discouragement on both sides : 'at no time from the beginning to the end of the Rebellion were the real friends of the Constitution more dejected. . . . Altercation, confusion, and animosity prevailed in the irregular and undisciplined Highland army, which it was not an easy matter to command.' Home himself, with Thomas Barrow, was made prisoner, and later escaped from Doone Castle in a romantic manner, displaying singular courage. Barrow, afterwards, told to Collins some of Home's Highland legends, so to Falkirk fight we owe Collins's beautiful Ode on Highland Superstitions. 'How sleep the brave who sink to rest' may, perhaps, be claimed as a tribute to the fallen of either party.

The day following Falkirk, January 18, was a deluge of rain. Johnstone was sent out to find the enemy's artillery, in the mist and deserted marshes, where lay the white stripped bodies of the dead. 'I remarked a trembling and strong agitation in my horse, which constantly shook when it was forced to put its feet on the heaps of dead bodies and climb over.' It was not yet used to dead men, like the horses of Rhesus in the Iliad. Except for Johnstone and his men 'none of us quitted our lodgings.' Yet, people certainly 'quitted their lodgings.' Home was brought in as a prisoner, with others, by Kilmarnock, and Charles, throwing up the window of his room, and supporting it with his hand (no sashes

then in Scottish houses), conversed with his officer.
Presently a soldier in English uniform, with the black
cockade, marched alone up the muddy street. Home
expected to hear a shot ; Charles, seeing the
prisoners looking all one way, turned in that direction, observed the English soldier, and spoke to
Kilmarnock. Instantly Kilmarnock ran downstairs,
attacked the soldier, who was now opposite the Prince,
struck off his hat, and trampled on the black cockade.
Then a Highlander ran up, and grappled with
Kilmarnock. He drew a pistol, the Highlander drew
a dirk, a crowd of the Camerons dragged Kilmarnock
away. The man with the dirk restored the hat to
its owner, and all marched off with him in triumph.
The soldier, in fact, was a Cameron deserter from
the English army, who was rejoining his clan. He
of the dirk was the deserter's brother. 'And in
my opinion,' said a Highland officer who explained
the scene, 'no Colonel or General of the Prince's
army can take that cockade out of the man's hat,
except Lochiel himself.'

A gloomier event occurred on the same day. A
Keppoch Macdonald, firing off his gun (as they
often did, despite orders), accidentally slew Æneas
Macdonnell, Glengarry's second son, who commanded
the Macdonnells of Glengarry. Though very young,
he was already married to a niece of Robertson of
Struan, and from him (for Young Glengarry, at this

moment in the Tower, left no issue) descended Scott's friend, the last chief of this once almost royal race who owned his family's lands. Though the brave and unhappy victim, with his last breath, begged that his slayer might not suffer, he was executed, 'and after all,' says the Macdonald narrator, 'they began to desert daily upon this accident, which had a bad effect upon others, and also lessened our numbers considerably.' It is said that the fallen chief was interred in the grave of Wallace's companion, Sir John Graham, near which the fallen English officers were also laid to rest.

The one chance of keeping the Highlanders together, now that some were discontented, and many satisfied with booty, was to follow Hawley to Edinburgh. Maxwell says that some were for dealing this blow; he and Johnstone agree that the siege of Stirling Castle was resumed on a promising report by Mirabelle, the foolish French engineer. Johnstone says that 'every one' was in favour of instant advance: perhaps what decided the matter was the impossibility of removing the artillery, as Maxwell suggests. Lord George is silent, though he would doubtless have blamed Sullivan, if he could. Johnstone argues with much truth, that artillery was, throughout, a ruinous and useless burden to the Highlanders. The Prince went back to Bannockburn House: the helpless attempt at a siege lingered on, men deserted more or less, and Cumberland was on his way north, while Hawley, who had been blustering, flogging, and hanging in Edinburgh, was reinforced by two regiments of horse, and one of foot.

Maxwell declares, ' relating the fact precisely as it happened,' that Charles determined to fight Cumberland at Falkirk, and sent Murray to Lord George, bidding him stay there. ' Lord George seemed to approve of everything, drew up a new plan of battle, with some improvements upon the first, and sent it next day to the Prince for his approbation ; the Prince was extremely pleased with the plan, and in the highest spirits, to think he was to have to do with the Duke of Cumberland in person.' But that very night Lord George and all the chiefs recommended retreat, on account of the desertions. I do not think that it is the *lues Boswelliana*, the favourable prejudice of the biographer, which makes me hold that, in this crucial moment of the campaign, the opinion of Charles was the wiser. In the matter of the retreat from Derby, it seems probable that military critics would agree in commending Lord George. A general can only act on his information. Lord George could not know the searchings of heart of the Duke of Richmond, for example, and the demands of other English officers for Hessians, ' or any one that will fight for us.' He could not rely on the Welsh : and it is certain, from a letter of ' Barry's ' to Balhaldy

(October 21), that the Welsh, and the partisans in the City, were only promising to rise *after* a French landing, of which there were no signs. Again, Lord George could not know the disorganised and rudimentary beginnings of the camp at Finchley. If he had advanced from Derby it would be merely on the unknown chances.

At Stirling everything was in a different posture, when, on January 29, Lord George wrote to Murray from Falkirk, enclosing a Memorial. Hay, who was in attendance on Charles, says that it arrived early, before the Prince had risen. If so, it arrived on the morning of January 30. Either the Memorial, or a revised copy, with additional signatures, is printed by Home. The Memorial avers that '*it is but just now* we are apprized of the numbers of our people that have gone off.' Were the desertions really so numerous as to necessitate retreat? On the 27th Lord George, writing to Tullibardine, had said that the army, being reviewed, 'had made a fine appearance.' Again, after a retreat which, Lord George says, was 'a disgraceful flight,' the army, reviewed at Crieff, was but a thousand short of its real strength, as Maxwell expressly declares. Thus, and moreover because the army did, till Culloden, cling together in the most surprising and creditable way, there is reason to doubt whether desertions had really been so numerous.

On the other hand, D'Éguilles vouches for large numbers of desertions. But he could hardly know more than what the chiefs chose to tell him. The Memorialists, insisting on the danger of giving battle, propose to master the forts on the North (which they did, to no purpose), hope to keep a force together till spring, and then expect to gather 10,000 men. Charles, according to Hay, who handed him the letter, 'struck his head against the wall till he staggered,' and exclaimed most violently against Lord George Murray. His words were, 'Good God, have I lived to see this day!' Probably Hay's anecdote is true.

Warren, in French service, who later rescued the Prince, and carried him to France, wrote to James (May 9, 1746, Paris) on the subject: 'I must say so unexpected a proposal to his Highness, who at that time thought of nothing less (an order of battle having been made ready a few hours before, and a firm resolution of waiting for an enemy) was bore with the greatness and constancy of soul the Prince is master of. However severe and unnecessary it might appear to him, he generally waived his own opinion. . .' This is not inconsistent with a moment of passion, before Hay, in his bedchamber. Charles, in fact, as Hay says, did send Sheridan to the Chiefs : ' to talk with you on the subject of your last night's memorial, as likewise to concert with you what measures shall be judged most proper to take at this juncture. I desire you may give entire Credit to him, and whatever shall be determined I shall readily agree to.'[1] Nothing could be more fair. Charles, with Sheridan, sent an expression of his own opinions He observes, with perfect truth, on the certain discouragement of his men, if a retreat is begun, and the proportionate elation of the English. He remarks on the increased difficulty of keeping Highlanders together in their hills. Their Lowland friends will be sacrificed. France and Spain will say that 'it is vain to send succours to those who dare not stay to receive them.' Charles, however, having expressed his opinion, adds, 'I am too sensible of what you have already ventured and done for me, not to yield to your unanimous resolution, if you persist in it.'

Even if composed by Sheridan or Murray, this letter is highly creditable to Charles's sense and spirit. His ideas were absolutely correct. The retreat, insisted on by the chiefs, was a blunder. His strength lay in the confidence of his men, and in the demoralisation of his enemy. At Prestonpans, Clifton, and Falkirk, his troops had invariably been successful. The English were now to have months in which to recover confidence, and learn tactics which Cumberland devised for resisting a Highland onset. His own men were to be reduced, as was inevitable, by famine. The

---

[1] State Papers, Blaikie, p. 77.

North had no adequate supplies, and often suffered from dearth. The English command of the sea provisioned their army, and cut off foreign aid from Charles. If the Cause was to be fought for at all, it must be where the Highland army could be fed. At Falkirk, in the neighbourhood of Stirling and Bannockburn, where Wallace and Bruce had defeated England; hard by the gates of the hills, open for retreat; on ground known, favourable, and encouraging by reason of recent victory: there the Clans should have made their stand against troops shaken by repeated disasters. Here alone the Lowland adherents could be saved from the gaols which Cumberland was presently to fill with Lowland gentlemen, abandoned by the decision of the leaders.

There was, really, but one alternative. Charles, and whoever of the Chiefs chose, might escape by sea. The clansmen might scatter and skulk in their mountain hiding-places, as in 1716. To retreat meant starvation, and a battle lost beforehand. No writing on the wall could be plainer. But the Chiefs were blinded. Charles again wrote, with fatal lucidity: ' I can see nothing but ruin and destruction to us all in case we think of retreat. . . . Has the loss of so many officers killed and wounded, and the shame of their flight still hanging on the enemy made them more formidable?' He added that he had no control, and must yield, ' but I take God to witness that it is

with the greatest reluctance, and that I wash my
hands of the fatal consequences, which I foresee but
cannot help.' Prophecy could not be better inspired.
Granting defeat at Falkirk, how could the ruin have
been greater then than after Culloden? And, at
Falkirk, the chance of victory, for men well fed and
confident, was infinitely greater than for men certain
to be starved and depressed in the famished North.
The one point in favour of retreat was the desertions,
and these seem to have been much exaggerated.
Charles was not, as at Derby, trusting to romance
and the chapter of accidents. His arguments, as a
leader of a desperate cause, seem unimpeachable.
Honour and the one chance of safety lay in a stand
at Falkirk.

The results of the rejection of his advice were
not only ruin to the Cause, but to his character
Blow after blow destroyed his confidence in Lord
George, and in mankind. Now, at least, he was
resolute, not obstinate : well advised, not rash. The
Chiefs persisted ; only avowing, in an unsigned note,
their fidelity to the Cause. On January 31 Lord
George was with Charles at Bannockburn till after
midnight. Dawn of February 1 saw the Highland
army in foul rout. The precipitate flight, 'by no
means a retreat but a flight,' is attributed by Lord
George to neglect of his orders, and the incapacity of
the Prince and those about him.

S

In a minute account (privately printed) and more briefly, in his Memoir for Hamilton of Bangour, Lord George tells us how his orders were not acted on, while he received no warning of a change in the arrangements. Stirling, he had decided, was not to be evacuated 'till further orders.' But if these were given, and if orders were sent to evacuate Stirling at daybreak, he only knew it by the explosion (however caused) of the magazine at St. Ninian's Church. He attributes the altered orders to Sullivan. Ker and the Macdonald narrator (on Ker's authority) also assign the hasty orders to Sullivan. Having been out scouting, Ker knew that Cumberland was not yet so near them as Falkirk. 'I believe the like of it never was heard of,' says Lord George. Maxwell lays the blame on the men. The Prince still hoped that the resolution to retire might be altered, but the 'common men,' who had discovered the secret of the retreat, made off spontaneously, including the troops in Stirling. At Crieff a council was called: Lord George asked who had been responsible. 'The Prince did not incline to lay the blame on anybody; but said he took it on himself.' This point, then, remains undecided, but Charles, in opposing retreat, was certainly wiser than Lord George.

The Jacobite host, most certainly by no fault of the Prince, was now in much the same position as

that of 1716, when the Chevalier's army retreated
from Perth, before the Duke of Argyll. More tena-
cious than his father, Charles did not slip away to
France by some eastern port. Nor was he hotly
pursued. Cumberland had slept in Charles's rooms
at Holyrood on January 30. He was inclined to
suppose that the Clans would never face him in the
field, and this impression was strengthened by their
flight from Stirling. At Linlithgow his men contrived,
by accident or design, to set fire to the ancient palace
of the Kings of Scotland. Charles was marching by
Castle Menzies, Blair Castle, Dalwhinnie, Ruthven
(where the fortalice of Sergeant Molloy was taken),
and so, on February 16, he arrived at Moy, where
he was entertained by Lady Mackintosh. The cau-
tious chief was with the English. Lord George,
with Lord John Drummond, took 'the coast road,'
going by Perth to Aberdeen, and reaching the Spey
when Charles arrived at Moy. Thence, by Elgin,
Forres, and Nairn, he went to Culloden, Forbes being
with Loudon in the North. The pair had left
Inverness on the 16th, with 1,500 men. Macleod,
with his clan, was of this party, which was to surprise
Charles at Moy. Lord Loudon, writing to Cumberland on the 22nd, says, 'a detachment which he had
sent to prevent intelligence, going a nearer way,
contrary to orders, fired about thirty shot at four men,
and threw the body along with Lord Loudon into

confusion, during which a great many dispersed, so that it was necessary to march back to Inverness.' This was the official account of the famous Rout of Moy. Before leaving Skye, Macleod's hereditary piper, MacRimmon, had composed a prophetic lament :

> Macleod shall come back,
> But MacRimmon shall never !

On the evening of the march a second-sighted friend had remarked (so Theophilus Insulanus, a Macleod, tells us) that the Piper's body seemed to shrink to the stature of a small child : a very bad omen. At Inverness, old Lady Mackintosh had heard of the intended surprise, and sent a boy, Lachlan Mackintosh, to give warning.[1] Running across country, the boy roused the household at Moy : the ladies wakened Charles, and hid his objects of value : he himself rushed out with his bonnet above his nightcap, and unbuckled shoes, down the side of the loch. Meanwhile the blacksmith of Moy, Fraser, with three or four men, watched the moor, and, seeing Macleod approach with his gang, fired on them, slew the prophetic piper, and, by cries to non-existent Camerons and Macdonalds, so shook Macleod's nerves that he fled with his company to Loudon's main body.

[1] Johnstone calls the messenger 'a dear girl.' Really he was a Mackintosh, and was taken into kitchen service. Thenceforward Johnstone frequently romances wildly.

They were all in a hurry to return to Inverness :
whence Loudon made haste to cross the ferry with
all his gallant men, except a small garrison left in
the Castle. The Castle surrendered on the 30th,
Loudon being now in Tain. He was driven up and
down the country, till, after trying Sutherland, he,
with Forbes and Macleod, finally fled to Skye, and
so is out of the story. Never was clan so discredited
as that party of the Macleods which followed its chief.

Charles's health suffered greatly from a cold caught
in his retreat from 1,500 men at Moy, and he resided
as much as possible at Inverness. From March 11
to March 20 he was ill at Elgin, at Thunderton
House, a place of Mr. Dunbar's. A Mrs. Anderson
nursed him, and tradition (in my own family, through
the late Miss Janet Lang, a descendant of Mrs.
Anderson) says that, when he asked how he could
repay her, she begged for a post in the Customs for
her son. She had been unhappily married and
unfortunate, and her desires were humble. It is
added that, in some inexplicable way, Charles found
means to gratify her ambition. The part of the army
which was not chasing Loudon like a partridge on
the mountains was now cantoned on the Eastern
coast, the only source of supplies : or was reducing
Fort Augustus, and failing before Fort William.
Cumberland had been delayed at Perth by slackness
in getting together provisions. His intelligence he

could never trust, and the Grants, like Dicaeopolis
in the Greek comedy, had actually made a treaty of
neutrality with the Jacobites. These circumstances
irritated the brutal temper of the Butcher. He had
judiciously garrisoned Blair Atholl Castle (under Sir
Andrew Agnew), with Castle Menzies, and other
points on the Highland Road, by which it was always
possible that Charles might give him the slip, and
get behind him as he moved on Aberdeen. This
strategy was favoured by d'Eguilles, to whom Charles,
at this time, confided his great distrust of Lord
George. D'Eguilles could not give his reasons in
writing for the suspicions which he shared with
Charles.

Lord George, meanwhile, raided into Atholl, where
his very reluctant attack on the eight-foot thick walls
of his brother's house failed for lack of artillery.
Cluny took part with great skill in this enterprise.
Lord George, by a march of thirty miles, took thirty
small posts, and three hundred prisoners, without
losing a man. Strathmashie saw, among papers at
this time seized, and copied, an order of Cumberland's
forbidding quarter to be given. The Prince of Hesse,
not liking a war in which no cartel protected prisoners,
took no active part in the fighting. His Germans
won golden opinions for good behaviour. Lord
George, however, retired before the Hessians, on
April 2, sending his men to the Spey, which (March

21–31) was guarded by Lord John Drummond.
Cumberland was making various reconnaissances from
Aberdeen, and lost a party of about a hundred in a
surprise at Keith. The Highlanders had triumphs
like those of Delarey and De Wet, but their numbers
were scanty, and they had no magazines of supplies.

But these gallant adventures were the last successes
of Charles. His funds were exhausted, though we
need not suspect, with Maxwell, that Murray of
Broughton was a thief. Indeed Lord George admits
that he managed the Commissariat well. But Murray
became seriously ill when Charles was at Elgin :
retired to Inverness, and, at least while Charles remained in Scotland, never saw him again. Hay of
Restalrig took his place, whom Lord George denounces as thoroughly incompetent. There was
grumbling in the unpaid army, and the *Prince Charles*
(the captured *Hazard*) was taken by the Mackays,
with 12,000*l.*, in the Pentland firth. Cromarty
was sent with a force to wring the money from
Lord Reay. Most of that force, Mackenzies, and
Macdonalds, under Barisdale, never returned to
Charles in time to be useful. They took Dunrobin,
the Earl of Sutherland fled, his wife either desired, or
pretended to desire, to raise the country for the Prince.[1]
But Cromarty, with a large party, was defeated by
the Mackays, and taken at Golspie, while Barisdale

[1] Her letter is in the Stewart MSS.

and his Macdonalds came up too late for Culloden. Meanwhile Charles (says Maxwell) ' appeared gayer even than usual : he gave frequent balls to the ladies of Inverness, and danced himself, which he had declined doing at Edinburgh, in the midst of his grandeur and prosperity. . . . All that could be done was to keep up people's spirits,' and it is to Charles's credit that he set so gay a face to adverse fortune. He had certain information, at last, that no French expedition would be sent, and he knew that Cumberland was advancing from Aberdeen. Drummond, who had but 2,500 men, and no artillery, could not hold the line of the Spey. Many of the army were scattered, for it was seed-time, and they were busy on their crofts. Among these were the brave Macphersons, who, summoned too late, arrived within six miles of Culloden on the 16th only to hear of the ruin of the Cause.

On the 14th Cumberland entered Nairn as Perth marched out, his rear protected by a small squadron, recently arrived, of Fitzjames's horse. Perth and Charles met at the Prince's quarters, the house of Culloden. On the 15th (we follow Lord George here), the Highlanders, expecting an attack, drew up on the open moor. Lord George did not like the position, and Ker was sent to view the ground on the other side of the Nairn, which seemed better fitted, by its hills and bogs, for Highland tactics. Sullivan was

absent, at Inverness. On his return the objection
was made that the enemy would seize Inverness if the
position beyond the Nairn was adopted. This view
was not far wrong, for, without Inverness, how was
the army to be fed? It became clear that Cumberland was resting his men (it was his birthday) at
Nairn. The Highlanders, Maxwell says, at once
began to scatter in search of food. 'The officers, as
well as the men, got but a biscuit each.' The Macdonald narrator also mentions the solitary biscuit. In
our century Mr. Chambers saw and tasted a relic of
the *viaticum* of the Cause. The last biscuit was made
of husks and the sweepings of a mill: to this had the
retreat from Stirling reduced the provisions of the
Clans. But better might have been had. The negligence of the Commissariat, under Hay, was ruinous,
as there were at Inverness supplies for a fortnight.

It was now two or three o'clock of the afternoon.
Many men had scattered to look for food. Cromarty,
Barisdale, Cluny, the Master of Lovat with part of his
clan, had not arrived: probably 2,000 of the whole
force were absent. A Council met, and a night surprise on the sleeping and probably beery camp at
Nairn, twelve miles away, was proposed: Maxwell
says by Lord George, most narrators say by Charles.
Lord George writes: 'His Royal Highness and most
others were for venturing it, amongst whom I was.'
At all events the expedition set out, about eight in

the evening.   All agree that, marching across country in the dark, progress was slow, and halts were frequent. About two in the morning Lord George, in the van, decided that the camp could not be attacked before daylight.   Statements differ as to whether Charles, on hearing this, exclaimed that Lord George had betrayed him.   This is Hay's account ; he certainly was present at the last hurried meeting to discuss the advance, and rode back to Charles.   Through Bishop Geddes, Home, many years afterwards, consulted Charles, in Rome.   He replied : 'Upon the army's halting, M. le Comte' (himself) 'rode up to the front to inquire the occasion of the halt.   Upon his arrival, Lord George Murray convinced M. le Comte of the unavoidable necessity of retreating.'   Home attributes Charles's reply to illusion of memory, after many years. The adventurer Watson, editor of Johnstone's Memoirs, appears to hold that Charles lied.   But Charles's remarks are quite reconcilable with facts.   In a letter, attributed to Lord George, given in the 'Lockhart Papers' and the 'Lyon in Mourning,' it is expressly stated that Hay joined the last halt, 'but nobody minded him.'   Hay would ride back to Charles, Charles would exclaim that he was betrayed ; he would then ride to 'the front' of the *retreating* column, would meet Lord George, and be convinced by his arguments.   Later, in his general indignation, he would alter his mind.   In 1759 he wrote to James, saying that Clanranald's men were in touch with Cumberland's outposts, and believed the attack to be feasible, had Lord George not retreated, contrary to his orders. But, in old age, and in the face of history, Charles admitted, in his answer to Home, that Lord George had convinced him at the moment. With many other suspicions, Lord George's disobedience rankled in his bitter years, but, when aged and beyond the stress of things, Charles told the historical truth. This, at least, seems a plausible solution of the problem.

Moreover, Ker of Graden declares that, after the end of the battle of Culloden, he sought out Charles, who 'inquired particularly about Lord George, and being acquainted that he was thrown from his horse in the time of action, but was nowise hurt, the Prince, in the presence of all there, desired Colonel Ker to find him out, and take particular care of him,' which, says Ker, shows that he then entertained no injurious suspicions. Ker's word is not to be doubted ; the Prince had no braver, better, or more loyal adherent. But, on later reflection, inflamed by the tales of others, and by Lord George's letter from Ruthven, a soured man and lost, Charles acted unworthily of himself as he had once been ; and in the spirit of his original, and not unnatural distrust of Lord George.[1]

---

[1] Neil MacEachain, who was later with Charles in the islands, avers that he bitterly blamed Lord George. But some of his other companions deny this : probably his moods varied.

Worse preparation for a battle there could not be than a night of hunger and fatigue. Returning to Culloden House about five in the morning, Charles himself is said to have found no food but bread and whiskey. Sixty hogsheads of claret, it was reported, had been drunk under Forbes's hospitable roof during the previous autumn, now the cupboard was bare, and the cellar was empty. Charles gave orders to have supplies brought from Inverness, but they arrived too late. His men, sleeping on the heather of the moor, were wakened to fight, and it is averred that many slept the sleep of exhaustion through the battle itself. The Highland army that was to be engaged mustered about 8,000 on the rolls, according to Patullo, the 'Muster Master.' But he reckons that not more than 5,000 took part in the fight, the Macphersons, Cromarties, Mackenzies, Barisdale's Macdonalds, and about half of the Frazers being absent, while stragglers were in search of food, or were asleep. Cumberland's army was officially reckoned at over 8,000 regulars, not including the Campbells, and militia or volunteers. Obviously the disproportion of numbers could not have been more unfavourable, while all other conditions would have been infinitely more favourable, had Charles been allowed to make a stand at Falkirk.

The Moor of Culloden as beheld to-day is so entirely altered in every respect, that the visitor can scarcely recognise the historical scene. Approaching

from Inverness by an ascending road, the way leads
through modern plantations to a comparatively narrow
open space. A great cairn on the north com-
memorates the calamity, the road passes over the
trenches dug to bury the dead, and woods cover the
right side of the position whence Lord George led
the charge. The names of the clans of the right
wing are carved on stones near where they fell, and a
slight rise in the ground leads to what is called the
Englishmen's field. Beneath it, in land still rather
marshy, is the Well of the Dead, where Macgillavray,
a gigantic hero of Clan Chattan, is said to have died
after slaying several men with his claymore. The
walls on the Highland right, which were occupied by
some of the Campbells, and partly pulled down by
them to let out the English cavalry, no longer exist.
But, far away to the west, lies the range of mountains to which part of the Highlanders fled across the
Nairn; on the left is the grey sea where the provision-
ships of the English lay; and northward are the
violet-tinted hills of Ross, from which came no aid.
These things we still behold as Charles beheld them :
a melancholy and memorable landscape.

Maxwell gives an account of the choice of alter-
natives which lay before Charles, when 'everybody
looked sullen and dejected; those who had taken
upon themselves to begin the retreat (from Nairn), as
well as those that had no share in it.' Perhaps, says

Maxwell, it would have been wisest to retire either beyond Inverness, or across the Nairn, till the scattered parties returned. Charles, he adds, disapproved of this, as ruinous to the confidence of the army. But how were the troops to be provisioned if Inverness was abandoned? As to a 'strong camp,' none had been constructed, nor were the Highland tactics good in defence: a charge was their sole idea of war. Lord George supposes that the army remained on the moor, as 'the enemy would have marched straight to Inverness,' the last source of supplies. Patullo, and many others, blamed Sheridan and the French, who had no stomach for a mountain campaign, and 'hoped, no doubt, for a miracle, in which light most of them had considered both the victory at Preston and that at Falkirk.' But the evidence of d'Eguilles is on the other side. Throwing himself at Charles's feet, he implored him not to fight. ' Many of his men were absent: many had left their targes at home. All were fatigued, many had not tasted food for two days. Let Charles cross the Nairn, and enter on a mountain campaign, awaiting French supplies on the west coast.' And on what, meanwhile, was the Prince's army to be fed? The want of food made fighting a necessity.

Very early, scouts reported Cumberland's advance. The clans must fight where they were. On the right were the Atholl men, Lord George's own, the

Camerons, and the Stewarts. In the centre Lord John Drummond commanded Clan Chattan, the Maclauchlans and Macleans; next the Macleans were Lochgarry's Macdonalds, Clanranald's and Keppoch's men, under Perth. Thus, contrary to their point of honour, the Macdonalds were on the left. Roy Stuart led the second line, French, Irish, Lowlanders, Gordons, and Ogilvies. Elcho had a handful of horse on the right, Pitsligo's remnant was on the left, and there were some fifty of Fitzjames's horse. Who made this disposition, so offensive to the clan pride of the Macdonalds? 'The Prince,' says Lochgarry, 'had agreed to give the right to Lord George and his Atholl men,' who, Lord George says, early in the campaign, were unduly under-rated. 'On this, Clanranald, Keppoch, and I spoke to H.R.H. upon that subject and begged he would allow us our former right, but he entreated us for his sake we would not dispute it, as he had already agreed to give it to Lord George and his Atholl men; and I heard H.R.H. say that he resented it much, and should never do the like if he had occasion for it.' The Macdonald narrator of the Lockhart Papers (probably Macdonald of Morar) says that 'our sweet-natured Prince was prevailed on by L.' (Lochiel, Lord George, or who?) 'and his faction to assign the honour to another on this fatal day, which right we judge they will not refuse to yield us back

again next fighting day.' These witnesses attest
the discontent of the Macdonalds, and though theirs
must be taken as prejudiced remarks, seem to show
that some one had influenced Charles. It does not
appear likely that Sullivan had any special interest
in the claims of either set of clans. Maxwell, who
was unprejudiced, agrees with Lochgarry. 'Lord
George had insisted that the Atholl men had the
right in Montrose's war, and made a point of it that
it should be so on this occasion. . . . The Prince
. . . found it easier to prevail with the commander
of the Macdonalds to waive their pretensions for the
once, than with Lord George to drop his claim.
However the Macdonalds in general were far from
being satisfied with this complaisance of their commander.' Lord George was again unfortunate ; his
advice made the injured Macdonalds no longer ' a
force in being.'

During the battle, the Prince was stationed on a
small eminence ' open to the centre of the first line,'
says an English account. A man was killed by his
side, says Ker of Graden. A huge flat-topped
boulder, behind the English lines, is said, locally, to
have been Cumberland's final point of vantage. It
is usual to stand on the top and curse the Butcher.
His front line, from the left (facing Lord George),
was made up of Barrel's, Monro's, the Scottish
Fusiliers, Cholmondeley's, and the Royals, with Lord

Ancrum's 'Ker's Dragoons' on the left; and Cobham's Dragoons, under Bland, on the right. Albemarle commanded the front line: the second line, Wolfe's, Ligonier's, Sempill's, Blyth's, and Fleming's, were under Huske. Mordaunt commanded the third line, Blakeney's, Battereau's, Pulteney's, Howard's, flanked on either hand by Kingston's horse. The guns were in the interval, between the battalions.

The English guns, well served, dominated the poor artillery of the inexperienced Highlanders, a useless incumbrance. The Campbells broke down the wall on the Highland right, permitting cavalry to advance on that flank. Here the clans, suffering most, grew impatient for a charge, and Ker and Graden carried the Prince's permission to advance. He also bade the Macdonald wing, the left, under the Duke of Perth, rush on, but they delayed. How far their irresolution meant a military strike, out of wrath at being placed on the left, can never be certainly decided. Lochgarry avoids the point, in a letter to young Glengarry, then a prisoner in the Tower. The left wing was more withdrawn than the right, which would make the Macdonalds come later into action, but they never came at all, and beheld the gallant but fatal attempt of the Camerons, Stewarts, Clan Chattan, Macleans, and of their own folk under Keppoch and Scothouse. *These* Macdonalds and Macdonnells fought like heroes, and the right and centre, with fire,

T

and wind, and snow in their faces, broke through Barrel's and Monro's regiments, were enfiladed by Wolfe's men (placed *en potence*), and though they fell in swathes under grape and musketry, yet the gigantic Macgillavray, and Gillie Macbean, with a handful of brave men, cut their way past the guns, only to die on the bayonets of Sempill's regiment in the second line. Keppoch fell wounded, rose, struggled on, and was shot dead. The Macleans, under Maclean of Drimnin, maintained, in this their last fight, the glory that they won at Glenrinnes (1594), and on many a stricken field. A broken and impoverished clan, their chief a prisoner, they were still the Spartans of the North; they died, but did not surrender or fly, and of 200 men, says Lochgarry, 150 fell. With Macdonnell of Scothouse some twenty of his following bit the dust. But the mass of Clan Donald, according to Maxwell of Kirkconnell, did not cover half the distance between themselves and the line of fire. How far they were reluctant to charge, as tradition avers, we can never ascertain. It seems probable that for various reasons of discontent, the clan did not display its wonted *élan*, but Mr. Ewald is perhaps not justified in saying that 'a more treacherous and disgraceful display of temper military history has never yet had to record.'

The first line being broken, 'the second line was but a handful in comparison of the Duke of Cumberland's army,' says Maxwell; 'however their countenance stopped for a while the pursuit of the enemy s cavalry, and saved abundance of men's lives. On the left the picquets brought off some of the Macdonalds, who were almost surrounded by Kingston's horse, and on the right Ogilvy's regiment faced about several times to the dragoons that followed, but durst neither attack nor pass the regiment.' Johnstone gives a similar but much more picturesque account. One English officer tried to take a Highlander, who cut him down, and made prize of his watch.

The Highland retreat was partly west, across the Nairn, partly on Inverness, where the fugitives were followed and slaughtered by hundreds : the French, under cartel, surrendering as prisoners of war. The question of Charles's own conduct has been debated. It was in no way timid or dishonourable, any more than Cumberland's own flight at Laffeldt. The report to the opposite effect is due to an error of memory. On February 9, 1829, Sir Walter Scott met Sir James Stuart Denham, nephew of Lord Elcho, the author of unpublished memoirs. Denham told Scott that Elcho rode up to Charles and asked him to lead a charge, retrieve the battle, or die sword in hand. Charles refused, and Elcho called him 'a damned cowardly Italian'—unmentionable person. No such story occurs in Elcho's Memoirs, and Sir James spoke from a confused recollection of what his uncle did

T 2

write.   On the other hand, Sir Robert Strange (who had executed cheap paper notes in Charles's lack ot money, and was later celebrated as an engraver) saw the Prince vainly trying to rally the Highlanders, as did Stuart Threipland.[1]   In 1750 Charles wrote a brief account of the affair (in the Stuart Papers) in which he says that he was ' led off the field by those about him.   The Prince then changed his horse' (a present from Dunbar of Thunderton), 'his own having been wounded by a musket ball in the shoulder.' Neil MacEachain, companion of the Prince, and father of Marshal Macdonald, gives the same story on Charles's authority.   Home cites a manuscript signed by the Cornet of the Guards, in which he says that he saw Sheridan vainly urge Charles to ride off, while Sullivan ' laid hold of the bridle of the Prince's horse, and turned him about.'

All the world has regretted that the Prince did not fall as Keppoch fell, leaving an unblemished fame, that he did not ride back, if it were alone, like d'Argentine at Bannockburn, and die with glory. But he turned late, and reluctantly, and like other defeated Princes and generals.   Johnstone blames him for sending ' six or seven aide-de-camps' to bid Lord George secure the wall on the right instead of going himself.   But Johnstone was not on that part of the field, and, in fact, Lord George did make his

[1] Dennistoun's *Life of Strange*, i. 63, and a Fingask MS.

dispositions to secure the wall, though they were not successfully carried out.

In his retreat, Charles crossed the Nairn with a handful of horse, 'pointing towards Fort Augustus' (which the Highlanders had taken), says Maxwell. He next, says Maxwell, consulted with Sheridan, Hay, and others; he then sent '*Young* Sheridan (nephew of Sir Thomas), who 'at first pretended to conduct them to the place where the Prince was to assemble his army again, but having led them about half a mile on the road to Ruthven, he dismissed them all in the Prince's name, letting them know it was the Prince's pleasure they should shift for themselves. There was, indeed, hardly anything else to be done. There were no magazines in the Highlands. The meal that had been brought to Fort Augustus had been brought back to Inverness, or embezzled by the people of the country. There was at that time a greater scarcity than usual in the Highlands. . . .' Elcho's account is that he remained when the horsemen had gone. Charles 'seemed only interested in the fate of the Irish,' whereas Ker of Graden mentions his solicitude for Lord George. Charles then told Elcho that he meant to go to France. Elcho answered that he was unworthily abandoning men who had sacrificed all for him, while he might live or die with 9,000 still in arms. He persisted, 'and I left him, fully determined never to have anything more to do with him,' a determination from which Elcho returned, after vain attempts to solicit a pardon from England.

According to Edward Bourk, the Prince's guide, Elcho accompanied Charles with Sheridan, Sullivan, and Alexander Macleod to Lovat's retreat at Gortuleg. What reception the old fox gave them is variously reported. By April 17 Charles reached Glengarry's deserted, and now ruinous, house of Invergarry, and thence proceeded to a cottage in Lochiel's country at the head of Loch Arking.

From Gortuleg Charles had sent to Cluny (the letter is in the possession of the Duke of Atholl) saying that he expected the clans to rally at Fort Augustus. Lord George wrote to Cluny that he could make nothing of this message, in the hand of Macleod, the aide-de-camp. The remains of the army had gathered at Ruthven, in Badenoch, knew nothing of a rendezvous at Fort Augustus, and, when Lord George received the Prince's note, he also knew that the Prince had retreated into Clanranald's wildernesses. Whether Charles and Lord George had misunderstood the arrangement or not, Lord George clearly thought that the Prince had purposely given the slip to him and to the remnant of his forces. This opinion he practically expressed, in an angry letter from Ruthven, on the day after Culloden. He censures Charles for coming over at all, ' it was highly wrong ; '

he attacks Sullivan and Hay, and gives his own 'demission.' Of the forces at Ruthven, their temper, and their supplies, Lord George says not a word. If Charles got his letter, he probably felt justified in retiring, as he did, on foot to Borradale and the sea. In any case united resistance at Ruthven or at Fort Augustus was impossible. Lord George writes in his Memoir, so often cited : ' Besides our defeat, there was neither money nor provisions to give ; so no hopes were left.' Johnstone says that Ruthven 'happened, by chance, to be the rallying point of our army, without having been previously fixed on.' He declares that Lord George sent Macleod to tell the Prince 'that a great part of his army was assembled at Ruthven ; that the Highlanders were full of ardour and animation ;' that a force of 8,000 or 9,000 might be depended upon, and so forth. This is certainly false. Johnstone adds, contradicting Ker, that on the 27th Macleod brought back a message from Charles, ' Let every man seek his safety the best way he can '—' an inconsiderate answer, heart-breaking to the brave men who had sacrificed themselves for him.'

Much of this is utterly untrue. Lord George sent no promises to Charles, not a hint of the state of the army. He sent reproaches and a resignation, but no intelligence. ' No hopes were left,' he remarks in his Memoirs. As to Macleod and the ' inconsiderate ' reply which he carried back from Charles, Mr. Blaikie says, 'this, if true, means that the A.D.C. (Macleod) must have gone from Stratherrick to Ruthven (about twenty-five miles) with the original letter, gone back at once with Lord George's message, by which time the Prince had got to Locharkaig, and again returned to Ruthven on the 20th, a very unlikely circumstance.' In fact, all was confusion, no trysting-place had been settled ; two, Fort Augustus and Ruthven, floated uncertain in the leaders' minds ; distances were great, roads were difficult, resistance to Cumberland was impossible. Lord George was repellent, and thus began the inevitable *sauve qui peut*.

The exact circumstances in which Charles failed to join the remnant of his army at Ruthven are important. We ask : did he desert his troops, and, if so, why ? The most obvious answer is that he had lost heart and hope, and (as Lord Elcho declares) was making straight for the first opportunity of a flight to France. This falls in with his dismissal of the gentlemen who had followed him to the Nairn. On the other side is the letter written at his command by Macleod to Cluny from Gortuleg, ordering a rendezvous at Fort Augustus. The most unfavourable view would be that this was a blind (compare Maxwell's account of the proceedings of *Young Sheridan*), meant to leave the impression that Charles had always regarded For⁴ Augustus as the rendezvous. But, if acted upon, the orders would draw Cumberland in Charles's direction, which would not suit his plan of escape. Supposing him to have been in earnest, and to have received Lord George's angry letter from Ruthven, it was not unnatural that it should make him determined to escape by sea. Lord George was still General, and it was his duty to make Charles acquainted with the numbers and situation of the forces at his disposal. He did nothing of the kind : his temper got the better of him. We do not know when, if ever, his letter reached Charles ; we only know for certain that Johnstone's story, the most unfavourable to the Prince, is entirely erroneous. According to Captain Stuart's official Journal of the Marches of the Highland Army, they reached Ruthven on the 18th, though Lord George dated his letter thence on the 17th ; the last entries are to Balmoral on the 19th, to Clova on the 20th. But these may represent Stuart's private movements ; if they stand for those of the army, its stay at Ruthven was but for one day.

In trying to understand the Prince's purposes, it seems necessary to consider Captain O'Neil's Journal, of which two copies exist in the 'Lyon in Mourning.' The Journal was severely criticised, at the time, by Highlanders. It is professedly written in defence of Charles against 'many scandalous libels.' O'Neil avers that Charles gave Fort Augustus as the rendezvous before the battle of Culloden, waited there all day on the 17th, and thence went to Invergarry, while O'Neil was left for two days at Fort Augustus to direct the troops that came up. Thence Charles only retired, O'Neil says, by six miles at a time, arriving at the sea in Knoydart on April 26.[1] But the Journal of Donald Macleod and other evidence prove that Charles arrived at Borradale, at the head of Loch Nanuach, in Knoydart, on the night of the 20th, and that his idea was to get the said Donald to carry letters to ask protection from Sleat or Macleod, his determined opponents. Donald met the Prince all alone in a wood, he declined to do his will as to carrying letters to Sleat and Macleod, but offered to sail with him to the Hebrides. Charles then, after remaining from the 20th to the 26th at Borradale, set forth, with Sullivan, O'Neil, Allan Macdonald, Donald Macleod as pilot, Edward Bourk 'a common chairman in Edinburgh,' and seven other oarsmen. A letter was sent from Boisdale, in Borradale, to Sheridan, enclosing a note for the chiefs. Charles tried to justify his conduct in going to seek French aid, and, by French influence, to procure better terms for the Highlanders. They were advised to keep together, and rely on the advice of 'the Duke of Perth and Lord George Murray, who, I am persuaded,

[1] For another version by O'Neil see the *Albemarle Papers*, vol. ii. p. xliv (New Spalding Club, edited by C. Sanford Terry).

will stick by you to the very last. . . . May the Almighty bless and direct you.'

According to Home, Lord George sent Hay to Charles at Borradale, 'to entreat that he would not leave Scotland, as Lord George had heard that he intended.' Murray of Broughton avers that he himself, very ill, and Lochiel, sorely wounded, were at this time at Loch Arkaig, and sent Lochiel's brother, Dr. Archibald Cameron, imploring Charles not to sail away. The Doctor met Hay, who declined to tell him where the Prince was, but finally said that he had already taken to the sea. This was disbelieved by Murray and Lochiel; they therefore sent another messenger, but he met Hay returning to Loch Arkaig.

Taking all the evidence together, it is plain that the instinct of self-preservation had now full possession of Charles: and very blind it proved. Had he returned to Lochiel at Loch Arkaig, he might at once have left for France in all possible security. For, on May 3, while the Prince, in distress and danger, was drifting about the wild Hebridean shores, two French ships arrived at Borradale, and landed 40,000 louis d'or, driving off the *Greyhound*, the *Baltimore*, and the *Terror*. Sheridan, Hay, Murray, and Lochiel heard of this event, and on board the French ships went the Duke of Perth, who died on the voyage, Lord John Drummond, Elcho,

Sheridan, Lockhart of Carnwath the younger, the much-reviled Hay, and others. Lochiel, from loyalty to the Cause and his clan, declined to fly ; Murray, from loyalty he says, from treachery say others, also remained on land. Thus Charles reaped the reward of his anxious, eager, and ill-directed haste, first, by missing what proved to be a certain chance of escape, next, by losing the 40,000 louis d'or, presently brought in a ship from France. He must now take to the heather, and endure the extremes of peril and distress.

CHAPTER IV

IN THE HEATHER

Lone places of the deer,
  Corrie, and Loch, and Ben,
Fount that wells in the cave,
Voice of the burn and the wave,
Softly you sing and clear
  Of Charlie and his men !

Here has he lurked, and here
  The heather has been his bed,
The wastes of the islands knew,
And the Highland hearts were true
To the bonny, the brave, the dear,
  The royal, the hunted head.

IN a biography of the Prince it is not necessary to linger (as it would be in a history of the period) on so well-worn a theme as the cruelties which followed Cumberland's victory at Culloden. His letters to the Government, throughout his expedition, teem with expressions of his desire to crush out the faintest embers of Jacobitism. He candidly expressed his opinion that the Celtic north and west might yet prove perilous to his family. In addition, therefore, to slaughtering the wounded, and crowding the gaols and hulks with prisoners who suffered extremities from cold, hunger, lack even of water, and want of surgical attendance, Cumberland gave orders for the actual 'destruction of the country.' Nothing like his measures had been known since the cruelties of Henry VIII. on the Border. Cattle were driven off, castles and cottages were impartially burned down, grain was destroyed. It is a Whig writer who tells us, in 'The Life of Barisdale,' that, in Knoydart, the very shell fish were not spared.

These facts do not rest merely on the Highland evidence for brutalities, carefully collected, sifted, and authenticated by Bishop Forbes. 'Parties were sent from Fort Augustus all round the Highlands. Wherever these came, they left nothing that belonged to the rebels. They burned all the houses and carried off the cattle,' says 'The Scots Magazine' for June 1746. The Magazine insists that 'even the well-affected' are not spared, and prints a letter from a minister: 'As the most of this parish is burned to ashes . . . there is no such thing as money or pennyworth to be got in this desolate place.' Occasionally the commanding officers were gentler than their orders. A kinswoman of my own, in Badenoch, was sheltering a wounded fugitive. She gave the English who visited her so good a dinner that their captain called her to observe that he had duly placed a light in the thatch of the house, and then drew off his men without looking behind him.

The House of Corriemonie, newly built, was spared, tradition says, because the English officer noticed a resemblance to his own escutcheon in the coat-of-arms carved over the door. But, as a rule, the effort was to annihilate all shelter, and all sources of food, while the starved and shivering people were flogged, to extract information which they did not possess. In proof of this I rely on unpublished letters from an English and, alas! from a Scottish officer in high command. These letters to Lord Albemarle are of undoubted authenticity; but to quote them at this distance of time, and to name the writers, may well seem invidious.[1] Cumberland's excuse was a forged addition to the Highland General Orders, declaring that No Quarter was to be given. The author of the forgery is unknown. The reign of terror, and the temptations of the French gold buried at Loch Arkaig, soon demoralised certain Highland gentry in the most deplorable manner. Of these men Macdonnell of Barisdale is notorious: he became a spy and informer; detected and punished by both parties. Other even meaner villains there were; some of them not yet forgotten or forgiven in Lochaber.

But the extremes of suffering, on the whole, only

---

[1] They are now to be found in Mr. Sanford Terry's *Albemarle Papers*. For a sight of some of them in manuscript I have to thank the kindness of Colonel H. Feilden.

brought out the innate and ineradicable loyalty of the clansmen to their fugitive leader. The reward of 30,000*l.* for Charles, dead or alive, did not even offer a temptation to the scores of people who might have earned the money. Of the chiefs and leaders, many, as Lochiel, Cluny, Lovat, Clanranald, and Glenaladale, held out in their fastnesses. In early May they tried to draw to a head at Murlaggan, but Lovat was evasive, Barisdale may have been treacherous already : he threw suspicion on Lochgarry, and the attempt nearly ended in the capture of Lochiel. Murray of Broughton was taken in his own country, whether by ill fortune, or by his own collusion. Carried to London he turned King's Evidence, and was allowed to live in the extreme of disgrace and universal abhorrence. Lovat, Balmerino, Tullibardine, and Kilmarnock were taken or surrendered. Tullibardine died in prison ; the others on the scaffold. Ogilvie and Ardshiel escaped to France ; Lord George, after adventures which have never been revealed, was equally fortunate. Strathallan did not survive Culloden. Cromarty and his son, Lord Macleod, were pardoned ; probably George II. was moved by the agonised entreaties of Lady Cromarty, who was about to be a mother. The good Pitsligo, lurking on his own property, owed his escape to the loyalty of his neighbours, and to his own presence of mind. The Chevalier Johnstone made his way to Lady Janet

Douglas at Drumsheugh, and hid under a haycock on what is now the site of the 'episcopalian' cathedral in Edinburgh. His adventures are amusingly told, whatever element of truth they may contain. An Act of Pardon, passed in 1747, was clogged by eighty exceptions. The estates of most of the leaders were forfeited, and placed under commissioners. Old Glengarry, after nearly throwing dust into the eyes of the Government, was imprisoned for years in Edinburgh Castle. He had been denounced to Government by some of his own clan and kindred, who accused him of keeping their pay for his private uses.

By such measures, in certain cases inevitable, in others mercilessly and indiscriminatingly vindictive, the Rising was stamped out. The prohibition of the Highland dress, the Disarming Act, the abolition of hereditable jurisdictions, the eviction of the Jacobites from farms on forfeited estates, and martial law in suspected districts, broke down all the old social order of the Highlands, all that, for six hundred years, had resisted English law and custom. Nothing was left but steadfast loyalty to the wandering *Righ nan Gael*, to Charles, who actually won more hearts in his distresses than in his gleam of triumph. Even allowing for the poetic and imaginative element in the reports of his Highland guides and preservers, it seems that Charles's conduct when 'in the heather' was brave, much-enduring, gay, considerate, and con-

U

tented.   It may even be held that he was happier,
when a proscribed wanderer, than at any other time
of his life.   He now trusted men freely : he was ready
to confide even in Sleat and Macleod.   He that had
been so melancholy, at Holyrood, was blithe when
wet, cold, hungry, and in the constant sight of danger.
He was born to love the open air, and to take pleasure
in the severest physical fatigues.   And he was now,
undeniably, king of his company : far more a Prince
than he had been among the jealousies of his Court
and his officers.

We left Charles as he was starting on his strange
expedition to the outermost islands.   The idea was
ill-considered.   In the intricate recesses and among
the almost untrodden hills of the mainland was his
best chance of hiding, and his best hope of rescue by
a vessel from France.   In the long straggling archipelago of the Lewis, Harris, North Uist, Benbecula,
and South Uist, he could not readily be found by
friends, while the sea was covered by English ships
on the watch, and militia and soldiers could 'net the
islands,' in the Greek phrase.   Charles, none the less,
was so eager to escape from the mainland that he
disregarded the weather wisdom of old Donald
Macleod, and started in the brewing of a storm.   'The
tempest was greater than any Donald had ever been
trysted with ;' thunder, rain, and wind darkened the
course of the boat, that had no lantern or compass.

Charles was anxious now to steer for the rocky coast of the salt loch, where death was certain, but Donald held on for the long course, and the open sea.

The night being pitch-dark they knew not whither they were driving, and especially dreaded making Skye, where the militia were on the watch. By peep of day they saw land, and went on shore at Rushness in Benbecula, having steered between Skye, and Canna, Rum, and Eigg. For all provision they had a pot and some oatmeal : Charles himself suffered from dysentery ; but neither illness, cold, wet, fatigue, nor bad food, seemed to reduce his strength. At Rushness they found an empty hut, the Prince slept on a sail laid on the ground : they killed a cow, and the pot came in useful, for the boiling. On April 29 they made a long voyage to Scalpa, a small isle on the east of Harris. Here Sullivan passed as Sinclair, and Charles as his son. Charles was most hospitably entertained for four days by a Mr. Donald Campbell. He informed the Rev. Aulay Macaulay, minister of Harris, and great grandfather of Lord Macaulay, who came hunting for Charles and the reward, that he would take sword in hand to defend the Prince from this clergyman and his party. 'They sneaked off the island, ashamed and disappointed at the loss of the money' (30,000*l.*), 'which they had already devoured in their thoughts, and divided to every man in his due proportion.'

Next day (May 1), Donald went to Stornoway, to hire a vessel for the Orkneys. On May 4 Charles heard that Donald had succeeded, and, with Sullivan, O'Neil (one of the Irish officers in French service), and a guide, he left Scalpa and landed in Harris. Odd homely anecdotes are told of his doings in Scalpa. He rose early, foraged about, and found two new-laid eggs, which he begged from Mrs. Campbell for his breakfast. Coming on a cow hopelessly bogged, he leaped into the black marsh, and dragged the victim on to dry land. On his march to Harris, by a blunder of his guides, they had a walk of thirty-eight Highland miles, over moor, marsh, and hill, before they came near Stornoway. Storm and mist beset them : and they sadly needed the brandy and bread and cheese which Donald, summoned from Stornoway by the guide, brought to the shelter where they lay.

To be done with an ungrateful topic, suggested by the brandy, it must be said that the Highland habit of dram-drinking is not so noxious as might be conceived, when men are taking severe exercise in a very rainy climate. Though Charles had shown some slight taste for wine in Italy, we never hear (except from Lord Elcho) that he was at all remarkable as a toper during his campaign. But his Highland guides, innocently expressing their admiration for one who could see their stoutest ' bowlsmen ' under the table,

who could begin the day with his ' morning ' of brandy,
and finish the bottle, without a touch of intoxication,
by supper time, prove that Charles confirmed, in his
wanderings, the habit which became his ruin.

' On a moor, all wet to the skin,' the Prince and
O'Neil ate and drank what Donald brought to them,
and were conveyed to the house of the lady of Kildun,
at Arnish, two miles from Stornoway in the Lewis.
Here Charles took off his shirt, which was dried before
the fire.   Donald went to Stornoway, to get ready
his vessel for the Orkneys.   But an alarm of Charles's
presence near Stornoway had arisen, through Lord
Macaulay's grandfather, a preacher in South Uist, and
a keen hunter of his rightful Prince.   The Mackenzies
of the Lewis, as retainers of Seaforth, were, if not
hostile, at least most anxious that Charles should
depart out of their coasts.   That night, however, the
Wanderer was too weary to leave Arnish ; but, on
May 6, the company, in a boat of Donald Campbell's,
sailed to the desert isle of Euirn.   Lady Kildun did
not wish to be paid for a cow they had slain, but
Donald was positive that ' deil a man or woman should
have it to say that the Prince ate their meat for
nought.'   They carried off some meat, meal, butter
between two lumps of bread, and plenty of brandy
and sugar.   On the desert isle they found dry fish,
left by the Stornoway fishermen ; and in an earthen
pitcher they brewed punch till the vessel was broken.

The Prince would give the toast of 'the Black Eye,' 'by which he meant the second daughter of France.' Perhaps he really meant Clementina Walkinshaw, whose eyes were of the darkest. He always spoke with affection of Louis XV., 'but, gentlemen, I can assure you that a King and his Council are two very different things.' The Prince was their best cook, using the butter skilfully, though Donald turned up his nose at the bread crumbs therein. Charles cooked a cake of the cow's brains : they ate on a stone for a table, sitting on the bare ground. A roofless hut, covered with a sail, served as a substitute for St. James's. When they departed, Charles wished to leave money to pay for the dry fish, but O'Neil and Donald persuaded him not to lay down this trail of his presence.

The good humour and resource of Charles, in circumstances so remote from the royal, won all hearts, and are the most pleasing of his traits.

On May 10 they meant to return to Scalpa, but their kind Campbell host was now in hiding. They were pursued by an English ship, found another in Lochmaddy, in North Uist, and on May 10 had to feed at sea on *dramach*, oatmeal mixed with salt water. 'The Prince ate of it very heartily . . . never any meat or drink came wrong to him, for he could take a share of everything, be it good, bad, or indifferent, and was always cheerful and contented in every condition.' On May 11 they put into Loch Uskevagh, lay in a hut, and feasted on crabs. On May 14 they went from Benbecula to Coradale, in South Uist, whence Donald was sent to get money and brandy from Murray, who was with Lochiel on the mainland. Donald was absent for eighteen days ; Murray would give no money, though he had 5,000*l.* of the French gold about him.

From May 15 to June 5 Charles abode in the forester's house in Coradale. Eight English vessels were searching the coasts, but Charles was enjoying himself. Grouse were abundant, and he anticipated the Twelfth of August. He shot flying very well, a novelty to the Highlanders. 'One day as they happened to go a hunting, the Prince, with his feusee in his hand, stood on a hill-side and whistled so exact that you could not distinguish it from a plover. Some gathered about him, of which he shot two on the wing, and two on ground.' His companion attempted the feat, but failed. His attire was sooty, a gift of the wife of old Clanranald, then re-siding at Nunton (Baile-nan-cailliach), in Benbecula. Charles was fond of fishing, lythe were plentiful, and so was brandy. He caroused with numbers of Macdonalds, mostly of the Sleat kindred, especially Hugh Macdonald of Balshair in North Uist. This gentleman acted as go-between for the Prince and Lady Margaret Macdonald, the wife of Sir Alexander of Sleat, who was then in attendance on Cumberland at Fort Augustus, ' kissing the hand,' he is reported to have said, ' of the puppy ' whom he had hoped to kick. If we believe a statement of Barisdale's, Sleat was also corrupting that chieftain, and persuading him to turn informer.

But while Sleat was thus engaged, his wife, Lady Margaret, was in correspondence with Charles. A daughter of the beautiful Countess of Eglintoun, she felt for the sorrows of a proscribed wanderer, made a plan for his escape, and sent him newspapers. Another of her agents was a Captain Macdonald who had been wounded in the foot at Culloden, but proved highly serviceable. Balshair, Charles, and the rest at Coradale, had a protracted carouse ; ' he still had the better of us.' He had to leave Coradale on June 6, as the red coats and Macleods were landing in the island, and the cruel Captain Carolina Scott was at his very heels. He therefore sailed to the isle of Ouia, off Benbecula, but, being pursued, returned to Coradale, and so skulked in various retreats till June 15, when they made for Loch Boisdale, in South Uist. For five days they were skulking. Donald left the party, and was soon arrested by Alan Macdonald of Knock, who has left a very bad name behind him in the Highlands. On the 21st the Prince, leaving Sullivan, and alone with O'Neil and Neil MacEachain, crossed the hills

to a hut near Ormaclett, about three miles from
Milton, then the home of Flora Macdonald, on the
west coast of South Uist. Flora was a stepdaughter
of Macdonald of Armadale in Skye, a captain in
Sleat's militia, but was now keeping house at Milton
for a brother of hers, Skye being her native island.
Charles, on this moonlit mountain journey, had with
him, in addition to O'Neil, the faithful Neil Mac-
Eachain, an educated man, and tutor in Clanranald's
family. O'Neil, in his narrative, omits MacEachain,
whose own record, by some means, got into the ' New
Monthly Magazine ' for 1840. According to O'Neil,
corroborated by Miss Macdonald herself, she ' happened to be ' in a sheiling on the hill on that night of
the full moon, June 21. O'Neil had previously been
acquainted with her, doubtless while the Prince was
at Coradale, and he asked her if the Militia were
to pass next day. She said ' not till the day after,'
and O'Neil, who had left the Prince at some distance
from the sheiling, requested permission to introduce
a friend. ' She, with some emotion, asked if it was
the Prince. I answered her it was, and instantly
brought him in.'

Here romance reaches a happy moment. The
full moon, and the late lingering daylight, showed to
each other two persons whose names live together as
innocently as immortally : the fair and beautiful girl,
brave, gentle, and kind, and the way-worn Wanderer,

the son of a line of Kings. About them were the
shadowy hills, below them the vast Atlantic plain.
It was the crisis of Charles's wanderings, and he
knew not how to escape from the hunters on the
island, and the cordon of vessels in the creaks and
along the shores. Here, in the doubtful lights and
in the dim shieling, he met his preserver. But the
interview can scarcely have been accidental : a young
lady was not out alone on the hillside, at midnight,
by pure chance. Undoubtedly the arrangement had
been made by Lady Clanranald, Lady Margaret
Macdonald, and others of the Sleat clan, with whose
honour and sense of pity it did not consist that
Charles should be taken by his pursuers, within their
bounds.

O'Neil says that he proposed a plan ; Miss Macdonald should get, from her stepfather, a pass for
herself and her servant to go and visit her mother in
Skye. The Prince put this before the lady, who
objected that the scheme would be ruinous to Sir
Alexander Macdonald of Sleat, whose retainer her
stepfather was. But O'Neil answered that Sir
Alexander, being at Fort Augustus, could not be
involved, while Flora would win honour and immor-
tality by so glorious an action. All this the lady
corroborated, in conversation with Bishop Forbes.
They parted, the Prince and O'Neil skulking in the
rocks in Coradale. Next afternoon they received a

message that ' all was well.' On the same day, Flora
and MacEachain were detained by the militia guard,
at a ford between South Uist and Benbecula, where,
at Rossnish, they had trysted to meet the Prince.[1]

---

[1] In all this part of the adventures, we are perplexed, more or less,
by the narrative of Neil MacEachain. This was published in the *New
Monthly Magazine* for 1840. The Editor stated that it was purchased
about 1820, with miniatures of Charles and Henry, from a hairdresser
in France, who was believed to be son of Neil MacEachain. Mr.
Blaikie says that Neil's only son who survived infancy was Marshal
Macdonald. But may not Neil have had a son born out of wedlock?
Neil's papers, says Mr. Blaikie, were lost during the French Revolution. I agree with him, on evidence of style and spelling, that the
Narrative is by a contemporary Highlander, and do not doubt that
Neil was the author. But we do not know at what time the paper
was written, and we cannot accept what Neil says, about events before
he joined the Prince in Coradale. I do not feel certain that he is right
in attributing the whole scheme of Flora Macdonald and Betty Burke
to Flora's stepfather, Hugh Macdonald. Neil says that Flora was
asleep in the shieling, that he himself wakened her, and that Charles
(after she had given him a bowl of cream) mooted to her the plan of
her stepfather. Her own account, given by Bishop Forbes, con-
tradicts Neil's version, that ' she joyfully accepted of the offer, without
the least hesitation,' and here O'Neil is in agreement with Flora. Neil
has a story of Charles's anger and despair when landed on what seemed
to be an islet, but proved to be a rock surrounded by water only at
high tide. ' He fell a scolding Neil as if it had been his fault : ' ' there
was no pacifying him at all,' till Neil offered to swim the strait and
bring a boat. Neil speaks of Charles's ' incomparable patience,' yet
often describes him as almost distracted by the terrors of his series
of sufferings. Charles scalded his hand in boiling milk, and ' cursed
the wife and her pot a hundred times, calling her a vile witch,' ' for '
(says he) ' she contrived it herself that we might burn ourselves.'
When dressed as Betty Burke, by Flora, ' he could not keep his hands
from adjusting his head dress, which he cursed a thousand times.' In

Very possibly this detention was collusive, for Armadale, Flora's stepfather, commanded the militia. He gave Flora a pass for herself, and Betty Burke, 'an Irish girl,' whom his wife (he wrote) would find serviceable in spinning. Now as no Betty Burke was with Flora, it is clear enough that Armadale knew who was to personate that spinster. On the 23rd MacEachain found Charles in Coradale, seized a boat, and conveyed him to Ouia. On the 24th they rowed to Benbecula, and reached Rossnish, the rendezvous, at midnight. On the 25th O'Neil crossed Benbecula to Lady Clanranald's house, Nunton, on the west coast, where Flora was. That day and the next were spent by Charles and MacEachain in the rain, devoured by midges, under a rock : at night they had shelter of a sort in a cottage. Both on their way thither, and in this hiding-place, they suffered accidents intolerable.

On the 27th, after various comings and goings, Lady Clanranald, Flora, O'Neil, a Mr. Macdonald, and MacEachain crossed the isle from Nunton, went to Charles's hiding-place, in a hut, and found him broiling kidneys on a spit. He placed Flora on his right hand, Lady Clanranald on his left, and they all

fact Neil, while attesting Charles's courage, avers that his temper and dignity broke down under fatigue, wet, cold, hunger, midges, and a series of provoking accidents, ending in the adventure of the scalding milk. Neil's paper breaks off in the middle of a word, just when the country people are censuring the unwomanly ways of Betty Burke.

' dined very heartily.' Next day (June 28) they learned that General Campbell had landed in Benbecula, and that Captain Ferguson, a peculiarly brutal sailor, was at Lady Clanranald's house at Nunton. She, therefore, had to hurry back, with the ready excuse that she had been visiting a sick child. This lady was soon afterwards arrested. Her health was bad, and her exertions for a Prince whose enterprise had ruined her family, were extraordinary. The rest of the party crossed Loch Uskevagh, and Flora insisted that O'Neil should now leave them. His life was safe, as he was not a subject, and was in French service, but it is plain that he was attached to Miss Macdonald, as well as devoted to Charles. Flora, however, was relentless. She had only a pass for one servant. O'Neil was later taken by Ferguson, who, he says, had him stripped, and was about to flog him. But Lieutenant MacGahan, of the Scottish Fusiliers, drew his sword, and threatened Ferguson, who desisted. O'Neil returned to France, after a period in prison, and is now out of the story. He was brave, loyal, and devoted, but, as we have seen, not an accurate narrator.

In the evening, on the north side of Loch Uskevagh in Benbecula, Charles donned the costume of Betty Burke, provided by Lady Clanranald : a gown of light sprigged calico (whereof a fragment is attached to the cover of the manuscript of ' The Lyon in Mourning '), a petticoat, a mantle of dun camlet, with a hood to cover the head in Irish fashion. They then set sail for Skye, in a clear sunset, which was followed by rain and tempest. The Prince sang several songs, which lulled Flora to sleep ; on waking she found him stooping over her to protect her from a chance stumble of a sailor who was obliged to go across to the other end of the boat. On the morning of the 29th, they made the point of Waternish in Skye, where they were fired on from a boat and were in sight of several English vessels. They rowed away, landed and rested for a while, and then crossed the wide bay, Loch Snizort, to Kilbride on the west coast of Skye. Here Flora left the Prince on the shore, and visited Lady Margaret Macdonald, at her house of Mugstot, which was hard by.

Never, probably, was the Prince nearer to destruction. In the house of Mugstot, conversing agreeably with Flora, when she arrived, was a Lieutenant Macleod. The sum of 30,000*l.* was waiting for the Lieutenant, in the person of a royal fugitive now wandering vaguely about, two or three hundred yards away. The officer had three or four men with him, and the rest of his command was not far distant. Meanwhile Mr. Macleod, much at his ease, was discoursing with Flora, in the drawing-room, about *la pluie et le beau temps*. The nerves of Lady Margaret Macdonald were unequal to the stress of the situation.

She left Flora with the gallant officer to a *tête-à-tête*, and walked into the garden with Mr. Macdonald of Kingsburgh.

Meanwhile she had contrived to send an express to Captain Roy Macdonald, entreating his presence. The wounded Captain jogged up, on a horse borrowed from his surgeon. Lady Margaret ran to him with outstretched hands, crying, ' Oh, Donald Roy, we are ruined for ever ! ' Her fear was lest the Prince should be arrested, to the eternal shame of her husband's family, so near her house. A brief consultation followed. All ways were dangerous, all paths were blocked. At last Roy Macdonald suggested that the Prince might tramp fourteen long Highland miles to Portree. But Lady Margaret could trust nobody save Donald Roy and Kingsburgh. Her husband's vassals thought that, Sir Alexander being a Whig, they could do him no greater service than to catch the Wanderer. Yet Lady Margaret called God to witness that Sir Alexander (in his heart) was no more a Whig than any other gentleman. Finally Roy Macdonald went to look for young Rasay (the plan being to smuggle Charles to his island).

Now, all this while, Flora was smilingly conversing with the lieutenant of Militia, and Charles, in petticoats, was prowling on the dim sea-shore, ignorant of his fate. But, as Flora herself declared, Neil

MacEachain kept strolling in a casual way from the house to the beach and back, comforting Charles. Flora herself knew nothing of the conference between Roy Macdonald, Kingsburgh, and Lady Margaret : her sole concern was to keep the Lieutenant happy, and no doubt the officer conceived that he was making a fortunate impression on the island beauty. Meanwhile Kingsburgh bade Neil go to the Prince, still loitering by the shore, and lead him (here I quote Neil) to the back of a hill, ' a long mile from the house of Mugstot, and there to wait till he came back to join them, and ordered that some light clothes should be packt in the form of a bundle, for the Prince to carry it on his back, as if it had been some of Miss Flora's baggage ; which done they set out for the hill, but they had not gone far when, tiring of his burden, which he carried very awkwardly, threw it from him, leaving it for Neil to carry or leave, as he should think fit. It was in vain that Neil insisted he would take it again, but he would never condescend saying he had carried it long enough.'

' When they came to the place of meeting, they sat down upon the side of a hillock, where they waited for Kingsborough. The prince, who was a long time silent and very pensive, ask'd Neil whether he had carried his case of knives from the boat ; Neil, who did not miss them till then, answered he had not ; " Then," said the prince, " you must return and look

for them."—" Shall I for the sakes of all the knives in
the universe, leave you here all alone?" reply'd Neil.
—" There will be no fear of me," said he, "do you
what you are ordered, for I must absolutely have it,
so no more words." Neil still opposed, but in vain ;
seeing him at last quite out of humour, and ready to
fly in a passion, went, leaving him there within a
gun-shot of the high road, without a soul along with
him.

'When Neil returned he found Kingsborough with
him taking a glass of wine, which Lady Margaret
Macdonald had sent by Kingsborough, together with
some few biscuits, of which he ate a little, and gave
the rest to Neil to keep for him till another occasion.
About an hour before sunset they set off for Kingsborough, where they were to be that night. Miss
Flora, who staid for dinner at Mugstot, that she might
not be suspected by Lieutenant Macleod, followed on
horseback at some distance, and was mightily diverted
to hear several of the country people with whom she
fell in upon the road, as they returned from the
meeting house at Mugstot, it being Sunday, make
their remark upon the behaviour of Betty Burke, her
maid, which name the prince borrowed, when he left
the Isle of Wist.

'Neil, who walked a little behind the prince, and
Kingsborough, hearing the subject the fellows were
upon, went slower till they came up and joined him,

X

but they, notwithstanding, continued to speak with the same freedom as before, of the impudence and assurance of Miss Burke, who was not ashamed to walk and keep company with Kingsborough, and was no less vexed than surprised how he took so much notice of her, when he never minded his mistress who was so near at hand. Betty very easie of what would be said of her, went on always at such a rate, that she very often got a piece before her fellow traveller, which gave occasion to some of the fellows to cry out, ' Curse the wretch do you observe, sir (meaning Neil) what terrible steps she takes, how manly she walks, how carelessly she carries her dress,' and a hundred such like expressions which they repeated over and over again.

' But what they most took notice of all was, when Kingsborough and his companion was come to a rivulet about knee deep which crossed the high road, to see Burk take up her petty coats so high when she entered the water. The poor fellows were quite confounded at this last sight, which made them rail out against Burk, calling her all the names in the world, and ask't of Neil if he was acquainted with her. Neil told them that he knew nothing about her further than to hear she was an Irish girl who met with Miss Macdonald in Wist, and upon a report of her being a famous spinster of lint, engaged her for her mother's use.

'The honest people soon after parted with Neil and Miss Flora, and made for their different homes full of astonish.'

Here honest Neil's narrative breaks off abruptly. He insists, always, on a kind of childish petulance and audacity in Charles. As to the 'case of knives,' Charles left a *nécessaire* of plate for field service on Culloden Moor. The loot fell to Lord Albemarle, in whose family it remains. The other 'case of knives' he was not unwisely anxious to retrieve, as it would have furnished a trace of his presence. Wet, and weary, and late did Kingsburgh, with his Royal guest, arrive at his darkling house. His wife had gone to bed, but was aroused by a maid, reporting that the laird had brought company home : 'Milton's daughter, and some company with her.' Mrs. Macdonald sleepily murmured that Milton's daughter was very welcome, and might make free with anything in the house. Presently her daughter rushed in, averring that 'a very odd, muckle, ill-shaken up wife' was with Kingsburgh in the hall. Finally Kingsburgh himself appeared, and bade the drowsy lady to dress, and get supper ready. The reluctant housewife arose, and met 'an odd muckle trallup of a carline' striding impatiently about the hall. The carline saluted Mrs. Macdonald, who felt the bristles of a manly beard. She ran to Kingsburgh, terrified, asking who this strangest of strangers might be. 'Why, my dear, it

is the Prince. . . .'   'The Prince!   Oh Lord, we are
all ruined and undone for ever!   We'll a' be hanged
now!'   'Hout, good wife, we will die but ance: and
if we are hanged for this, I am sure we die in a good
cause.'

Next, the lady was troubled about supper, and
courtly fashions.   But roast eggs, collops, bread and
butter, and two bottles of 'that poor creature, small
beer,' were a royal regale for the Wanderer.   Then
came the brandy: 'I have learned in my skulking
to take a hearty dram,' said the Prince, filling up a
bumper.   And then he had, at last, a smoke out of
a clean pipe: his old broken cutty he had furnished
with a stem, the leg bone of a bird.   Then came
punch, and the indefatigable Charles would fain have
made a night of it, but Kingsburgh seized the bowl,
that was broken in the struggle, and so this festive
and undefeated Wanderer was induced to go to bed,
to the first clean bed he had slept in for many weeks.
After Charles had slept nine good hours, Mrs.
Macdonald led Flora into his room, and begged for a
lock of his hair.   He laid his head in the lap of his
preserver, who cut the lock.   'I have heard Mrs.
Macdonald say,' writes Bishop Forbes, 'that when
Miss Flora at any time came into the room where the
Prince was, he always rose from his seat, paid her
the same respects as if she had been a queen, and
made her sit on his right hand.'

While Charles had been marching from Mugstot to Kingsburgh's house, and while he had there been so kindly treated, Roy Macdonald had been riding about in search of Young Macleod of Rasay. He missed Rasay, but found Rona at Portree, and, walking with him in the fields, asked where his father was? With reluctance Rona explained that the elder gentleman was in Knoidart: but he consented to row over to Rasay, and thence bring a proper boat to carry the Prince to Rasay from Portree. Boats had been so carefully secured by the Militia, that Rona was obliged to take 'an old shred of a boat, which he found in a fresh-water loch near Tottrome.' The distance from Portree to Rasay is only three miles, but whoever has fished in the old shreds of boats on secluded Highland lochs knows the dangers of Rona's little voyage.

While Roy Macdonald and Rona were arranging these things, on Monday, June 30, the Prince, still dressed as Betty Burke, was parting from Mrs. Macdonald of Kingsburgh. She gave him a little silver 'mull,' or snuff-box, with two hands clasped together upon the lid of it, and the common motto, 'Rob Gib,' which means 'stark love and kindness.' The party marched, and, in a wood, Charles quitted the costume of Betty, and dressed in Highland costume. Kingsburgh later destroyed 'the female rags and bucklings,' except the sprigged skirt, whereof, as has been said, a patch is preserved in the cover of the manuscript 'Lyon in Mourning.' Having resumed the kilt, and 'got the claymore in his hand,' Charles embraced and parted from Kingsburgh. Both wept, and drops of blood fell from the Prince's nose, 'ordinarily it happens to me,' he said, 'in parting with a dear friend.' Flora rode to Portree by a different path, and at Portree Charles met Malcolm Macleod, and young Macleod of Rasay. Here he took leave of Flora with much kindness. I have not discovered, in the manuscripts, any proof that he later corresponded with her, but a ring, said to be his gift, with hair under a crystal, is in the possession of one of her descendants.

Both Flora and Kingsburgh were arrested, and carried to London. The noble behaviour of Kingsburgh in refusing to fly, and giving himself up, when he was freed, by a mistake, at Inverness, is well known. He refused to profit by an error which would probably have ruined the officer who made it. He was protected to the best of their ability by Lady Margaret and Sir Alexander Macdonald. Flora had a kind of triumph in London, where the natural modesty of her bearing won every heart : and not least that of poor Frederick, Prince of Wales, who exerted himself in her service. Her later adventures, her marriage, her meeting with Dr.

Johnson, her emigration to America, her wound received in a sea-fight during her homeward voyage, after her husband had fought in the lost cause of English ascendency in America, are well known. Her stainless memory will be fragrant while white roses bloom.

Early on July 1, Charles, with Malcolm Macleod, Murdoch Macleod of Rasay, and John Macleod, younger of Rasay, landed in that island. Thinking it too small for safety, he doubled back to a place near Scorobreck in Skye, hard by Troternish. Here they lay in a byre, and had very scant commons. Next day, by a forced march over very difficult country, accompanied by Malcolm Macleod, he travelled to Mackinnon's lands. He himself carried the baggage, and passed as Lewis Caw, supposed to be a servant of Macleod. He declared that his private perils affected him little, what grieved him, 'struck to his heart,' was the sorrows of his brave followers. Near Strath, in Mackinnon's country, Macleod went on to the house of his sister, who had married a Mackinnon. Here Charles played his part as a shy serving man very well. But Mackinnon's maid demurred to washing his feet and legs; 'He's but a low country woman's son,' quoth she. Mr. Mackinnon now came home, and gladly accepted his dangerous responsibility. It was here that Charles diverted himself with Mrs. Mackinnon's baby, 'carry-

ing him in his arms, and singing to him.' They did
not mean to let the old Laird into the secret, but the
Chief, with great courage, took all on himself, and,
with John Mackinnon and four boatmen, carried
Charles to the mainland. He made presents of a
silver shoe-buckle and some guineas to Malcolm
Macleod.[1]   Malcolm was shortly afterwards arrested,
and suffered much from the cruelties of Captain Ferguson.   But he returned from London in triumph, in
Flora Macdonald's coach.

On July 5 the fugitives arrived at Loch Nevis, on
the mainland, where their boat was pursued by
another full of soldiers.   Rounding a point, they
leaped on shore, climbed a hill, and escaped (July 8).
They then took boat again, and landed at a little isle
near Scotus, or Scothouse.   John Mackinnon met old
Clanranald, who, aged and overcome with many
sorrows, declined to be of any service.   They therefore walked to Morar, where Macdonald of Morar
was dwelling in a bothy, for his house had been
burned.   The party slept in a cave, and made for
Borradale (July 10).   Here the Mackinnons left the
Prince : they were arrested by Ferguson, and
threatened with torture.   One of the boatmen was
flogged, in Kingsburgh's sight, ' till the blood gushed

---

[1] A miniature of the Prince in uniform is also among the family
relics : I happened to find a replica of this miniature in a shop at
Peterborough : it is reproduced in *The Companions of Pickle.*

out at both his sides.' Letters from English officers prove that this was their regular practice.

Charles rested at Borradale with Angus Macdonald (July 11–12) while Angus sent his son to summon Glenaladale, whose narrative is now followed.[1] On July 15 Glenaladale joined the Prince, and a place of hiding was fixed on in the glens of Morar : ' Mac-Eachaine's Refuge,' near Locheilt. On the 18th they learned that Clanranald's country was begirt by a cordon of troops. They made for the braes of Arkaig, in constant danger : the English camps were pitched within half a mile of each other, and sentries were stationed within call of each other in every direction. Happily they had met Donald Cameron of Glenpean, a valuable guide in that country. They made night marches, seeing the English campfires everywhere, and, on July 21, slipped between two sentries, and out of the cordon. Their path involved the descent of a very steep rock, where Charles slipped, but managed to save his life by catching at a tree. After other perils, they happily met a Glengarry man, whose father had just been shot by the English.

On July 22 they reached Glenshiel, and ' beaked before the sun ' on a rock, through a day of great heat. ' We were all seized with such a drought that we were all like to perish before sunset.' At nightfall,

---

[1] See Mr. Blaikie's *Itinerary*, p. 56, Note 5, for an error of five days in Glenaladale's dates.

according to John Macdonald, they went staggering
to a burn, 'and drank water at no allowance.' Here
they met a boy, who brought them milk. Glenaladale,
who carried the purse, gave the boy some shillings,
but dropped his purse, and did not miss it till he had
rejoined the Prince, who was at a short distance off.
Glenaladale returned for the purse, but found that all
the gold was missing, forty louis d'or. They hurried
to the cottage of the boy's father, who threatened the
lad with hanging. The little rogue then gave up the
gold, which he had buried.

Happily Charles had waited apart, during this
interval, and so escaped a small patrol, into whose
arms he would otherwise have run. In this event,
and in the accident of the enemy chasing towards
him the Glengarry man who served as guide, Charles
recognised 'the hand of Providence.' They now
made for wet hill-tops and fastnesses towards Glenmoriston, and on July 24 arrived at the famous cave
of Coiraghoth in the braes of that district. Herein
dwelt eight honest men : two Macdonalds, three
Chisholm brothers, a Macgregor, a Grant, and a
Macmillan. 'A fine purling stream' ran by Charles's
bed of heather, through the cave, and here Charles
rested for three days. On July 28 he made for
another cave, now unknown, and there dwelt for
four days.

Finding the Campbells were near, Charles moved

to a shieling in Strathglas, and sent messengers forty
miles to Poolewe, to seek tidings of French vessels.
On August 7 he learned that the ship had sailed to
Lochiel's coast, and turning southward to Glenmoriston again, Charles, on August 14, forded the Garry.
On the 15th a messenger from Cameron of Clunes
suggested 'a very fast place' where Clunes would
meet them. Here one of the Glenmoriston guard
relieved the party much by shooting a fine stag.
On the night of August 15 Lochgarry joined them :
he had been fighting a little guerilla war 'for his own
hand.' They now walked down Loch Arkaig side,
where they remained for two or three days, while
Charles sent for Lochiel. On August 20 Archy
Cameron arrived, Lochiel being still disabled by his
wound. Some French officers also came, with
despatches. Then followed days of peril and constant change of hiding-place, till, on August 27,
Lochgarry and Archy Cameron, who had gone to
Lochiel, returned, to guide the Prince into Badenoch.
Lochgarry's voice had been all for war, and he
believed he could raise 2,000 men. Charles approved,
but Lochiel and Cluny did not : and Charles resolved
to join them in Cluny's celebrated wattle hut on Ben
Alder. He parted here with the last of his Glenmoriston friends, to whom he gave twenty-four
guineas.

On August 30 he met Lochiel on the Ben Alder

range of hills.   Lochiel was lying at a small shieling :
he at first took Charles and his five companions for
enemies, and brought twelve muskets to bear on them.
But the Prince and the rest were recognised in time,
and Lochiel hobbled out to meet them.   He would
have kneeled to his Prince, but Charles exclaimed
that there might be eyes on them.   He was gay and
hearty, after his weeks of distress and labour.   Food
was abundant, minced collops were dressed, healths
went round.   Presently they removed to a foul smoky
shieling, in the recesses of Ben Alder, and on September 5, with Cluny, retired to his cage, the old-
fashioned wattled hut, green and grey on the grey
and green of the cliff-side Letternilichk, ' the slope
of the slab of stone,' overlooking Loch Ericht.   Here
they had comforts enough, and a cordon of Cluny's
sentinels.

On September 6 two French vessels, under
Colonel Warren, with young Sheridan on board,
touched at Loch Nanuagh.   This is the Sheridan
who remained in Charles's household at Avignon,
during the twenty years of his incognito, and who,
in 1766, rejoined him at Rome.   Charles had sent
Cluny and Archy Cameron to Loch Arkaig, most
probably to bring back the buried treasure.   In
this effort, if they attempted it, they failed, but they
met John Macpherson, who came from Cameron
of Clunes, with news of Colonel Warren's ships.

The messenger was sent on to the Cage, another summoned Macpherson of Breakachie and John Roy Stuart. As John Roy entered the hut, Charles peeped out from under a plaid, so astonishing his friend that John Roy fell back into a puddle of water. On the 14th they all reached Corvoy, where they practised shooting at bonnets tossed into the air : ' in which diversion his Royal Highness by far exceeded.' Then, marching and hiding, they reached Achnacarry, where they slept, after drinking toasts in brandy, brought actually from Fort Augustus, and, on the 17th, reached the head of Loch Arkaig, where they banqueted on beef and bannocks.

On the 19th they 'arrived at the shipping,' where they found the worthy Barisdale, who had come on board as a spy. Him, with his son, they welcomed but grimly, and put under hatches. Barisdale was one of the worst of men, but it was not fortunate for him that so many Camerons, with his cousin and enemy, Lochgarry, were the companions of the Prince at this juncture. Despite their high spirits, just before their departure, and in sight of safety, it was a melancholy company that bade Scotland good-bye. Charles ordered Cluny to stay, and conduct his affairs at home, leaving a list of persons who were to be relieved out of the buried treasure. At home, in a hundred dangers, preserved only by the inviolable and sleepless vigilance of the children of his tribe, remained Cluny : himself (if the ancient laws of Celtic hereditary custom had existed) the Legitimist King of Scotland ; the representative, through the House of MacHeth, of the blood of Lulach.

Lochiel and Lochgarry received (as we shall see) such posts of honour in French service as Charles could procure for them. About 1754 Young Lochgarry took service with England, never forgiven by his father, who finally entered the service of Spain, leaving his curse on any of his sons who acknowledged the Elector. The family has lost its lands, though now represented by one of the first of Sanskrit scholars. After their Odyssey of adventures, the house of Lochiel still retains the old lands, and the affection and respect of Highlands and Lowlands : while, at the close of services even more arduous, Clan Vourich yet boasts a Cluny, to represent that ancient Celtic royal line, compared with which the Stuarts are *parvenus* and interlopers.

Charles, his adventures ended, sailed with a company of gentlemen, to some of whom Fate finally relented. To him she was relentless. Leaving Lochnanuagh the Prince left his good days behind him : left his high spirits and indomitable ardour of endurance. Fortune did not reserve for him one happy hour. War and wanderings in the mountain air he was born to excel in, to him the air of palaces and convents was fatal. From Roscoff, in Britanny, on October 10, the gallant and loyal Warren reported to James his happy arrival ' this moment, within four leagues of Morlaix, at half an hour past two in the afternoon ; t'is scarce to be imagined what a crowd of dangers run thro', by sea and land.' *Per tot discrimina rerum !*

CHAPTER V

HOPE AND DESPAIR (1746–1766)

> Oh, it's hame, hame, hame,
>   And it's hame I wadna be,
> Till the Lord call King James
>   To his ain countrie ;
> Bid the wind blaw frae France,
>   And the Firth kep the faem,
> And Lochgarry and Lochiel
>   Bring Prince Charlie hame !
>
> Let the rivers stop and stand
>   Like walls on either side,
> Till our Highland lad pass through
>   With Jehovah for his guide !
> Dry up the river Forth
>   As Thou didst the Red Sea,
> When Israel cam' hame
>   To his ain countrie !

DURING the whole of Charles's expedition and adventures, it seems that his father, in Rome, had but the scantiest news of him. After Culloden, James roamed, lonely and anxious, through his desolate palace : ignorant of the fate of his son. Henry, whether at Boulogne or elsewhere, was wretched in France, and the letters between James

and him harp on the weary and puzzling old theme :
the supposed estrangement between the two Princes.
We see no proof of this estrangement. Henry had
been in affectionate correspondence with Charles,
during the invasion of England. He had done his
best to urge on the dilatory French. Just before
Culloden he had sent to Charles young John Macdonnell, of the Scot House family, a soldier in
Spanish service, with 2,000*l.* in gold. Macdonnell
arrived when all was over : part of the money was
stolen from him by the Mackenzies of Laggie and
Kilcoy, the remainder was paid over by Macdonnell
to Murray of Broughton.[1]

Thus Henry had done all that he could do, yet
he and James keep playing on the old string of
the political, though not personal estrangement, supposed to have been caused by Strickland. While
Charles was running all kinds of risks, while he
was actually lurking with his faithful Glenmoriston
men in the cave of Coiraghoth (July 25), James,
in Rome, was writing thus to Henry. 'So for
God's sake, dear Child, be on your Guard, and whatever the Prince may happen to do or say that might
be disagreeable to you, bear and suffer everything
with as cheerful an air towards him as you can.
The Cardinal's and Obryen's advice may be of use to
you on such occasions, and above all inform me of

---

[1] See, in *Companions of Pickle*, 'A Gentleman of Moydart.'

everything ; it will be a less evil that you should let yourself be deprived of every servant you have, and allow yourself even to be ill used for a time, than that there should be any disunion betwixt you and your Brother, which would be the ruin of you both, whoever was in the right, for the consequences would be the same, and the world can easily judge of public appearances, whereas by suffering everything with patience, besides the interiour comfort that conduct will give you, nothing can be more capable of opening the Prince's eyes. . . . You may be sure I will not suffer you should be oppressed, and that one way or another I hope I shall always be able to draw you out of such a situation with decency, but then all will depend on your own patience and moderation.'

The outlaws of Glenmoriston, the only people then with Charles, were not likely to be intriguing against Henry. While the Prince's life might hang on the crackling of a dry bough, or the falling of a stone in a corry, here were his father and brother absorbed in a petty set of intrigues! Old Sheridan, as we saw, escaped from Scotland in May. He was now in France, and to him James wrote sharply. He had not written directly to James, since his escape. All that he had to say he had told Murray (Dunbar), he had no recent news, and was being attacked for deserting the Prince, till he exhibited Charles's written orders to leave him. To Sheridan also James kept grumbling about Strickland, but Sheridan, in reply, announced the death of that unlucky gentleman at Carlisle. James now recalled Sheridan to Rome, and Henry was left in the society of Graeme, Kelly, Carnegy, and others, who were not in his favour. James warned Henry against an open rupture, or *éclat* with Charles (August 1), while Charles was lying hidden in a shieling in the Braes of Strathglas. Meanwhile Elcho, in Paris, had been on bad terms with Sheridan, till the Prince's tutor very reluctantly set off for Rome. Manifestly Charles was about to return to a disagreeable state of affairs. On October 10, having landed at Morlaix, he wrote thus to Henry :

Dear Brother,—As I am certain of your great concern for me, I cannot express the joy I have (on your account) of my safe arrivall in this country. I send here enclosed to lines to my Master just to shew him I am alive and safe (being fatigued not a little, as you may imagine). It is my opinion you should write immediately to ye French King giving him notice of my safe arrivall and at ye same time excusing my not writing to him myself immediately, being so much fatigued and hoping soon to have ye pleasure of seeing him. I leve it to your prudence the wording of this Letter, and would be glad no time should be lost in writing and dispatching it, as also that ye should consult nobody without exception upon it but John Greme and Sr. Thomas, the resans of which I will tell ye on meeting. *Note bene.* It is an absolute necessity I must see ye F. K.

as soon as possible, for to bring things to a write head. Warren ye bearer will instruct ye of the way I would wish you should meet me at Paris. I Embrace you with all my heart and Remain your most Loving

Brother. CHARLES P. R.

John Graeme, from Clichy, now announces (October 17) the safe arrival of the Prince, in perfect health and high spirits :

Tho' the fatigue, the want of all necessarys, and the dangers he has undergone are beyond imagination, yet he looks as well as when I had the honour to see him more than two years ago. Nothing was ever so tender as his first interview with the Duke, which I am sorry I was not witness to, having mist him on the road in the night time and found them together on my return next morning. It is an unspeakable pleasure to me to see how much they love one another.

O'Brien now went to concert an interview between Charles and Louis XV. Macdonnell of Barisdale was consigned to prison for his treachery, while Charles, who had gone to Paris, ' remained very private there.' Charles had not known Henry, at first ; Henry found him ' fatter and broader,' and received him with affectionate raptures. Louis refused, O'Brien reports, to see Charles ' in a public way,' but the Princes supped at Fontainebleau, with Louis and Madame de Pompadour, and gave entertainments, at Henry's expense.

Charles's biographers publish a glowing account of his reception at Court, from an English pamphlet. He is said therein to have gone straight from Paris to Versailles, where Louis embraced him with many compliments. The truth is that he really remained private in Paris for some time. When he did see Louis, says O'Brien, no reference was made to business. The pamphlet tells how Charles, ten days later, made a brilliant public progress to Versailles; in one coach went Ogilvy, Elcho, Kelly, and Glenbucket, Charles following in another with Lord Lewis Gordon, and Old Lochiel. Stafford and young Lochiel rode beside the Prince, who wore rose-coloured velvet, lined with silver, diamonds in his hat and shoes, and all his orders. 'He glittered all over like the star which, they tell you, appeared at his nativity.' All this may be true, for Mann heard the news in Florence; moreover we have the bill for the hire of the horses. Certainly the Princes, as O'Brien reports, were received with applause at the Opera (October 31). But on the very same day Henry was writing in cypher to James, making a tale of complaints.

The situation is easily understood. Charles was enjoying life and his laurels: Henry could neither drink nor otherwise divert himself in a 'popular' way. He disliked Charles's friends; he probably displayed his religious devoutness; and he held by O'Brien and Cardinal Tencin, whom Charles thoroughly distrusted. Reason enough was his to disbelieve in ministers who had deserted and disappointed him. But his plan of treating them cavalierly, like a hardy Highland chief, was fatal. He could do nothing directly with Louis, which was his purpose and desire, and, for three years, he broke himself on the French politicians. They again and at once disappointed his expectations. In November Cardinal Tencin showed O'Brien a statement of what they proposed to do for the Prince. He was to receive from Louis 12,000 francs monthly, and a house for himself and Henry. James had warned Charles, even before he heard this news, that he would need ' patience and fortitude.' But Charles told O'Brien that he could not believe that the French proposals had ever been really made.

D'Argenson on this *wrote* the proposal. Charles, much against O'Brien's wishes, sent the following reply, neither accepting nor rejecting : it illustrates Charles's method of ' falling foul ' !

. . . J'ai reçu la lettre dont vous m'avez honorer, en datte d'hier, que j'ai communiqué sur le champ à Abbadié [the P.] qui m'a dit ces propres mots, qu'après toutes les bontés et amitié que Le Roy de France luy a témoigné et dont il manque de parolles pour exprimer sa reconnaissance, *il est fort surpris que le Marquis d'Argenson ayant depuis tant de jours les ordres de Roy en son égard, vous en aquitté*

comme vous faittes et ne luy avé pas donné connaissance mot
pour mot, en quoy il ne tiendra jamais bon ce qui lui viendra
d'ailleurs.

Was ever Minister in this manner wooed by a
dependent and guest of his Master? D'Argenson
had a kind of sentimental admiration for Charles :
probably he was not allowed by O'Brien to see the
Prince's note. And was ever a pious monarch, like
James, told by his son that the ministers of his chief
ally were 'vermin'? Charles next informed James
that he would give an 'Ordiance' (audience) to his
Majesty's old friend, Madame de Mézières (*née* Oglethorpe) 'the next time I intend to make penance.'
This lady was regarded, both by James and the
Prince, as a reckless and feather-brained conspirator.

The causes of Charles's irritation are not hard to
discover. While the French Court was offering a
liberal provision for him and his brother, he had been
imploring Louis to grant him something very different.
Thus, on October 22, just after his landing, he wrote
from Fontainebleau to the King. 'The reason why
I did not speak to your Majesty about my affairs
last night, was because my brother was present, and,
loving him tenderly, I was anxious to avoid giving
him cause for jealousy.' He then asks Louis to grant
him a private interview. On October 25 he again
asks for an interview : he has drawn up a statement
of his ideas. He wanted to meet Louis secretly in

the rooms of d'Argenson. Now Louis, later, conducted a whole foreign policy of his own, without the knowledge of, and contrary to the notions of his Ministers.[1] But, at present, he did not mean to submit himself, like Cluny, to 'the soothing close applications, which an angel could not resist,' of the Prince. Charles's Memoir represented that the penal measures of England against his adherents would be the ruin of Scotland, unless he could instantly return with French troops. With 18,000 or 20,000 regulars, he could conduct an enterprise which he would confide to Louis alone. This project had been Charles's reason, or excuse, for trying to leave Scotland immediately after Culloden. But the French Court would listen to no such proposals. Charles informed Louis that any suggestions of measures (such as a pension) for his private benefit had never come from him. He had asked only for aid in an expedition, and to such requests he had received no reply. He is grateful for the kindnesses of Louis. Meanwhile he means (the paper is undated) to retire from Paris, where, as things are, his presence can only encourage false hopes in his friends at home. This attitude, as we shall see, he maintained with energy.

It appears that he was encouraged, perhaps guided, by the example of Lochiel. Louis had

[1] See *Le Secret du Roi* by the Duc de Broglie.

been assisting the exiled companions of the Prince, with pensions proportionate to their military rank. Lochiel, Brigadier and Colonel, received 4,000 *livres* yearly, Lochgarry had 3,000, Ogilvy 4,000, Maxwell of Kirkconnell 1,800, and all had commissions in the French army.   Lochiel, writing to James on January 16, 1747, expressed his reluctance to accept the regiment and pension which Charles had procured for him.   His arguments are the same as those of Charles to Louis.   Scotland will be ruined, he says, the Highlands will be 'depopulated' if France does not send an expedition at once, and with this expedition Lochiel desires to go.

It was Lochiel who begged that Charles's application to France might be 'only to procure the necessary assistance.'   Charles made these applications persistently, but, in January 1747, had to tell Lochiel that they were urged in vain, but that a regiment in French service would be given to the Cameron chief.   'I told H.R.H. that Lord Ogilvy or others might incline to make a figure in France ; but my ambition was to serve the Crown, and serve my country, or perish with it.'   If a regiment was procured for him, he must accept it, 'out of respect to the Prince ; but I hope your Majesty will approve the resolution I have taken to share in the fate of the people I have undone, and if they must be sacrificed, to die along with them.   It is the only way I can free myself of the reproach of their blood. . . .' It was noble, and worthy of Lochiel, this resolve ; which was also the resolution of the Prince. But to his requests Charles received no reply ; while to Lochiel James could only write with helpless pity and unavailing sympathy. The purpose of Charles was excellent, but his manner, towards the Ministers of Louis, was childish and deplorable. A few months ended the sorrows of Lochiel, who died in 1748.[1]

The last months of 1746 were partly occupied with marriage projects. O'Brien mentions the idea that Henry should wed Mademoiselle de Mazarin, and Charles, the third daughter of the Duke of Modena, an impecunious prince. These matches O'Brien thought inadequate. James, however, reckoned the Modena marriage better than none at all. Charles was of opinion that Henry should marry as soon as possible, but Henry was not a marrying man. James (November 22, 1746) wished to recall Henry to Rome, or to send him into Spain, to avoid a quarrel. It may have been at this time that Cardinal Tencin suggested to Charles the surrender of Ireland to France, the Prince replying, 'All or nothing, *point de partage.*'[2] The Cardinal's idea was quite intoler-

---

[1] A portrait, said to be that of Lochiel, exists at Callart, in Mamore. But it is dated 1762, and cannot represent this famous Chief.

[2] In 1901 the Duc de la Tremoille published some letters of the

able, of course, and Charles (November 27) described him to James as 'a rogue and a rascal,' hated by Louis, who lacked the force of character to dismiss him. Of O'Brien (on whom James mainly depended) Charles gives no better account. D'Argenson, even, does not escape censure, though he failed from lack of power, not lack of will. The very kindest sentiments about Henry are expressed. 'My opinion is I cannot as yet marry unless I get the King's dauter which is in vain to ask at present, and am afraid will always be the same.' He proposes the daughter of Prince Radzivil for Henry. Meanwhile Henry laments that Charles still attacks him, 'in a loving way,' for his strict mode of life. He regrets his own 'unfortunate sensible [sensitive] temper.'

On November 28 James announced old Sheridan's death from apoplexy. He added a long complaint of Charles's affection for Sheridan (selected as he was by James himself) and Strickland. Providence had removed these evil ones : let this be a

Prince to Anthony Walsh and George Kelly (*Une Famille Royaliste Irlandaise et Française*). For a copy of this work I have to thank the Duc de la Tremoille, a descendant of Walsh. The period of the letters is *circ.* 1758. Unluckily but few of the cypher names in the correspondence were known to me, but Mr. F. H. Blackburne Daniell has discovered the cypher at Windsor Castle. Thence it appears that, in September 1758, the Prince refused to cede Ireland and Scotland to France, in return for French assistance. On this point he remained patriotic. (*English Historical Review*, No. 69, January 1903, pp. 121, 122.)

warning.   Charles keeps both him and Henry in the
dark as to his plans.   This is, doubtless, the result of
bad advice from designing persons.   In truth, Charles
was probably well aware that whatever James knew
was known, by return of post, to the English Government.   This fact, vouched for by Walton's letters
from Rome, is noted by Charles on a scrap of paper.
' Nothing to be said to Rome, where all is known.'
But he never told James this reason for his secrecy,
in so many words : and, till his father's death, Charles
showed a want of confidence which James, though he
lamented and blamed it in every letter, never allowed
to destroy his affection, nor interrupt his long-suffering
kindness.

His position and conduct are most pathetic.
Personal ambition was dead in the suffering King : he
reminds Charles that he had only waited the proper
moment to abdicate in favour of his son.   But the
Prince's obstinacy was engaged ; his natural affection
dwindled, and presently he could tell himself, not
wholly without justice, that his father and brother
had deserted and betrayed the Cause.   Hence arose
his ' system :' that of a secret and secluded life, without communicating his whereabouts to his father.   ' I
will always love you, I will always believe you love
me,' says James, at this date.   ' You may be sure I
shall never order anything to interfere with the
measures you may take in your affairs, as long as I

shall think fit to suspend the directing of them myself.' He endeavoured to shake Charles's confidence in his own old servant, George Kelly, relying on tales told to him at Rome. He denounces Charles's associates as a ' gang,' and sees him, as indeed he was, ' on the brink of the precipice.'

Charles's only wise policy was to submit to France, but against that his heart revolted. Charles replied, ' with tears in his eyes,' not so much for his old friend, Sheridan, as for ' the expressions of your Majesty's goodness.' He wished to obey, but humbly thought that Kelly had been misrepresented. James called him indiscreet, but, in 1721, an English minister had, in fact, applauded Kelly's discretion, and reckoned him much superior to Atterbury. Charles's ' ears are open to everybody,' and against Kelly he has not heard one word. He trusts Henry as much as possible, but the confidence is not reciprocal, and he fears that Henry is prejudiced against him by evil advisers. But, as usual, Charles sends no account of his plans, alleging that he needs a new cypher. Now James, most indiscreetly, sent copies of Charles's letter and of his own reply to O'Brien in Paris, who, as he knew, was detested by the Prince. There could be only one end of these proceedings : an entire break up in the exiled family.

On February 3, 1747, James wrote to Charles a long review of his whole behaviour from the time

when the eternal Strickland intervened, in 1742, down
to the Prince's refusal of a French pension, in 1746.
He especially fears that Charles is seeking English
popularity by neglect of the Catholic religion. ' I
have already been too long in hott water on your
occasion, and that without profit or advantage to any
of us.' In the end of January, or beginning of
February, Charles had carried out his idea (announced
by him to Louis XV.) of retiring from Paris. He
wrote to Henry from Lyons, and Henry (February 3,
1747) told him that James meant to send himself to
Spain. Charles (February 9) replied from Avignon :
indignant that James and Henry had decided on the
Duke's journey to Spain without apprising him. He
himself, while in Scotland, had intended to visit the
Spanish Court, doubtless (as Mr. Ewald points out)
on the strength of advice from Charles Wogan, given
in a letter of December 10, 1745. Charles now informs Henry that, in leaving for Avignon, his real
point was Madrid. As he had never hinted at this,
either to Henry or James, he had little reason to
blame them for concealing their intentions from him.
But this never occurred to the Prince. He counsels
Henry not to go to Spain, ' as everybody will imagine
we do not act in concert, and consequently have no
confidence in each other.' Everybody would have
been perfectly right in that conclusion. Charles had
not even trusted young Sheridan with his purpose :

Sheridan was to carry the letter to Henry and return with his answer.

So began the game of Hide-and-Seek which Charles was to play from 1749 to 1766. He had told Edgar, who told James, that he was leaving Paris, but not *where* he was going. He had told Henry that he was going to Avignon, as he did, but only for a few days. Henry (February 15) replied to Charles that he had informed him about his projected Spanish journey, as soon as he heard from James, whose letter he had forwarded at once.

The natural bad results of the game of Hide-and Seek at once declared themselves. In Rome, James (February 17) only knew that Charles had gone to Avignon. Had Louis, he asked, expelled the Prince ? James did not know : he was 'in cruel anxiety,' but, like a kind father, he sent to Charles a sum of 15,000 livres. There was another inconvenient consequence of Charles's disappearance. Balhaldy and Sempil (who were always James's trusted agents) had now some expectation of bringing Louis to the point of sending forces to Scotland. But as Charles had broken with Sempil and Balhaldy, they were obliged to communicate with James, through Lochiel, and James had to write to Charles, at Avignon, a letter which was certain not to find him in that papal city. Indeed, while James was addressing his letter to Avignon Charles was at Barcelona, trying to get permission to see the King of Spain. Meanwhile, Lochiel was addressing Charles, whom he also believed to be on the Rhone. His absence from Paris was ' matter of the greatest affliction' to Lochiel and his other friends. They expected peace to be made between France and England, and England was sure to insist on the expulsion of Charles from France. This would be more easily acquiesced in by France, as the Prince was no longer in the territory of Louis. Then there was the chance that Sempil and Balhaldy, though Charles disliked them, might now get Louis to lend some troops, and Sullivan might be employed in the negotiations, as Louis and Sullivan already had some sort of secret understanding. All these plans were frustrated by Charles's mysterious disappearance.

There really were no grounds of hope ; but, if there had been, Charles was lost to the knowledge of his friends. He was trying to discover whether Spain would not make, in his favour, a joint expedition with France, and lend him arms, and other supplies. At Guadalaxara (March 6–14), he was soliciting the royal family of Spain. He told James the story of his misadventures : how he was smuggled into a coach, ' with a great many ridiculous precautions,' and carried to see the Spanish Minister, who entreated him to go away at once. He retired to his inn, where, at midnight, Caravajal came and took him to see the King and Queen. They were very civil, but insisted on his departure, and, after another interview with Caravajal, Charles was obliged to leave the scene. He returned to Paris, where (March 26) he announced to Clancarty his intention of living as privately as possible. Here,—some one writes anonymously to Murray (Dunbar),—the Prince's credit for sobriety was 'a little blemished,' on account of the convivialities of his confessor, an Irish cordelier named Kelly (not George Kelly), 'a notorious drunkard.' Meanwhile Sullivan had been in Rome, and was returning with a letter from James, who announced (April 17) that he wished Henry to come to him. He also acknowledged a present of a 'China box, really very pretty,' which the Prince had sent.

As for Charles, he conceived the idea of proposing for the hand of—the Czarina of Russia! This was brave! James Keith had fled from Russia rather than marry the august lady. Charles also spoke ill to James about Lord George Murray. James defended Lord George, and said what it was natural to say about the amazing Russian marriage. The Czarina would not even allow the Earl Marischal to reside in her country, so closely was she allied with England. It was hardly probable, then, that she would accept the Prince's 'blunt proposal.' As for Lord George, he had asked James to offer to

z

Charles his apologies for any personal failures of his
in courtesy ; and James confesses himself touched.
' I can scarce remember that ever any one made such
an act of submission as he has done.' Lord George
was going to Cleves, and only desired to pay his
respects to Charles ; but, when he came on this errand,
he was insolently rebuffed ; in a manner, as James
said, ' unchristian, unprincely, and impolitic.'

Thus, within one year of Culloden, Charles had
offended every human being whom he ought to have
respected, and who could help him. James, Henry,
Lochiel, O'Brien, Sempil, Balhaldy, Lord George,
and the French ministers, had all been mystified, or
insulted, or otherwise alienated. Punishment came
in a moment, and the blow was mortal. On April 29
Henry stole away from Paris, leaving a letter for
Charles. He wanted to see his father, ' if it were
but for a fortnight.' The change of air would be
excellent for his health. Like Charles, he had been
refused permission to make a campaign with the
French army. He is departing secretly, he says,
because he knows that Charles would never let him
go. He will return at once, if he can be useful.
Henry was *sournois*. He never meant to return : he
meant to secure his future, and ruin the Cause in the
opinion of England, by taking a Cardinal's Hat.
D'Argenson says that he fled in circumstances of distinguished treachery. He invited Charles to supper,

had his house lit up splendidly, all his servants were ready, but *he* had secretly made off at five o'clock in the afternoon. The Prince, waiting till midnight in the empty house, was in mortal anxiety lest his brother might have been assassinated. Charles did not hear from him till three days later. If this anecdote is true, Henry must have caused his letter of April 29 to be delayed in delivery.

Charles now vowed never to return to Rome, but rather to take refuge in some hole in a rock, says d'Argenson. To this resolution he was constant : not even to see his dying father would he visit Rome, till James expired in 1766.

Charles had often mystified his family, but he never put such a trick on them as this of Henry's, and not for twenty years did he forgive his brother. With d'Argenson he believed, contrary to all probability, that England had bribed Cardinal Tencin and O'Brien to urge Henry into taking the Cardinal's Hat. Few things suited English policy better, but Henry had always been conscious of a 'vocation.' Moreover he despaired of Charles, so he feathered his own nest comfortably with benefices. On May 14 James replied to a letter in which Charles had spoken his mind about Henry's flight. He himself, he says, had known nothing of the Duke's intentions. James now said no word of Henry's clerical ambitions ; but, on June 9, told Louis XV. that he and his son had consulted the Pope, and that his Holiness had promised a Cardinalate.   On June 13 James sent the same news to 'his dearest Carluccio.'   He and Henry, he remarks, had foreseen that Charles 'might probably not approve' of this sudden promotion.   James himself did not know the Duke's intention before his arrival in Rome, but he would have advised the step, 'had he not had the vocation he has' because he 'could not enjoy tranquility and happiness in any other state.   You will understand what I mean without my enlarging further on this so disagreeable article.'   The inference as to Henry is pretty obvious. James then speaks of Charles's lack of money.   Later (July 4), he cannot understand Charles's indignation against Henry, which is intelligible enough.   All the party were heart-broken.

There was a certain Irish priest, Myles Macdonnell, who had recently complained to James that George Kelly had suppressed (naturally, for Charles never tolerated such things) a conspiracy to seize or slay the Duke of Cumberland in London.   This Myles now wrote again, to tell James that Henry's behaviour 'is a mortal deadly stroke to the Cause.' Theodore Hay sent the same information to Edgar. 'Everybody looks upon it' (the Cardinalate) 'as of much worse consequences than the battle of Culloden.' George Innes, Principal of the Scots College in Paris, wrote to Edgar that, 'from the Prince to the lowest of his subjects, all are unanimously crying out against what is done.' Charles returned to Saint-Ouen, and attempted to induce the Earl Marischal to join him, and manage his affairs. The Earl, who was at Treviso, refused. The letters between James and Charles were now rare and brief, though Charles sent his miniature, and remarked that his 'bust in marble is much admired for its being singularly like.' On Old Year's day Henry wrote from Rome to Charles, with protestations of affection. The Prince made no reply. James, early in 1748, wrote a long remonstrance of the usual kind. Sempil, who was at Rome (February 16, 1748), sent James a paper in which George Kelly was accused of being the ruin of the Cause : Sempil himself having at first recommended Mr. Kelly to the Prince ! One of the Ministers of Louis, M. de Puisieux, had excused the indolence of France on the plea that Kelly was not a *persona grata*. George was a much more honest man than Sempil and Balhaldy, whom the Earl Marischal had detected years before ; and, in fact, talk about Kelly's favour was a mere transparent excuse for French neglect of Charles. In no circumstances would France have aided Charles : the private notes of d'Argenson make that a matter of certainty.

Early in May 1748 Charles warned James that a Peace was now much talked of : it would, of course, be fatal to his hopes. The plenipotentiaries soon met at Aix-la-Chapelle. In July d'Argenson writes, 'The Prince is amusing himself with love affairs. Madame de Guéménée almost seized him by force : they quarrelled after a ridiculous scene. He lives with the Princesse de Talmond : he is furious and obstinate in everything. He wished to imitate Charles XII., and stand a siege in his house, like Charles XII. at Bender. Madame de Talmond has dissuaded him : it is thought that a retreat will be found for him in Switzerland.' Charles, in fact, was now on the very brink of the precipice. In other words, a crisis was approaching, with which all his recent conduct and experience rendered him unfit to cope. His behaviour, when the conditions of the Peace of Aix-la-Chapelle made it necessary for France to refuse her hospitality, amazed equally his enemies and his friends. Many months before, James had said that the extraordinary conduct of Charles could not be the result of mere caprice. It must be part of a system deliberately considered.

That system, in James's opinion, was to win the goodwill of England by neglect of himself, of the Catholic religion, and of the Court of France. England loved neither France, the Pope, nor the Pretender, and Charles might have been advised, by Kelly, Sullivan, young Sheridan, and the rest of the 'gang,' to disregard France, his father, and his faith. This theory might help to explain the Prince's be-

haviour, during the discussion at Aix-la-Chapelle.
But it is certain that most of his *entourage* were as
much puzzled and dismayed by his proceedings as
James himself, or the ministers of Louis.   By braving
the French king, Charles was imperilling, not only
his own prospects, but the daily bread of his friends
and gentlemen, who cannot have advised him in his
behaviour.

What, then, were his motives in a course which
seems almost if not quite insane ?   In the first place,
there was the influence of women.   They literally
'pulled caps' for the Prince, says d'Argenson.   In a
singular drama which this now fallen Minister left in
manuscript,[1] he introduces the Princesse de Talmond
and Madame d'Aiguillon, fighting like fishfags over
the object of their admiration.   Madame de Talmond
was a Pole by birth, a Jablonowski, a cousin of the
Queen of France.   As she married M. de Talmond
in 1730, she must have been several years older than
Charles, and was probably about forty in 1749.
Voltaire ascribes to her

> Le goût qu'on ne trouve qu'en France,
> Et l'esprit de tous les pays.

Madame du Deffand admits her beauty, wit, and
vivacity ; but adds that she has the vanity of the

---

[1] Published by the Duc de Broglie.

Poles, is jealous, capricious, unhappy, absurd, and always affected. 'She is feared and disliked by all who live in her society. Yet she has truth, courage, and honesty. . . . She pleases, she provokes, we love and hate her, seek her and avoid her.' She was Charles's mistress, probably ; was certainly his Egeria, and is said by d'Argenson, to have 'governed him with fire and fury,' and encouraged him to brave the Court of France.

Madame d'Aiguillon, on the other hand, was a hostess of the *philosophes*, was the bosom friend of the celebrated Montesquieu : and was berhymed by Voltaire. ' Her wit is like her face, brilliant and out of drawing,' says Madame du Deffand. Profuse in her expenditure, eager, energetic, and impetuous, she never was the Prince's mistress, but was not the wisest of advisers.

There are traces also of an affair with Madame de Montbazon, whom Charles compromised, it appears, by firing off two pistols, on what occasion is not known. He was flattered, at this time, by English-women, who came over from London, merely to gaze at him in his box at the Opera. All the world knowing that he would certainly be compelled to leave France, the general sympathy was with him. He dressed splendidly, affected an air of gaiety, and is said to have ordered a service of plate, worth 100,000 francs, for a party to which he invited Madame de

Talmond and the rest of his French friends.[1]   He
went to Court, laughed or hummed a tune when
the Peace was talked of, and was thought capable of
fortifying his house and resisting any attempts to
remove him.   He declared, says d'Argenson, that he
possessed letters in which Louis vowed that he
would never desert him, and d'Argenson supposed
that such letters might really exist.   He rejoiced
openly in the victories of the British fleet, and had
medals struck, in silver and copper, with his head,
and, on the obverse, ships, and the motto *Amor et
Spes Britanniae.*   The sums paid for these medals
are entered in his accounts.

The source of his supplies is mysterious : from
France he would not take money for himself.

On November 3, 1747, he had expressed his
surprise at receiving some 25,000 francs, with a
promise of 70,000 more, in drafts on the Royal
Treasury, from Tencin.   The Cardinal was un-
authorised to interfere, he told the Minister, and his
father's subjects would be justly offended.   ' The
Cardinal is accused of having a hand in my brother's
recent behaviour, for which I can never be consoled.'
He returned the money.   Probably he received
English subscriptions, and Major Kennedy, in 1748
managed to send to him some 6,000*l.* of the French
gold buried near Loch Arkaig, after Culloden.

---

[1] Newsletter sent to a sister of Clementina Walkinshaw.

Many of his adherents appear, from his accounts, to have been supported by Charles himself. However he got the money, he had busts, pictures, and medals of himself done, and told the Prince de Conti that, though the British fleet might be his enemy, he was its friend ; and that the glory of England was his own. All this behaviour may have aimed at popularity in England, and in France, where the public detested the policy which submitted to the expulsion of the heroic guest of the country.

It is thus that d'Argenson explains Charles's behaviour. But not thus can we explain the scandal which he caused by trying to break into Madame de Talmond's house, when her husband refused him admission. In fact Charles had made up his mind to be what d'Argenson calls a *tête de fer*, and to set his own will against the resolve and the necessities of France. This idea appears in his scribbled notes, ' Maximes d'un Homme sauvage.' He would be a Wild Man, and return, for his part, to Rousseau's State of Nature. Against the conclusions of the Peace of Aix-la-Chapelle, he published a Protest. The document he despatched to Louis (July 10), to de Puisieux, the Minister, his enemy ; and to Montesquieu. He complains that Montesquieu has not given him his book ' on the Romans.' ' There should be better relations between authors, and I hope that my way of dealing may procure for me the con-

tinuance of your good will.' Montesquieu had a
Jacobite housekeeper, oddly enough, and was an
acquaintance of the Jacobite Lord Elibank, the
friend of David Hume, John Home, and Dr. Carlyle.
He replied, applauding the eloquence of Charles's
manifesto : especially his noble expressions about
his brave Highlanders. He averred that, were
Charles not so great a Prince, he himself and
Madame d'Aiguillon would secure his election to the
Academy !

At this time and later Charles took some interest
in the *philosophes* and their systems. But, for the
present, France was constantly urging him to leave
the country. An asylum was found for him in the
Canton of Fribourg : he was to have guards and a
pension. De Gèvres was frequently sent to him
with the King's commands to depart. He turned
his back on de Gèvres, and threw down in contempt
a kind of blank cheque which the King had offered.
The French court now applied to James : a copy of
his letter was handed to Charles by the Duc de
Gèvres on December 4. James herein told the
Prince that he was gaily breaking with France. 'As
your father and your King I command you to obey
his Most Christian Majesty instantly,' and to leave
his territory with a good grace. Resistance will
only ruin the Prince's reputation. Charles, according
to d'Argenson, replied to de Gèvres with a threat of

suicide. On December 9 he was warned that he must leave Paris in three days. His chief supporters in Paris withdrew from him. On December 11 he was arrested, as he was entering the Opera House. Louis had signed the order, murmuring, ' Poor Prince : how hard it is for a King to be a friend ! ' [1]

The English narrator, whose paper was published in 1749, says that Charles was informed of the order for his arrest, but only cried somewhat hastily, ' Pish-pish, an idle rumour ! They know that I will obey my father.' The Duke de Biran, of the Guards, was charged, it is said, with the management, and provided silk cord (or black ribbon) to bind the prisoner hand and foot.

The reason for this measure (which absolutely horrified the world and d'Argenson) was the fear that Charles might draw his pistols and fire on others or on himself. Twelve hundred of the Guards invested the Opera House to prevent a popular tumult: troops were lining the streets ; scaling ladders, for an attack on Charles's house, and even surgeons were provided. A warning voice in the street informed Charles of his danger, but he went on, was seized by several men, hurried into the kitchen

[1] Of the details of this event there is a long account in the Lockhart Papers. D'Argenson also is minute and copious, and I have seen a manuscript description, cited above, in a letter addressed to a sister of Clementina Walkinshaw.

court of the Palais-Royal, and taken into the rooms of
Marsolan, surgeon of the Duc d'Orléans.   Vaudreuil
there told him that he was arrested : he was searched
and bound.   His sword, a brace of pistols (which he
was in the habit of carrying as a precaution against
assassins), and a knife were taken from him.   He was
then carried, head foremost, ' like a corpse ' into the
coach, which drove off to Vincennes.   Three of his
gentlemen, including, it seems, Sir James Harrington
and Henry Goring (younger son of Sir Harry, the
conspirator of 1721), were hurried to the Bastille.
D'Argenson reports that Charles said to Vaudreuil,
' Mon cher Monsieur, vous faites là un vilain métier.'
Again, he said, ' France promised me an asylum : if
I had only a morsel of bread I would share it with a
friend.'   The English narrator avers that Charles was
placed in a miserable den, high in the donjon of
Vincennes.   D'Argenson says that he had a noble
apartment in the palace of the King, a good bed, and
a good supper : which is more probable.   He refused
to be waited on, saying that he had long ago learned
to be his own valet.

For several days Charles was closely guarded,
showing, says the English narrator, ' as much temper
and magnanimity as any man could show in the
height of prosperity, and even in his prison he
appeared the monarch of the universe.'

There was much public indignation at this usage

of a guest of France.   D'Argenson declares that the
Dauphin wept: the English narrator makes him
remonstrate with Louis 'in full levee.'   A servant of
Madame de Talmond had been arrested: the lady
wrote to Maurepas, 'Sir, the King's laurels are in
perfect flower, but, as the imprisonment of my lackey
cannot add to their glory, I pray you to release him.'
Libels and lampoons rained on the King and his
ministers.

> Tu triomphes, cher Prince, au milieu de tes fers,
> Sur toi, dans ce moment, tous les yeux sont ouverts.

If Charles wished merely to attract all eyes, and win
sonorous sympathy, he had certainly succeeded.
Walpole wrote to Mann (December 15), 'I don't
know whether he be a Stuart, but I am sure by his
extravagance he has proved himself of English ex-
traction!'   This was what Charles desired: he was
playing to the English gallery, from which he won a
round of ephemeral applause, all that he gained in
return for the loss of the concealed but useful protection of France.   On Sunday he was set free, under
the condition of leaving France.   The Earl Marischal
thought that he had also pledged himself never to
re-enter French territory : this is uncertain.   According to D'Argenson, an official accompanied him only
as far as Fontainebleau.   The English narrator says
that he was conducted to Pont Beauvoisin, on the

Savoy frontier : thence he went to Chambéry, and so to Avignon, the Papal city. His head, as he wrote on December 16, 'was still on his shoulders.' Stafford and young Sheridan were with him. Harrington and Goring were forbidden to come within fifty leagues of Paris, where Goring, however, constantly ventured himself, though in great dread of 'that horrid Bastille.' How Goring was rewarded we are to see.

Charles arrived at Avignon in the uniform of an officer in an Irish regiment. He appeared at the bedside of Murray (Dunbar), who was now out of James's favour, and he stayed with Mrs. Hay (Lady Inverness) till the house of the Marquis de Rochefort was got ready for him. He wrote to James on January 1, 1749, 'in perfect good health, notwithstanding the unheard-of barbarous and inhuman treatment I have met with.' It is now that Mr. Ewald places the arrival of Miss Walkinshaw. He relies on a statement of Walton's that 'The Pretender has learned with much vexation that the same Dulcinea who has so greatly disturbed the mind of his son, and was the cause of all his wildness at Paris, has joined him at Avignon, where she lives as his mistress, with much publicity.' But *that* Dulcinea was Madame de Talmond, and D'Argenson (whom Mr. Ewald never cites) says nothing about her flight after the Prince. She was sent to her place in

Lorraine, and it is not known that she went to Avignon.

England remonstrated with France on Charles's residence within the old walls of the Papal city on the Rhone, a nest of Jacobite exiles. But France would not interfere with the Pope. Charles, according to Walton, soon quarrelled with the ecclesiastical authorities of the town, because he was introducing the pastime of boxing. The Pope being threatened with the bombardment of Civita Vecchia, ordered the patron of the Fancy to withdraw.

Charles did not disobey. On February 24 he sent Sir John Douglas to the Landgrave of Hesse Darmstadt, with a proposal for the Landgrave's daughter. ' Unluckily I have not a crown to offer her at this moment, as she deserves, but I trust to have one, some day.' He also drafted, and probably sent, a letter to the King of Poland, saying that he had just arrived, bringing with him the daughter of the Landgrave, his wife! These were astonishing projects, as, of course, the Landgrave never dreamed of giving his daughter to a Prince without a roof to cover her head. Except the Estates of the Pope, where he would not go, not an inch of European soil was open to him.

On February 28, 1749, Charles rode out of Avignon, with Henry Goring, and, for many years, was lost to the eyes of his father and of Europe. A chapter might be written on the perplexities and conjectures of diplomatists.[1] Now he was said to be in Poland, now he was invited to the opening of the Radcliffe, in Oxford, when Dr. King delivered a veiled Jacobite oration, in Latin ; repeating *Redeat Ille*, and so forth. The party of Frederick, Prince of Wales, and the Parliamentary Jacobites met at a tavern in Pall Mall, a hundred and twelve in number—and nothing came of it. Charles was proclaimed, as King, at a strike of pitmen, in Newcastle. Harmless travellers were spied on, in Berlin ; in Russia Lord Hyndford hoped to catch the Prince, and carry him to Siberia !

Meanwhile, what was Charles doing, after the night enveloped him, as he left Avignon on February 28, 1749 ? If we could trace all his travels for the next five years, we should open a chapter of romance as remarkable as his Highland adventures. In many a strange disguise he visited many an unlooked-for place, always in peril of arrest, imprisonment, or even assassination. Though there are blanks in our knowledge, a close criticism of the Stuart Manuscripts reveals much that is curious, and that (before the publication of the present writer's ' Pickle the Spy ') was wholly unknown to the biographers of the Prince.

In March 1749 Charles must have gone to the

---

[1] A full account of these, from the State Papers, will be found in the author's *Pickle the Spy*.

A A

last place where he was likely to be welcome, Paris.
Thus, on March 6 he informed Waters, his Paris
banker, that he 'would *call* for letters.' He was
corresponding with Major Kennedy, in French
service, one of the MacUlrig Kennedys settled in
Glengarry's country. A portrait of this gentleman
shows him wearing the Glengarry tartan. He was
now engaged in getting a part of the gold buried at
Loch Arkaig, and conveying it to the Prince. There
had been hidden, originally, about 35,000 louis, and
Kennedy had helped Dr. Archibald Cameron in the
task of concealment.

Charles's reason for trying to return to Paris was,
doubtless, to arrange a system of correspondence
with Kennedy, Lally-Tollendal, his English adherents,
and other friends. It was necessary that Waters's
Bank should be only a kind of clearing office for the
letters, and that Waters should not know where
Charles was really concealed. On April 3 he was at
Lunéville, in Lorraine, the capital of Stanislas, ex-
King of Poland, and father of the Queen of France.
In Lorraine were the estates of Madame de Talmond,
and it is probable that the Prince was protected by
her, or by her influence, if she happened to be in
Paris. On April 3, then, at Lunéville, Charles
drafted, in very bad French, a Project for his arrival
in Paris. He was to go to Dijon, and Goring was
to go towards Paris, in a chaise bought at Lunéville.

But at Ligny, Goring was to desert his chaise and ride, leaving in some way the impression that the chaise was to make a return journey to Paris. How this was to be managed does not appear, but Charles was to arrive as if by accident, and was to seize the chance opportunity of a chaise returning to the French capital. Probably Goring was really to arrive at Ligny from the Paris side, without having visited that town. Then, after some jugglery with a trunk, Goring was to go to Dijon, and wait there, Charles entering Paris in the chaise which was returning thither. On the confused draft of this plan occur some names and addresses, including that of

> *Mademoiselle Ferrand,*
> *Grande Rue Varenne,*
> *Faubourg St-Germain,*
> *Paris.*

This young lady was at the moment, and till July remained, personally unknown to the Prince. But she was destined to serve him very faithfully and secretly. She was suggested as an ally by an unknown correspondent, signing ' T,' or anonymous : almost certainly Madame de Talmond.[1] Between her and that imperious lady, a great deal of jealousy was to arise later.

By April 10 Charles had probably entered Paris,

[1] See Preface.

and settled some matters with Waters. He next wrote to Mrs. Drummond, probably a relation by marriage of Balhaldy, and made her his channel of communication with the Earl Marischal, then residing at Berlin, with his brother, who had entered the service of Frederick the Great. D'Argenson supposed Charles to be in Sweden at or about this time. But, on May 20, he learned that the Prince had been concealed in Paris, by Madame de Talmond, for eight days, and this is not improbable. Thence, says D'Argenson, the Prince followed her to Lorraine, and it was held that Maurepas might have been dismissed from office because, as a friend of Madame de Talmond, he had connived at these arrangements. But it was certainly *from* Lorraine that Charles had entered Paris. 'Assuredly,' says D'Argenson, 'the Prince acted very ill in breaking his word of honour to the King, when he promised to leave the realm ; and he is greatly discredited by returning to a country whence he had been so brutally expelled.' On April 26 Charles was at Strasbourg : he seems to have sent Goring to Berlin, asking the Earl Marischal to meet him at Venice. He himself was there on May 17, but, on May 25, he was commanded to go away. He tried an appeal to Maria Theresa, without success.

'What can a bird do that has not found a right nest?' he notes on a scrap of paper. 'He must flit

from bough to bough.' What bough he perched on
next we know not : on June 3 he wrote to Montesquieu, and, by June 30, he was in Paris again. He
then wrote to Mademoiselle Ferrand, saying that she
would be surprised by his letter, as he was not
fortunate enough to know her, but Mrs. Routh (wife
of an Irish colonel in French service) would explain.
Mademoiselle Ferrand had written an account of
Cartouche, the celebrated robber, and it was as a kind
of Cartouche that Charles (so he put it) invited her
sympathy. Her part was to receive, from Waters,
the letters directed to ' Mr. John Douglas.' It is probable that now, or soon afterwards, Charles became
the guest of Mademoiselle Ferrand, or Des Marres,
and of her friend, Madame de Vassé, in the Convent
of St. Joseph, in the Rue Saint-Dominique. Years
later, Grimm wrote to Catherine of Russia that these
ladies had sheltered the Prince. At the Convent he
was under the same roof as Madame du Deffand, the
famous wit whose superannuated tenderness was
destined later to annoy Horace Walpole. Montesquieu, and Bulkeley, a very reputable Jacobite, were
often among her guests. Madame de Talmond also
had rooms in this retreat. By a secret staircase
Charles used to visit his Princess at night. In the
evening he would lurk in an alcove of the rooms of
Mademoiselle Ferrand, where he heard much good
talk, and a great deal of conversation about himself.

These facts were not known till long afterwards, when Madame de Vassé revealed the secret to M. de Choiseul.

She had, she said, been obliged to turn out the Prince at last, because he and the Princess used to quarrel, and alas! come to blows. Grimm learned his facts from an intimate friend of Madame de Vassé, This part of Charles's adventures is, perhaps, the most singular of all. His French Flora Macdonald, Mademoiselle Ferrand, was a very extraordinary woman. She appears to have been of Norman birth, daughter of M. Ferrand des Marres. Madame de Vassé, apparently a young widow, was daughter of M. de Pezé. These two ladies always spoke of themselves as 'sisters.' In Charles's letters and notes, Mademoiselle Ferrand appears as 'Mademoiselle Luci,' her friend is named 'La Grande Main,' or 'G. M.' Only by an accidental oversight or two, in the secret papers of the Prince, were we enabled to discern the real names.[1]

The ladies lived on the most intimate terms with Condillac, the philosopher, whose existence was quiet and has left few biographical traces. But the Dedication, to Madame de Vassé, of Condillac's 'Traité des Sensations,' shows how much he owed to Mademoi-

---

[1] Miss V. A. Simpson, by a minute study of D'Hozier, found out the real name of Mademoiselle Luci. She has since copied, in an undated packet of Stuart MSS., points which I notice in the Preface.

selle Ferrand, who had died, in 1752, before the work
was published. 'I consecrate my book to her
memory. . . . May it be the monument of your
friendship, and preserve it unforgotten!' Yet so
forgotten are the ladies, that only Grimm's gossip
preserves a record of their existence, and the chief
authorities on French art have vainly, though gene-
rously, sought for a portrait or miniature of ' Mademoiselle Luci' (Mademoiselle Ferrand) or of La Grande
Main (Madame de Vassé). Condillac attests 'the
keenness, the just balance, of Mademoiselle Ferrand's
intellect, and the vivacity of her imagination.' He
appears, at one time, to have had doubts about the
purely sensational origins of our knowledge, as in the
theory of Locke. Mademoiselle Ferrand suggested
to him the illustration of the animated statue, whose
closed channels of sense are opened, one by one.
' She enlightened me on the principle, the plan, and
the most minute details of the book . . .' but 'she
did not observe that she was becoming an author.'
Had she lived, her sensitiveness was such that she
would not have allowed Condillac,— *le philosophe* as
Charles and the ladies called him,—to acknowledge
his obligations.

He attests 'the intellect, the loyalty, and the
courage, which formed these ladies for each other.'
That Mademoiselle Ferrand was charming, is partly
attested by the jealousy of her which tormented

Madame de Talmond.   But there is not a trace
of an intrigue between Charles and his protec-
tress.   Her motive was human charity, and, while
she was unconsciously leaving her mark on the
philosophy of the century, she was also sheltering the
homeless head, and the desperate fortunes, of the
last of a line of Kings.   She died before Charles
could suspect her, or break with her, the best and
kindest of his friends.

Desperate indeed were the fortunes of Charles.
Kennedy had been arrested in London.   An officer
in French service, he was soon set at liberty, and
made his way to the Prince, to whom he presented a
good pair of English pistols.   But it was not much
of the Loch Arkaig gold that Kennedy could bring.
Young Glengarry, in the winter of 1749, and Archibald Cameron, had, to an extent not easily ascertained, meddled with the money.   Other Highlanders
secured shares ; Young Glengarry was accused of
forging James's name : Cluny was distracted by
claims, just or unjust, and 'even Lochaber con-
sciences' (wrote the English commander at Fort
William) were shocked by the treacheries of families
that followed, brothers and cousins betraying each
other.[1]

Charles, in poverty, sent Goring to England (July
31, 1749) to see the managers of the Jacobite party, and

[1] Cumberland MSS., Windsor Castle.

get what money he could.   Balhaldy, later, also visited
London, and found the party in a tremor.   To Goring
they had insisted that Charles must make his peace
with France, and dismiss his advisers.   The Prince
promised to give up Lally, Graeme, Oxburgh, and
Kelly, and he received 15,000*l.*, to which Goring's
brother, Sir Charles, probably còntributed gene-
rously.

D'Argenson had news of this affair.   Poor George
Kelly, at Avignon, on November 16, informed Charles
that, 'as an honest man,' he could not remain in his
service.   Oxburgh had written to Kelly, saying that
the Earl Marischal was the Parson's enemy, as was
known through Floyd, a friend whom the Earl later
recommended to David Hume.   Kelly, in fact, had
always wished the Earl to undertake Charles's affairs,
as he and Oxburgh both declare.   But Kelly had to
go : he returned later.   Of his money Charles sent
15,000 livres to his household at Avignon, Sheridan,
Stafford, and the others.   He supported his gentlemen there for many years, in fact till he became
titular King, in 1766.

It is not to be supposed that Grimm is correct
in thinking that the Convent in the Rue Saint-
Dominique was Charles's only ' nest.'   On November
22, 1749, for example, he was at Lunéville, in Lorraine,
where he wrote, or perhaps only copied, some information about his own movements.   He cannot have

been far from Paris on December 19, when he sent Goring to get 'his big muff and portfolio.' Many notes of this period (1749–1750) are drafts of angry or affectionate *billets* to Madame de Talmond. Thus on January 25, 1750, he drew up a formal little treaty, promising 'to retire from her territory' (her rooms probably), 'at any hour of the day or night,' when she so commanded. 'If you want to protect me, you must not make my life more wretched than it is.' Probably he was in bad health, as diplomatists reported : he writes, 'Pray take care of the young surgeon, M. le Coq, and see that he wants for nothing. As the lad gets no money from his relations, he may be in need.' The Prince (May 18, 1750) requests Mademoiselle Ferrand to procure for him 'Joseph Andrews' in English, and 'Tom Jones' in French. In 'Tom Jones' he may have been amused by the adventures of Sophia when mistaken for Jenny Cameron, and by the festive and futile Jacobitism of Squire Western. Even so good a Whig as Fielding would have been pleased, had he known that his books were assuaging the melancholy seclusion of 'the Young Pretender.'

At this period Charles had hopes from England, and Scott, in the introduction to 'Redgauntlet,' seems to think that there really was a strong revival of English Jacobitism. Scott had seen many of the Stuart MSS., being a member of a commission ap-

pointed to examine them. Conceivably some papers
then extant are now missing ; [1] but the collection as
it stands does not justify the belief that the English
Jacobites intended more than some kind of political
coalition with the party of Frederick, Prince of
Wales. At all events, as early as 1750, Charles was
projecting a visit to England. 'Ye Prince is determined to go over at any rate,' he wrote on May 3.
' He assures that he will expose nobody but himself,
supposing the worst.' Harry Goring's brother, Sir
Charles, was to send a ship to Antwerp, in August,
and there were dealings about weapons with Mr. P.
of D. (perhaps Mr. Patullo of Dundee, late 'muster-
master ' in the Highland Army). ' The great affair
of L.' (London ?) is to be attempted.

Probably this affair was to be a mob-rising and
an attack on St. James's Palace, as in the Layer plot,
in the past, and the Elibank plot, in the future.
Charles secretly deposited 186,000 livres with Waters,
and distributed little silver tokens with his own
profile, reduced from the medal with the inscription,
Laetamini Cives. The same head appears, with no
inscription, on a seal used by Waters. The head
is very like the profile of Queen Victoria on her
early coins. Charles's agent in Antwerp was Mr.
Dormer, a son of the fifth Lord Dormer, engaged in

---

[1] See preface to volume i. of the Historical MSS. Commission's
edition (1902).

commerce. On June 3 Charles bade him procure 26,000 muskets and other weapons. On July 2 he asked James for a renewal of his commission as Regent: the document is now in the Royal Library. James, in reply, called Charles 'a continual heartbreak,' but Edgar sent him two heads of the King on engraved stones.

Of all Charles's plots, this is the most mysterious. For what army did he want 26,000 muskets? The Highland chiefs did not even know where he was. In England, as Æneas Macdonald wrote from Boulogne in September, 'not three persons of distinction are of the same sentiments as to the methods of restoring the Royal family.' As far as Æneas knew, the scheme was for the English Jacobites to side in opposition with the followers of ' Fred,' Prince of Wales, crown him, call a Free Parliament, and see how the country would take it! Probably the mere restlessness of hope deferred took Charles in disguise to London. He left Antwerp on September 12, was in London on the 16th, and left for Paris on the 24th. He reached his 'nest,' probably in Lorraine, on the 30th, and his notes express doubts of the good faith of ' the Lady,' who may have been Madame de Talmond.

At this time Dr. King, of St. Mary's Hall, Oxford, was a Jacobite manager. Later, on the accession of George III., he deserted the Cause, and in his Anec-

dotes he observes that once, when the Prince had
been taking tea with him in London, his servant remarked on the visitor's likeness to busts of Prince
Charles, sold in Red Lion Square.   Possibly the Prince
was concealed at Lady Primrose's, but nothing is certain.   Hume, in his letter to Sir John Pringle, says, on
Jacobite report, that Charles was admitted to the
Anglican communion, ' in the New Church in the
Strand,' in 1753.   In June 1753 Archibald Cameron
left a statement to the effect that, when he last saw
Charles, the Prince bade him tell the party that
he was a member of the Church of England.   This
does not fix the date of the Conversion, but Hume
was wrong, for one of the Prince's notes runs,
' To mention my religion of the Church of England
as by law established, as I have declared myself
when in London the year 1750.' [1]   The Conversion
was known to Lord Denbigh, and Sir James Harrington, in the autumn of 1752, but it never was proclaimed in such a way as to reach the English people.
Thus it never had any effect, except on a few
Jacobites such as worthy Bishop Forbes, and indeed
the Prince's change of faith came too late.   In 1744
or 1745 it would (as Dr. Carlyle said at the time)
have won the Lowland Scots, but it would also
have estranged France.   For several years Charles
was Protestant enough to despise ' Papists,' as his

[1] A draft of his declaration (1759) on this subject exists in manuscript.

scrawls of notes indicate, and Republican enough to despise Kings. But his religion was always 'to seek,' as Lord Elcho has said in the Forty-Five. He later, in Italy, conformed decently to the creed of the Pope : he had gained nothing by deserting it.

We shall never know details about this audacious raid on London in 1750. We have shadowy glimpses of a disguised Prince, with a price on his head, drifting through sultry empty Pall Mall, visiting the Tower, beholding the palaces which are 'by right his ain,' fluttering the dovecotes of respectable Jacobitism, and forswearing the faith for which his grandfather and his father had lost, or refused the crown. How great a risk he ran, to how little purpose ! Long afterwards (December 6, 1783), Charles told the tale of his adventure to Gustavus III. of Sweden, and Sir Horace Mann reported it to Fox. Charles had viewed the Tower with a Colonel Brett, and thought that a gate might be blown in with a petard. He met about fifty of his followers in a room in Pall Mall ; two names are given in cypher, those of the Duke of Beaufort and the Earl of Westmorland. He offered to head a rising if 4,000 men could be mustered. How nervous the English Jacobites must have felt !

Only an increase of gloom could arise from this view of all that, to his mind, was his by right. ' God had given him bitter waters to drink.' He strayèd back to who knows what secret hiding-place, to the *Reine de Maroc,* as he calls his mistress, Madame de Talmond. She left him ; mistrust awoke ; on September 26 he wrote to tell her that he, too, was leaving his *triste solitude.* He had given Mademoiselle Ferrand orders to forward no letters : to Waters he says that he will disappear till January 15, 1751. He vanishes. From some place unknown he complains of Madame de Talmond, in notes to Mademoiselle Ferrand, and one letter was shown by Mademoiselle Ferrand to the elder lady, which annoyed Charles, but he and his Princess were reconciled for a while. Till March 1751 the Prince's hiding-place is unknown. But Goring was certainly working for him in Prussia, and, on February 10, 1751, Lord Albemarle, English ambassador in Paris, reported that Charles had been very civilly received by Frederick in Berlin, but had not succeeded in the suit (which was certainly offered) for the hand of his sister. Frederick, too, had played at Haroun Alraschid, in his day, and curiosity, sympathy, and irritation against George II. may have induced him to see the wanderer.

Could we only follow with certainty the Prince's adventures at this time, in London and in Berlin, could we see 'our dear wild man,' as Edgar called him, in Pall Mall or with Frederick, no part of this unparalleled career would be more interesting. *Premit nox alta !*

It is a prince 'of dark corners,' and of many

disguises : now as a lacquey, now as an Abbé, now as a Brother of Orders Grey, now as a bearded man with blackened eyebrows, now with a face painted to indicate small-pox, he drives in a chaise to dusky auberges, or is smuggled into noble houses, convents, palaces. What was he doing at the convent of English nuns at Pontoise, where he left his watch behind him ? Goring alone knew his retreats ; Goring and perhaps the Principal of the Scots College in Paris. He was lost to the philosophical Mademoiselle Ferrand, to Madame de Vassé, and to the ' Queen of Morocco,' as to his banker and, of course, to his father. So he followed, all alone, the will-o'-the-wisp of ambition, the glimmer of the airy crown, the hand of the Invisible Princess. Wherever Charles may have been between October 1750 and February 1751, in March he was in Paris, at the *bal masqué* in the Opera House. This was probably an audacious flying visit, for presently he must have been in seclusion. He asked Mademoiselle Ferrand to procure for him Racine's 'Athalie' and Richardson's ' Clarissa Harlowe.' He did not read much when actively engaged.

Mademoiselle Ferrand, in replying, informed him that an acquaintance had been telling Condillac that he knew the Prince's hiding-place ; the lady also advised him against certain psychological books which he wanted to buy. These, she said, were trash. Goring was sent on futile errands to Sweden and Berlin, but nothing was really being done. In October Mademoiselle Ferrand had a severe illness, and fell under the jealous suspicion of Madame de Talmond. The ladies addressed each other in letters of stately but hostile courtesy: and copies of these epistles exist in Charles's own hand. He looked, as he says in one of his notes, on Frederick the Great as his most hopeful ally. 'There is nobody whatsoever I respect more as ye K. of Prussia; not as a K. but as I believe him to be a clever man.' Mr. Carlyle's hero justified this estimate, but he was rather too clever to let Charles marry his sister, as the Prince desired.

The Prince was now to secure a new adherent. This was Alexander Murray, brother of Lord Elibank, the friend of David Hume, Dr. Carlyle, John Home, Smollett, and most of the Scottish wits. The ruined tower of Elibank still stands on Tweed, near Ashiesteil. The district is near Traquair and Broughton, and Lord Elibank was intimate with Lord Traquair. He kept out of the affair of 1745. In 'Humphrey Clinker' Smollett praises him for the universality of his accomplishments, and the humanity of his nature, 'over and above the entertainment arising from the originality of his character.' Dr. Carlyle's account of his matrimonial infidelities does suggest a certain unbecoming levity; and his senile

amorousness, later, just after the death of his rich
and injured wife, was decidedly eccentric. None the
less Elibank was a man of wide reading, and, though
believed to be a Jacobite, of great caution. It is
therefore not easy to understand why, in 1752, this
ornament of Society entered into a kind of Fenian
plot to seize the Royal family, and proclaim the
Restoration. Home, Hume, Carlyle, and Smollett
would have been astonished indeed had they known
what was brewing under Elibank's wig, while Elibank
would have been no less amazed, had he known that
the Government was aware of every step in his plot,
revealed, as it was, by Young Glengarry.

The beginning of this wild adventure was the imprisonment of Lord Elibank's brother, Alexander
Murray, in the summer of 1751. He was charged
with violence and intimidation at the famous Westminster Election. Murray declined to beg pardon of
the House on his knees, and therefore was not released till the close of the Session, when he was
escorted by the mob to Lord Elibank's house in
Henrietta Street, Strand. In July 'Dixon' (un-
identified) assures Charles that Murray is zealously
his friend, and can raise 500 men for his service in
Westminster. Murray was certainly devoted to
Charles personally, if his letters are to be trusted,
though his character is impeached by Lord Elcho,
his enemy for family reasons.

Murray was not the only hopeful recruit. In August 1751 Frederick, obviously as an insult to King George, sent the Earl Marischal as his ambassador to Versailles. Thither the Earl went with his 'pretty little Turkess,' as Voltaire calls his brother's captive, Mademoiselle Emetté. Judged by her portrait, the girl was not likely to be a temptation to the old Earl's virtue. A Tartar valet, Stepan, accompanied the Earl, and he had a retinue of odd pagans, black and brown, whom he educated but did not attempt to convert. Charles was not too sanguine now, though an old friend, rather a cold friend, was at Versailles. 'They mean to sell us as usual,' wrote the Prince.[1] In spite of his distrust as to French or Prussian aid, Charles set to work to win the Earl Marischal. Goring was despatched to see the Earl privately, and a meeting was not easy to arrange. Goring was under sentence of imprisonment in the Bastille, if he was found within fifty leagues of Paris. Though the Earl's appointment to Versailles was an insult to England, still he did not wish to be detected

---

[1] Dr. King, in his *Anecdotes*, accuses Charles of borrowing money in Paris from a lady far from wealthy, when he had plenty of gold in his strong-box. On September 15, 1751, he certainly borrowed 1,000*l.* from Lady Montagu, and, on December 1, he certainly left 2,500 louis d'or, and 130 guineas, in a strong-box, also he left 'a big box of books,' with Madame de Vassé. But, of course, Dr. King may refer to some other circumstances, and Lady Montagu does not seem to have been in Paris when Dormer paid over her loan to Charles.

in the company of the equerry of a Prince who had defied the Court of France. The Earl suggested a garden famous for its fruit as the place of rendez-vous : Goring preferred to come to the Tuileries gardens, when ' literally dark,' in the disguise of a lacquey, or of an Abbé. Charles must have needed, at this time of stealthy adventure, a wardrobe as varied as that of Monsieur Le Coq, the detective in the novel. The Earl accepted this arrangement, granting fine weather, for suspicion would be aroused if an elderly ambassador walked a midnight garden in torrents of rain. Charles was ready to meet the Earl himself, so he must have been in or near Paris, but the old diplomatist did not want to know the Prince's place of abode. He had promised that, if he ever did know, he would inform some one to whom he was ' unwilling to lie,' probably either James or Frederick.

On other occasions meetings with Goring were arranged at one of those lace-shops where Molière used to sit and observe the fashionable customers. The Earl also suggested Madame de Talmond's house, or perhaps her rooms in the Convent of Saint Joseph. Meanwhile Lord Albemarle, the English ambassador at Versailles, told his Government that Charles had travelled through Italy and Spain as a Dominican friar ! Though the Earl Marischal had probably orders to sound the Jacobites, time went on with no change in the Prince's affairs. He was very poor: Waters would not lend money: in March 1752 the French servants of the useless household at Avignon were dismissed, and the coach in which Sheridan and Stafford used to take the air was sold. Madame de Talmond was more and more jealous of Mademoiselle Ferrand. Probably this rather absurd jealousy caused the quarrels between the Prince and the Princess, which made it necessary for Madame de Vassé to withdraw her protection from Charles. He had to leave his alcove and his secret staircase in the convent, and by April 1752 was in Ghent, choosing a house, and trying to raise money. His account with Dormer was much overdrawn: Madame de Vassé declined to lend; and she also displayed the greatest repugnance to executing some commission which Charles desired her to perform. Even Goring was mutinous: nobody would have anything to do with the matter of a certain *demoiselle*.

Now Charles, as we saw, had been separated from his mistress, Madame de Talmond, and he probably wanted feminine society. He remembered his old flame, Miss Clementina Walkinshaw, whom he had met at Bannockburn House in 1746. Had she then, as Lord Elcho declares, been his mistress? In a letter written by Miss Walkinshaw, from Boulogne on June 3, 1760, she remarks (apparently to Andrew Lumisden, James's secretary), 'I do not choose to say any more to you, but that before 1745 I lived in

London, in great plenty, was between that and the 1747 undone, and am now in a strange poor place, starving indeed. . . . I was bred to business about White Hall, and could be of use to Him, were there not unluckily an obstacle in the way, which has done Him no service, and me great hurt. . . .'

All this is mysterious : what is the 'business about White Hall?' was the 'undoing' moral or financial ? Another account of Miss Walkinshaw was, in 1774, presented to the French Court by her daughter, Charlotte. After speaking of Clementina's promise, made in 1746, to follow Charles 'where providence might lead him,' the memorial says that she obtained the rank of a canoness in a *chapitre noble* of the Netherlands : where Charles was in 1752. An envoy came from Charles, reminding her of her old promise, and, moved by pity and passion, she went to Douay. Charles was then at Ghent, and arranged to meet her in Paris.[1] All this fits in, as regards dates, with Charles's residence at Ghent, in May 1752. It also fits in with Madame de Vassé's refusal, in May 1752, to execute an unnamed commission about a *demoiselle*. Moreover, the situation is illustrated by angry letters of June 1752 between Charles and Goring. Charles accuses Goring of 'pretending to give laws in everything I do.' Goring answers, 'Believe me, Sir, such commissions are for

[1] Archives of French Foreign Office, 81. f. 94. 1774.

the worst of men, and such you will find enough for money, but they will likewise betray you for more.' The letter contains obscure references to 'Lady P.' (probably Lady Primrose, who was then in France) and to Charles's wish to dismiss a French agent who knew the secrets of the party.   There is some work to be done which honest men, George Kelly, the Earl Marischal, and 'Campbell' (Alexander Murray) would refuse.[1]   Goring asks why he should be ordered to do work which these gentlemen would decline.   'If any accident should happen to you by the young lady's means' (Miss Walkinshaw), 'I shall be detested and become the horror of Mankind, but, if you are determined to have her, let Mr. Sullivan bring her to you here, or anywhere, himself.'

All these letters imply that Goring refused to be Charles's envoy to 'the Canoness,' as the Prince styles Miss Walkinshaw.   Her sister was in the Household of Frederick, Prince of Wales.   The family called her 'their faithful Walky,' and it was feared, by the Jacobites, that Miss Walkinshaw would betray the Prince's secrets, through her sister.   This, perhaps, is the 'obstacle' referred to in Miss Walkinshaw's letter of June 1760.   There was no just ground for sus-

[1] I myself think that Campbell is a pseudonym of Alexander Murray.   He speaks of his brother, where Lord Elibank is apparently intended, or even named.   But there are certain difficulties as to handwriting.   A note of Charles's refers to his suppression of a plot of Campbell's, in which poison was to be used!

picion, but Goring could not play Pandarus of Troy. He stayed with Madame de Vassé, in the country, and left the part of Pandarus to Sullivan, so tradition says, or to another. In any case Charles had his way, to the increase of his troubles.

In October 1752 Mademoiselle Ferrand died. She had long been in bad health. Charles, writing to an unknown correspondent, expresses his regret, and sends his brief condolences to Madame de Vassé on November 10. This is a notable date, for it had been intended as the day for the execution of the Elibank Plot. Our information about this affair is mainly derived from the letters of a spy of the English Government. For reasons which I have elsewhere set forth in full, I am compelled to identify this spy Pickle (he chose the name from 'Peregrine Pickle,' published in 1751), or Alexander Jeanson, or Roderick Random, and so forth, with Alastair Ruadh Macdonnell, eldest son of John, the chief of Glengarry.[1] This gentleman was born about 1725, being the son of Glengarry, by his first wife, a Miss Mackenzie. According to Wodrow, in his 'Analecta,' Glengarry consigned his wife to a lonely islet, where she refused food, and died. He then (about 1727) married a daughter of Gordon of Glenbucket, by whom he had issue. According to Murray of Broughton, Alastair was oppressed by his father and step-mother. He

[1] See *Pickle the Spy*, and *The Companions of Pickle*.

was educated, as we have seen, at James's expense, in the Scots College in Paris. He obtained a commission in the French army, was engaged, early in 1745, in the intrigues of Murray of Broughton, went to France, in June, with a message for Charles, and, in November, was taken prisoner on board a French ship, and lodged in the Tower. He was released in 1747, and, in October, tried to obtain his pardon by abandoning the Cause, and his rank in French service. He failed, and, in June 1749, went over to London.

Here he was so reduced that he sold his sword and shoe-buckles. According to Mrs. Archibald Cameron, writing to Edgar in 1754, Glengarry in 1748, or 1749, had offered his services ' in any shape they thought proper' to Henry Pelham, who told Campbell of Lochnell at the time, and Lochnell was Mrs. Cameron's informant. Probably his services were then declined. He returned to France, and, in November or December 1749, visited Cluny in Badenoch, and obtained a large sum, partly from Cluny's treasure, partly out of money that had been in the hands of Murray of Broughton, with whom Glengarry (1749) was on good terms. He now visited Rome, and he and Archibald Cameron quarrelled. Alastair accused Archy of embezzling 6,000*l.* ; Archy accused Alastair of forging James's name. Certain informers in Lochaber charged Alastair with betraying them, and expressed their desire to betray *him*. In 1751, 1752, Alastair lived in York Buildings, Strand, and was not molested by the English Government, though he gave himself out as James's English agent, and then, and later, corresponded with James, and with his secretary, Edgar. Alastair now came and went between France and England, as the English Government knew, and he especially frequented the Earl Marischal, 'whose coach is often lent him,' writes a spy from Paris.

Now, on November 2, 1752, begin the letters of Jeanson, or Pickle, to the English Government. They are written in a feigned hand, in which it does not need an expert to detect that of Glengarry. Every peculiarity of Glengarry's spelling (and they are many) is a peculiarity of the spy's, and all he says of himself, as a spy, is true of the Macdonnell chief.[1]

On November 2, the spy writes from Boulogne, you'l soon hear of a hurly burly, but I will see my friend or that can happen.' On November 4, at Boulogne, he informs Henry Pelham (apparently) that Charles has been in Berlin, and that Frederick will countenance a new plot. Scotland is not to move till London 'pulls off the mask.' Later, on April 5, 1753, Glengarry, writing to Edgar, says that 'the tenth of November last was the day fixed,' but

[1] Experts agree on this point.

that 'frivolous excuses retarded this great and Glorious blow. Thank God, the Prince did not venture himself at London, though he was upon the Coast, ready at a call to put himself at their head.'

Here a curious little piece of evidence comes in. An old house, near Godalming, now the Meath Home for Incurables, is, or was, said to be haunted by the ghost of the Prince! The reason apparently is that, at this date, the house (which belonged to General Oglethorpe) was unoccupied, till, in the late autumn of 1752, the sister of the General, Madame de Mézières, came from France, and took up her abode there. The lady (a sister of Miss Oglethorpe, erroneously spoken of by Thackeray as the mistress of James in 1714) was a wild conspirator, usually regarded as a bore by James and Charles. But it seems highly probable that she (not Lady Primrose as Lord Elcho states) did, about this time, shelter the Prince in the house near Godalming, convenient to the Portsmouth Road. From his wanderings at night about the grounds, would easily arise the legend as to his haunting ghost.[1]

To return to Glengarry's letter of April 5, 1753, the plot was that he should head 'above four hundred brave Highlanders' in London, and, after 'the blow' was struck, should raise the Highlands. The English

---

[1] See 'Queen Oglethorpe.' *Blackwood's Magazine.* The facts were discovered by Miss Alice Shield.

Government knew all this from the spy, who, in December 1752, drew up, or dictated, a statement in London, which gives the outlines of the plot. Charles, in September 1752, had despatched Alexander Murray to bring Lochgarry and Archibald Cameron to Menin. He sent them thence to the Highlands, where there was to be no rising till General Keith (the Field Marshal) landed in Scotland with Swedish troops. Cameron of Fassifern (brother of Lochiel) and Cameron of Glennevis were other agents. Both men were arrested more than once, namely in 1751 and 1753. The spy himself was to have met Charles at Ghent, in November or December 1752, but came across him at Furnes, and was ordered by him to London. ' I waited of Lord Elibank, who, after the strong assurances of the Young Pretender, surprised me to the greatest degree, by telling me that all was put off for some time, and that his brother had repassed the seas in order to aquent the Young Pretender of it, and from him he was to go straight for Paris to Earl Marischal.' Mr. Hepburn of Keith, and Elcho's younger brother, Mr. Charteris, were in the secret, and Lord Elcho gives a more or less correct account of it in his manuscript Memoirs.

' The Jacobites believed that Pickle would have a number of Highlanders, even in London, to follow him,' says Pickle himself, and Glengarry told Edgar

the same story. The spy was more explicit later, as
to the plot, which lingered on ; 'if ever any attempt
is to be made, it's a night onset.' Lord Elcho attributed the delays to the timidity of Murray, who
went to London with his accomplices, and then lost
heart. This plot, however, was not wholly laid aside,
Charles never suspecting that Young Glengarry had
revealed all to Harry Pelham. Perhaps the most
curious feature of the wild conspiracy is, that the
Prussian ambassador at Versailles, the Earl Marischal,
knew all about it ; and, though he took no active part,
did not think it his duty to put down a scheme so
unworthy. Probably he guessed that it would never
come to a head.

About the Prince, in 1753, little is known except
through Pickle's letters. On March 15 he wrote to
his employers from Paris, where he had suffered from
pneumonia, with a relapse after the *bal masqué* at the
Opera House. There he met the Prince, and was 'a
little piqued that he did not inquire after me during
my illness!' This was, indeed, ingratitude, but
Charles, later, gave him a fine gold snuff-box. Rather
later Pickle went to London and handed in a statement to Henry Pelham. He had been with the
Earl Marischal, who knew about the plot from
Goring. The Earl 'doubted not they might succeed,'
but could not help, as he 'was quite a stranger to the
different posts and manners for placing their Guards.'

James Dawkins (the archæologist who rediscovered Palmyra) had brought to Charles 4,000*l.* from England. Charles had been trying to win officers of the Scots regiments in Dutch service, to aid in the night onset. Two of these heroes are introduced by Smollett into 'Peregrine Pickle.'

The end of these schemes was the arrest of Archibald Cameron, in the Highlands, on March 20, 1753, and his execution, in June, on the old charge of his accession to the Rising of 1745. As Scott says, in the introduction to 'Redgauntlet,' 'The Ministers thought it prudent to leave Dr. Cameron's new schemes in concealment, lest by divulging them they had indicated the channel of communication which, it is well known, they possessed to all the plots of Charles Edward.' Probably Sir Walter knew 'the channel,' Young Glengarry. For his capture, Dr. Cameron blamed Samuel Cameron, a brother of Glennevis. But Pickle was the chief 'channel of communication.' He and Archibald Cameron were at deadly feud, caused by their dealings with the Loch Arkaig gold. Cameron had not really, as Horace Walpole writes, 'a commission from Prussia to offer arms to the discontented Highlanders.' But he was to promise Swedish troops led (with Frederick's connivance) by Marshal Keith. Frederick had, on the Earl Marischal's suggestion, seen James Dawkins, who, with Dr. King, and the Earl of Westmorland, was a chief of the English Jacobites. But Frederick wrote to Marischal that the plot was too crude. ' It will be for my interest to encourage them in their design underhand, and without being observed.' The English Government, through various channels, was aware of Frederick's attitude.

The arrest of Archibald Cameron alarmed Charles, and he consulted the Earl Marischal as to a safe place of retreat, such as Basel. By a misunderstanding of Alexander Murray's he conceived that the Earl recommended Cologne. But Marischal feared that there the Prince might be kidnapped, put in a boat, and carried to Holland. He wandered about to Coblentz, Frankfort, and, in July, to Liège. Later, in August, he sent for 'G.,' and Glengarry answered his call, meeting him at Ternan. Charles showed Pickle Lochgarry's list of friendly clans (9,650 was the roll-call), and a memorial from Lochgarry was also given to Pickle, and by him to his employers. Charles had been hunted about in Flanders by a Jewish spy, and was disguised as a Capuchin !

We are almost tempted to fancy that Smollett must have encountered Charles, disguised as a Capuchin, Miss Walkinshaw, and the Hebrew spy, as they trapesed through Flanders. But it was before this date that Peregrine Pickle, in the Ghent diligence, met a female adventurer—a very handsome black-eyed girl—a Capuchin, and a Rotterdam Jew. Indeed this part of the Prince's romance is more suited to the pen of Smollett than of Sir Walter. Charles travelled with Pickle (the spy, not Peregrine) to Paris, where Miss Walkinshaw was, about to become a mother. 'The Pretender keeps her well, and seems to be very fond of her.' Charles had abandoned all hope from Prussia : so says the spy.

From this moment the Muse of Biography would fain avert her gaze from the career of the unhappy Charles. Of him no gallant act, no brilliant adventure, nay, scarce a single kind or generous deed remains to be recorded. And he had still more than thirty years to linger upon earth : *De vivre et pas vivre, c'est beaucoup pis que de mourir :* 'To live and not live is worse than death,' he wrote among the scraps of notes which he was wont to pen. For Charles, the best hope had always lain in a life of exertion under the open sky. Now for years he had been 'sedentary,' as he says, mewed up in cloistered retirement ; brooding over his wrongs, wrongs from France, Spain, Prussia, from all Europe ; wrongs from father and brother, friends and adherents. All the world had injured him : he was lectured by his party about his private life : his equerry rejected his commands as wicked and dishonourable. His 'system,' that extraordinary system of secrecy and incognito (first suggested to him by D'Argenson) was disapproved of on every hand. Weary of literature, he had fallen back on wine; and wine had so affected him that every good quality of his original nature was now replaced by its reverse. This is a notorious consequence of that morbid passion for alcohol which rarely, if ever, exists, except where there is an injured brain. Of Charles as he had been, remained only secretiveness, and recklessness: his kindness and clemency were changed to cruelty and callousness: his generosity to avarice. The moment came when even the loyalty of his adherents turned from him in absolute despair, not of the Cause, but of the Prince.

Examples of Charles's ruined character are only too common and familiar. Miss Walkinshaw's child, Charlotte, was baptised at Liège on October 29. On November 12, Charles wrote to Goring, who was in the worst health, '*I have wrote to Avignon for to discard all my Popish servants. . . . My mistress has behaved so unworthily that she has put me out of patience*' (these words are underscored), 'and as she is a Papist too, I discard her also!!!' The underscoring of this and other notes of November 12, indicates violent excitement. Charles expressed deep concern as to Goring's health, but even Goring was unable to remain in his service. The 'humanity, I ought to say tenderness,' which, according to Lord Pitsligo, Charles showed to 'everybody,' in 1745, was gone, with the death of his original self. He was being hunted from town to town, and his supporters, Dormer and young Edgar, insisted that he was easily tracked, as he took about with him his mistress and the little child. He carried away his objects of art, left at Lunéville, and D'Argenson says that he was seen selling his pistols to an armourer. His very wardrobe was of the scantiest: a shabby battered man called one day at the house of Madame d'Aiguillon: the servants recognised him: it was the Prince.

Early in January, Goring, in Paris, began a series of letters of admonition. English adherents are wearied by Charles's requests for money. They insist on the dismissal of Miss Walkinshaw; and blame the discarding of one Dumont, who knows too many secrets, and may imperil Mac (Glengarry?), Mead, and Dawkins. Goring himself fears 'that horrid Bastille.' The dismissal of the Catholic servants will not even conciliate bigots. 'Some of them went through all dangers with you in Scotland.' Goring has often been 'hard put to it,' when asked by friends to cite even a single instance of any one poor follower whom Charles has relieved. Goring refuses to dismiss the poor loyal Catholic Highlanders: 'give such comitions to somebody else.' 'For God's sake, Sir, have compassion on yourself.' Goring then asks leave to resign, as his life is threatened by his disease. Charles, so far, took advice, and did not dismiss his poor followers Goring returned to the charge. If Charles persisted that it was the 'duty' of his English friends to send money, they would send none.

Charles was now driven by spies from place to place, till he reached Paris (April 14, 1754) to consult the Earl Marischal. But the Earl abandoned him. He was a friend of Goring's, and Goring (May 5) again sent in his resignation. Charles did not accept it, and (May 16) Goring closed the correspondence in such an epistle as even exiled princes are not wont often to receive. Charles, he says, had dismissed him cruelly, by a verbal message, and had left him penniless in Paris, where the Bastille awaited him. He had served 'at the hazard of his life, and to the entire destruction of his health.' He would serve no more. The Earl Marischal declined to hear Charles, except through Goring. He rebuked the Prince for casting doubts on the honour of that faithful servant. He accused Charles of threatening to publish the names of English adherents who had lately advised him to put away Miss Walkinshaw. How, then, can the Earl expose others to such treatment? 'I appeal to your own conscience, and I may to the world, if I can.' Charles replied, 'My heart is broke enough, without that you should finish it. . . . Anyone whosoever that has told you I gave such a message to Ed. as you mention' (the threat of publishing names) 'has told you a damned lie. God forgive them. I would not do the least hurt to my greatest enemy (were he in my power), much less any one that professes to be mine.' Unhappy Prince! 'my heart is broke enough.'

The Earl was not to be moved. Returning soon to Berlin, he carried with him poor Goring, who presently died in Prussian service. Dr. King has left, in his Anecdotes, the story of how a Mr. Macnamara endeavoured to induce Charles to dismiss his Clementina: how Charles, professing no great regard for her, declined to be dictated to, and how Macnamara exclaimed, 'What has your family done, Sir, thus to draw down the vengeance of Heaven on every branch of it, through so many ages?' The family, in fact, had done a number of things of an unjustifiable kind, but most families, or at least most royal families, have been equally misguided. Having broken with England, Charles was in dire need of money, and (September 4, 1754) summoned Cluny to him, bidding him 'bring all the effects whatsoever that I left in your hands, also whatever money you can come at.' Cluny, who had been in hiding for eight long years, probably could 'come at' no money. Nor was he ever able to discover certain articles of plate, and family relics, for example a diamond ring, the property of Charles II., when Prince of Wales, which Charles had left in his keeping. On his death-bed, years later, Cluny attested, on his oath, his innocence as regarded these objects, lost or mislaid in the confusions of his wandering life.

When, on August 15, 1755, a Scottish remonstrance about Miss Walkinshaw was made, it was signed by

> C. M. P.
> H. P.

probably Cluny Macpherson and Henry Patullo. The remonstrance expressed the fears of his friends that the Prince might be tracked by his 'movements in a family way.' If he refused (as he did) to leave his mistress, his friends would be compelled to conceive that there was truth in the aspersions of James Dawkins, lately Charles's envoy to Berlin. Dawkins declared that Charles ' was entirely abandoned to an irregular debauched life, even to excess, which brought his health and even his life daily in danger, that in these excesses he had no guard either on his conduct or on his expressions, and was in some degree devoid of reason.' For all this, and much more, Dawkins said that he had the evidence of Henry Goring : and Lord Elcho corroborates him, in his Memoirs.

Charles listened to Cluny, and bade him put his ideas into writing. He then merely replied that he was 'conscious of his conduct and despised the low malice' of his accusers.

At this period (1755–56) Charles was residing, under the name of Dr. Thompson, at Basel. The Earl Marischal, retired from diplomacy, was acting, for Frederick, as Governor of Neuchâtel, where he protected Rousseau. Even Charles, poor as he was, contributed to the support of that needy philosopher, 'Monsieur Rousseau,' as his accounts prove, unless there were *two* Rousseaus accepting money. But the Earl was on no terms with the other patron of the author of the 'Confessions.' On May 28, 1756, the English Resident at Berne, Arthur Villette, sent information about the Earl and the Prince. Some one who knew well, had given intelligence orally. The Earl declined to see Charles, and mentioned him 'with the utmost horror and detestation, and in the most opprobrious terms.' His view of the Prince was confirmed by Lord Elcho, who said that Charles's attendant (Murray?) was as weary as Goring had been of his service. Villette also mentioned the envoy from Scotland, whose remonstrances had been so ill received.[1]

The outbreak of the Seven Years War now encouraged Jacobites who hoped to fish in troubled waters. Among these was Lord George Murray, still ready to fight for one who had insulted him. But

[1] Ewald, ii. 253. From State Papers.

Charles's mood, and mode of life, destroyed their expectations. In May 1755 Charles had an interview with the Duc de Richelieu, a friend, but James heard that it was unsatisfactory. Charles's conduct made it impossible for James to treat with friendly powers, whose friendship, of course, merely took the form of desiring to hamper England. The Prince's poverty compelled him to dismiss his poor Highland servants, and even his valet, Morrison, who had been a prisoner at Carlisle. They went to James in Rome, and were dismissed with a little money. On January 30, 1756, Walton reported that Louis XV. was to give Charles the hand of a daughter of France ! In a tract called 'Testament politique du Maréchal Duc de Belle-Isle' (published in 1762) it is said that Charles declined the proffered leadership of the attack on Minorca (April 1757), saying, ' The English will do me justice, if they think fit, but I will no longer serve as a mere bugbear.' This showed a just appreciation of French policy.[1]

A little light is here thrown on Charles by the published letters of a wretched Irish spy, Oliver Macallester. This degraded adventurer was a hanger on of Lord Clancarty's, and probably published his verbose book with the purpose of blackmailing that

---

[1] A few letters of the Prince to Walsh, at this date, have been published by the Duc de la Tremoille. They merely exhibit Charles as sulky and secretive.

nobleman. Clancarty had railed against high and low, from Louis XV. and Charles to Lochgarry. He confirmed, to Macallester, all that Dawkins and the Earl Marischal said against the Prince, with whom, however, he dined on occasion. On July 1, 1756, Charles was so broken in spirit that he applied for money to Louis XV. 'If I knew a Prince more virtuous than you, to him I would appeal.' Frederick the Great, in 1757, heard that France meant to invade Ireland, but that Charles would take no part, unless the Courts of Vienna and St. Petersburg guaranteed the French proposals. One lesson he had learned, distrust of France, and, in 1759, he declined to join any French invasion which had not London for its objective.

All through the spring, summer, and autumn of 1759, France was dealing with Charles, through Alexander Murray and his deadly enemy, Clancarty. For once James was consulted, and sent his new secretary, Andrew Lumisden, to visit various Courts. Charles was at Bouillon, the home of his cousin, the Duc de Bouillon, where he lived in the society of the President Thibault, the guardian of his child. He reconciled himself with Madame de Pompadour. He had been on ill terms with her, about 1748, and, according to Pickle, had declined to answer her letters. He was in correspondence with the Duc de Choiseul, and the Maréchal de Belle-Isle, but he did not trust them, nor did they trust him. Finally, according to Mac-allester, Charles went to Brest, 'damning the Marshal's old boots, which always were stuffed full of projects.' On October 8 Murray reported that his brother and the Scottish Jacobites would not stir if a landing was made in Scotland, but not in England. Then came a hasty note on the defeat of the invading force under Conflans by Admiral Hawke, in Quiberon Bay, and that hope followed all the other dreams.

The French still purposed an invasion, and Alexander Murray still told Choiseul that Charles would never embark, except for an attack on London. What Pickle knew of the schemes was at the service of the Duke of Newcastle, but Glengarry, his *alter ego*, died on December 21, 1761, and Pickle's letters cease : since 1754 he had been of no use, and was much disappointed by the ingratitude of England.

Meanwhile James's health was utterly broken, and, in 1760, he made the most touching appeals to Charles. He longed to see his dear son, who might visit Rome in perfect secrecy. He sent 12,000 livres for the expenses of the journey (March 3, 1760), but Charles was deaf to his entreaties. On April 3 Charles informed Edgar that he was ' suffering from nerves.' Those around him also suffered. His adherents pressed him to see his father. He refused. In June or July 1760 Miss Walkinshaw fled from him, taking her child with her. Her letter on June 3,

already cited, looks as if she fled in June, but, on
July 25, Gordon, the Jesuit, from Paris, reports that
he has taken lodgings for the fugitives, and that Miss
Walkinshaw absolutely declines to return to Charles.
On July 20 Miss Walkinshaw had hired a coach,
and disappeared.   Her idea was to enter a convent,
where her child might be educated.   Charles, on July
20, appealed to the Maréchal de Belle-Isle, for aid in
the recovery of his child : but appealed in vain.   To
Gordon he writes, ' I shall be in ye greatest affliction
untill I guett back ye child, which was my only
comfort in my misfortunes.'   In his Highland distresses he had consoled himself by playing with the
baby of a farmer's wife.   The letter of a servant,
' Jones ' (probably Stewart, the Prince's valet), gives
a picture of the pursuit of Clementina :

From Jones the servant.

31st July.

. . . They (Gordon and Bodson) both came to my
room and told me to go to the Lady's lodgings and see to
amuse her untill such time as they had an order to take up
the chylde.   I went to her lodgings but she was gon out, I
waited untill she came back.   She seemed much surprazed
at seeing me.   I reasoned the matter with her but all to
no purpose.   She told me that she would sooner make
away with herself than go back, and as for the Chylde she
would be cut to pieces sooner than give her up.   I stayed
in the Lady's Room untill ten and a half.   She sent for a
coach to go out.   I asked her if she would allow me to

accompany her and the Chylde. She told me yes, wee set
out and at a little distance from the lodgings, the coach
stopt, there came a gentleman well-drest and two others
. . . and told the Lady to come out and to go with the
other coach. I came out allong with them. I asked the
Lady if there was place for me ; the Gentleman answered
in Ruff manner 'No Sir, go about your business if you
have any.' They set off in a coach and four horses, which,
Sir, seemed to me to be hired horses, the Gentleman was a
Frenchman as far as one could judge. I followed them as
far as I was able but lost sight of them.

The letters show, and Macallester reports, that
the search was urged vigorously for a month. But
Louis protected the fugitives, who were safe in a
convent, pensioned by James.

This was a new and unpardonable grievance.
Charles, brooding over his wrath against France and
his father, sulked at Bouillon. James (September 8)
explained that he had approved of Clementina's purpose of withdrawing, and educating her child, but
only if she had Charles's permission. From England,
adherents kept imploring Charles to reform his
'vicious habits;' otherwise they must resign all hopes.
Charles now dismissed Alexander Murray, suspecting
him of being auxiliary to Miss Walkinshaw's departure. Murray (December 29) sent a letter from his
brother, Lord Elibank, and added: 'Your Royal
Highness is resolved to destroy yourself to all intents
and purposes. Everybody here talks of your conduct

with horror, and from being once the admiration of
Europe, you are become the reverse. Think what
cruel anguish these reports give to me, and the few
here that are truly attached to you. . . . You have
banished all your father's subjects. . . .' Charles
banished everybody. James, on December 29,
unbosomed himself to the Maréchal de Belle-Isle,
contrasting Charles's affectionate conduct, before
1745, with what he had now become. He implores
Belle-Isle to induce the Prince to visit Rome. Early
in 1761 Murray, from London, informed Charles that
his adherents were about to publish printed protests
against the Coronation of George III. If Charles
remains obdurate, they will approach the King of
Sardinia, who was, failing Charles, the rightful heir.
To this had the White Rose fallen ! That Charles
visited London, and saw the coronation, is a story of
the Earl Marischal's, of which no proof has been
discovered.

Miss Walkinshaw (February 13, 1761) wrote to
her 'dearest Prince,' excusing her flight. 'You
pushed me to the greatest extremity, and even
despair, as I was always in perpetual dread of my
life from your violent passions. . . . It is reported
that you are not yourself, that your head is quite
gone.' Indeed 'he was not himself:' we need not
multiply evidence and even medical warnings, of
which a profusion exists in the Stuart Papers. It

is strange that Charles preserved these melancholy records.

Charles made one reply to all remonstrances. He wrote to Gordon, who had spoken plainly, condemning his neglect of all exercise, and abstinence from all solid food. On these points Charles was silent; his words are :

Charles's reply to Gordon.

18 January.

. . . My attachment to our country is strong, but my Scotch Blud is to high after all ye Insultes to apply more to them that Refused a Little Childe in my Concine (*sic*). I shiver to think of a reporte that ye Scotch Regiments are to be reformed. The Olde Gentilman is ye only man that can remedy such an Infamy. Hee should I think to be father of his Subjects so to do all that is possible to pare (parry) the Stroke, Being more in power than even the first of his subjects.

Here we have the insane obstinacy of the dipso-maniac; the man of ruined brain, who is always in the right, when all the world is wrong. The Prince's concern for his disbanded adherents proves that, on one point, he had 'Scotch blud.' On February 18, 1764, he was informed of Cluny's death, and of his dying oath regarding his innocence as to Charles's missing plate and jewels. Lady Cluny and her daughter had returned to Scotland, and would answer for the plate 'with their heads,' of the trinkets

subject I can't conceive that he can think that the justice of his claims will force an acknowledgment, if the Baron therefore intends to come here and live quite incognito under another name, I believe there will be no difficulty, but beg him to reflect only how far it will be consistent with his dignity or decency, how much easier it would be for him to succeed in this affair if he was here at his father's death being duly acknowledged as presumptive Heir, and imparting to the Prince (the Pope?) the news of that melancholy event, they would be quite at a loss how to deny his succeeding to his father's Honours. . . . After all I have said and done in vain, I quite despair of everything, my only comfort is the consciousness of my having omitted nothing either to convince or persuade the Baron to do what is for his true interest. . . .

Among many other difficulties, was Charles's desertion of his father's Church. To return to the Church, publicly, would merely shock every one, argued the Cardinal. People would think it a farce. With everything unsettled, Charles left Paris on December 30, 1765. James died at 9.15 p.m. on January 1, 1766, 'without the least convulsion or agony,' writes Lumisden, 'but with his usual mild serenity in his countenance. . . He seemed rather to be asleep than dead.' He had a royal funeral, and 'there remaineth a rest for the people of God.' Henry now resigned to Charles his pension of 20,000 crowns from the Pope, and all James's savings, which, by James's will, were his own. The Cardinal also moved in every direction for Charles's acknowledgment as

King, by the Vatican, but moved in vain. On January 23 Lumisden met Charles, 'who charms every one that approaches him,' writes the loyal secretary. Charles himself, on January 27, wrote thus to Lady Webb :

I am arrived here with a great deal of trouble and for what I do not conceive but the pens (pains) of my journey, which might have been spered had I not been led into it by ye satisfaction of seeing yet before I cross ye seas ye King my Father. You may always depend that I shall never forguet the unwearied zeal you have to serve me. So remain your sincere friend.

C. R.

What seas did he expect to cross ? The Channel, probably ! Indeed he had taken little by his journey : he could have signed himself C. R. anywhere. He wrote kindly letters to Thibault, President of the Court at Bouillon. He 'wishes he had his dear Thibault to amuse and comfort him.'

Charles had 'come home,' at last. After twenty-two years, first of gallant adventure, then of darkling conspiracy, then of ruin, he was again in the old scenes, a poor, despised, forsaken, unacknowledged, exiled King. There is no unhappier fate, no more cruel catastrophe. What he should have done, after 1746, it is not easy to decide. He might have lived a decent if despised life at Rome, as an exiled Prince, a gazing stock for curious tourists. But he had, as Horace Walpole says, begun by 'resolving to be very resolute,' and his sense of the injustice of Fate, of France, and of his father, combined with a wild but ineradicable hope that he would yet be summoned to England, made him detest the idea of returning to the Eternal City. The only alternative of which he could conceive was a life of lurking, where his active spirit and body were first devoured by indolence, and then ruined by the desperate resource familiar to extreme poverty and extreme despair.

Necessarily all the bad passions of his nature, suspicion and senseless obstinacy, and pride, were forced into flower ; while courtesy became insolence, and an almost extreme clemency was converted into the cruelty which does not shrink from brutality to women. A posthumous loyalty still cherishes a belief in 'exaggeration' by enemies. We are told that 'it was an age tolerant of hard drinking.' It was not tolerant of solitary and shameful excesses : and the charges rest, not on the slanders of enemies, but on the remonstrances of heart-broken friends. About such a character and such a life as Charles's had become, silence is the best record. He was no longer, for years he had not been, of the faintest political importance. But he might still be a father, and his son (it was fancied) might still be a thorn in the side of England. So he was tempted by France into marriage, and a brief account of the squalid history of that union must be reluctantly given.

CHAPTER VI

CHARLES III

Red roses under the Sun,
  For the King who is lord of lands
But he dies when his day is done.
For his memory careth none
  When his glass runs empty of sands.

White roses under the Moon
  For the King without lands to give ;
But he reigns with the reign of June
With his rose and his blackbird's tune,
  And he lives while Faith may live !

WHEN Charles came home, at last, to the city of
priests whither he had vowed to himself that he would
never return, Jacobitism was a dead thing. Born in
England, and 'glorying in the name of Briton,' the
young and handsome George III. had found the
relics of the old Jacobite party ready to come in, and
be forgiven. Dr. King,[1] the Jacobite orator with his
Redeat, was presented by Lord Shelburne. The
great charge against the new monarch alleged that
he was little better than a Jacobite himself, on his

---

[1] From the Duc de la Tremoille's papers one gathers that this
Oxford don had been conspiring as late as 1758–59.

own account. Had he not chosen a Stuart, Lord
Bute, from a family of royal though illegitimate
origin, for his Minister ?   Were not the Scotch
(naturally rebels) filling the best places in the State,
the Army, and the Navy?   Was not Smollett,
the semi-Jacobite author of ' The Tears of Scotland,' editing a ministerial newspaper, ' The Briton ' ?
Wilkes, in the ' North Briton,' kept harping on these
horrors, and insisted that Lord Elibank ought not to
be one of the Sixteen Scottish Representative Peers.
The English Government knew more about Lord
Elibank than did Wilkes.

Except such survivals as the Scottish nonjuring
Bishops, and the Oliphants of Gask, who had been
scheming a marriage for Charles, or ' Cousin Peggie '
as they called him, Scotland had gone over to the
rising sun.   The Highlanders were fighting the battles
of England, under the Master of Lovat, young Lochgarry, and other leaders of the Forty Five.   The
fresh struggle was not to be a contest between rival
dynasties, but between the old and the new, the
Crown and the People.   Charles, in Rome, was an
anachronism.   Yet the English Government, and
their diplomatic agents kept up a pother about ' the
Pretender,' as if he were either still dangerous, or still
capable of being made useful as a bugbear.   In fact
the officials had an insatiable curiosity about the
' Pretender,' and his mode of life.   From Florence,

Horace Mann was writing copiously about Charles to the last. Was there any danger that England might be insulted, endangered she could not be, by Charles's recognition by the Vatican? The Cardinal did his best to secure for his brother the empty honours formerly given to James. The Papal Court determined not to grant them, and Charles, as he wrote to Lady Webb, found that his long wintry journey had been undertaken to no purpose.

On February 24, 1760, Webb wrote to him in great distress. He had heard that the King's life was no better than that of the Prince had been. 'On all sides his adherents are saying that it is useless to help him any longer.' Yet one sign of grace Charles gave : on April 15 he wrote courteously and affectionately to his old Egeria, the Princesse de Talmond, *veterum haud immemor amorum.* ' Mon tendre amitié pour vous, Madame, était toujours gravé en mon cœur.' A year ago, Horace Walpole had visited her in her apartments at the Luxembourg. He found her old and devout, in a darkling chamber, surrounded by cats, and by pictures of Saints and Sobieskis. Now she and her wayward friend were reconciled at last, and the stormy days were over. At this date there was much affectionate correspondence between Henry and Charles. The old wrong of the flight from Paris and of the Cardinal's hat was forgiven. As matters had turned out, the ecclesiastical wealth of Henry was the support of Charles, and, except in the one step of taking holy orders, the Cardinal was the best friend that his brother ever had. Being now in public view, and able to take his old favourite exercise of shooting, Charles improved both in health and conduct. He continued many of the pensions to adherents which James had been wont to pay. When he wrote to his friends, Thibault, the Webbs, and others, his letters were not only kind, but grateful. Yet Webb had spoken with a moral vigour of censure which many men would not easily have forgiven.

Charles did not forgive Miss Walkinshaw. He never named her, or inquired about the child of whom he had been deprived. Miss Walkinshaw was a rebel! ' His passion must still greatly cool before any application can be made to him in your behalf,' wrote Andrew Lumisden, secretly to the lady.[1] Lumisden was still secretary, and had a hard and difficult post. The Cardinal was much vexed, in February 1767, by a story that Charles and Miss Walkinshaw had been married. There seems never to have been any ground for this belief. Living with Charles, in hiding, as his wife, and named by his assumed name, Johnson or the like, Miss Walkinshaw might conceivably have had a claim, if these things

[1] MS. Letters and Notes of Lumisden.

had occurred in Scotland. Perhaps she did flatter herself that she had a claim. But the Cardinal writing through Lumisden to Waters the banker put pressure, doubtless financial, on Clementina. She reluctantly signed a formal document, to the effect that she never had been Charles's wife.

Charles, at this date (February 1767), wrote a perturbed and confused letter to Henry, saying that it was absolutely necessary for him to remain at Rome, and show himself out of mourning, 'and, I may say, of ragged clothes, as well as my servants.' He complains of ' my situation, that cannot be amused with quails, or any diversion whatsoever.' For he must not seem insensible of his state, or content with shooting and other trifling diversions. 'What is in my breast cannot be divulged until I have occasion. God alone is judge. I have but one view which is my duty before God and Man.' He cannot 'enter in innumerable things that my roving the world and experience have shown me.' Apparently he had again fallen under his old ruling vice. ' He has singular tenderness and regard for me,' wrote the Cardinal, 'and all (that) regards myself, and as singular an inflexibility and disregard for everything that regards his own good. . . . I am persuaded we should gain some ground as to everything, were it not for the nasty bottle, that goes on but too much, and certainly must at last kill him.

Stafford is in desolation about it, but has no sway, as, in reality, no living body has with him.' [1]

Lord Elcho arrived in Rome, to dun for his 1,500*l.*, which Charles was ready to pay, as soon as he was crowned ! Hamilton, from Naples, reports that Charles's life ' is now very sober and regular ' (May 12, 1767) but retired. He reckons Charles's income from Henry at 3,000*l.* a year : 'it is said.' He quotes a letter from an English lady, who met the King. ' He looks good-natured, and was overjoyed to see me ; nothing could be more affectionately gracious. I cannot answer for his cleverness, for he appeared to me to be absorbed in melancholy thoughts, a good deal of distraction in his conversation, and frequent brown study. . . . He told me time lay heavy on him.' [2] For this reason he was privately reconciled to the Pope, by his brother's intervention. (May 1767.) Perhaps he now saw more of society, but, in December 1767, he finally broke with Lumisden, and, apparently, with his other gentlemen. They had refused to accompany him in his carriage, when he was in no condition to go abroad. The Cardinal applauded the conduct of his suite, and, by Bishop Forbes, was suspected of wishing to remove Protestant companions. Laurence Oliphant of Gask

[1] Letters in possession of the Rev. F. Hopkinson. Cited by Mr. Ewald, ii. 246.

[2] Ewald, ii. 252.

gave the Bishop his information. Charles had now only two 'subjects' with him, Mr. Wagstaff (apparently a Nonjuror) and Stewart, a servant. Hay of Restalrig, the unlucky secretary at the time of Culloden, had been dismissed with Lumisden. The Bishop had sent to Charles a cake from Scotland. He placed it in a drawer, saying 'no teeth shall go upon it but my own.'

These futile, faithful Scots kept hoping that Charles was still a Protestant, kept trusting that he would marry, if possible a Protestant Princess. He replied that he had tried and failed, referring, it was thought, to Goring's mission to Berlin. In 1770, Charles began to bestir himself a little, with an eye to marriage. He had refused to marry, when James desired it, during his incognito. Why, he asked, should he become the father of beggars, of sons who might receive such treatment as his had been from France? At this time, though he stooped much, and though his face was red and bloated, he is described by an English lady as having 'a noble person and a graceful manner.' The best portrait is the beautiful miniature by Ozias Humphrey, now in the possession of the Duke of Atholl. A larger sketch in two crayons, published in the Culloden Papers, was doubtless done by Humphrey, at the same date. The face has an irritable expression, but is not weak. In January 1770 the prospective bridegroom was in treaty with the Duc de Fitzjames, for the hand of a girl of seventeen, Marie Anne, daughter of the Duc de Deux-Ponts. From letters of Caryll, Charles's English correspondent, it appears that the wooer wanted a subscription to be raised for him. Caryll thought the time inopportune, and hinted that a more important design was in contemplation.

On May 29, 1771, Charles wrote from Rome a long letter, in French, to Mr. Mansfield. He meditates a secret journey to Paris, and asks for a passport for 'Mr. Douglas' and one servant. Pisa will be his first stage, as if he meant to take the waters; which he had done in 1770. Henry, as usual, is to know nothing of the journey. A marriage was in view. But Charles learned that dowry and pin money must come out of his own very limited funds: Henry could not help. And Henry declared that Charles's hope of regal recognition at Rome was absolutely out of the question. Charles went to Paris, as we know from other sources, and thence to Siena, and so back to Rome again. All his effects in the custody of Waters, he had deposited at the Scots College.[1] From her convent at Meaux, the daughter of Miss Walkinshaw remonstrated with Charles on his 'cruel indifference.' The Duc d'Aiguillon was approached, for some matrimonial scheme.

---

[1] From a communication by Monsieur Kerallain it seems that Gordon sent these things to Monsieur Kerallain's ancestor in Brittany.

The whole story of the intrigues connected with Charles's marriage is embroiled. The despatches of English diplomatists are ill informed : they were hoodwinked by the French. The Stuart Papers are here incomplete, and it seems that the missing portions have found their way into Lord Braye's collection.[1] It was on September 26, 1771, that Horace Walpole wrote to Mann in Florence, bantering 'so watchful a cat' on 'letting its mouse slip at last, without knowing into what hole it has run.' Charles had always wits enough to baffle Horace Mann. He left Siena for Paris on August 18, and was certainly in Paris as early as August 29, 1771. He lodged at the house of a tailor named Didelot, Hôtel de Brunswick, off the Rue Saint-Honoré, being incognito by his own desire. The persons who undertook for him were the Duc de St. James and Ryan, an Irish colonel in French service, who acted as plenipotentiary. The Duc d'Aiguillon was also concerned, and the King of France was in the scheme, permitting Charles to travel without a passport, promising subsidies, and even expressing a hope that the Pontiff would grant Charles his coveted royal honours, as enjoyed by James.

The first matrimonial advances were made to ' Miss Speedy.' But 'the young person,' as a letter

---

[1] Historical MSS. Commission. Tenth Report. Appendix VI. The papers were bought by the Baroness Braye, at Rome, in 1842.

informs Charles, burst into a passion of tears at the bare idea of leaving home for the arms of the King of England. The Stuart Papers leave Miss Speedy's real name obscure, but a cypher in Lord Braye's MSS. proves that she was Marie Louise Ferdinande, daughter of the Prince of Salm-Kynburg, a maiden of eighteen. Charles's agent declared that to persevere, and coerce Miss Speedy, would be the height of barbarity. We may congratulate this very sensible young lady on her resolute refusal.

Meanwhile Ryan got general orders to negotiate a marriage between Charles and any suitable Princess or Countess of the Empire. He set out on his mission, like Wogan, long ago, and about the end of September the English Government became aware that Charles was in Paris. Colonel Blaquière, the secretary to the Embassy, visited D'Aiguillon, who abounded in explanations. He had heard of the intrusion, and at once sent to ask what Charles meant, and what was his business. He found that it was an affair of a marriage, and bade Charles to quit the kingdom instantly. 'He desired the Duc de Fitzjames to see the Pretender safe across the Alps, and by this time the two must have arrived in Italy.'[1] The narrative of the Marquis de Fitzjames, in Lord Braye's MSS., proves that D'Aiguillon did not adhere to the strict truth. Charles was expected in Paris, subsidies

[1] S.P. France, 525, Oct. 1, 1771. Ewald, ii. 267.

were promised (I do not find that they were paid), and hopes were expressed of Papal recognition. Charles himself asked for the company of the Marquis, not the Duc, de Fitzjames on his return to Italy, 'and therefore his most Christian Majesty has given the Marquis leave to accompany him, and has expressed his satisfaction at his doing so.'

On December 30, 1771, Ryan, who had been at Brussels, found that the Princesse de Stolberg and her daughter Louise, a canoness of a noble Order at Mons, were 'willing.' Louise had 'a good figure, a pretty face, and excellent teeth, with all the qualities which Your Majesty can desire.' The Princess also offered, as an alternative, her third daughter, aged fifteen (so the Duc de St. James reports), if Charles preferred so juvenile a bride. But Fitzjames thought that Louise, the eldest, a maiden of eighteen, was more suitable. Charles answered that he chose the elder, who might travel to Bologna by the Tyrol. By February 24, 1772, 'Stewart' (the Marquis de Fitzjames) was trying to raise funds at Versailles for the marriage. There were difficulties about theological and legal arrangements which Charles (March 18) said had been drawn up by three theologians, two of them Cardinals. But Louise overrode the difficulties, being 'very impatient to assume her distinguished position.'

The young lady was no involuntary Andromeda,

sacrificed to the monster. Young as she was, this
Princess was by no means ignorant of the world, and
she knew very well what she wanted. In her book
'The Countess of Albany,' Vernon Lee says 'the match
had been made up hurriedly,—most probably without
consulting, or dreaming of consulting, the girl.' Our
sympathy with the bride would be intensified if we
believed in this theory. But we have seen that ' Miss
Speedy,' the Princess of Salm, *was* consulted, and that
nobody 'dreamed' of forcing her inclinations. Louise
was consulted, and, so Charles's agents assured him,
was impatiently anxious to join him. Indeed, after
declaring that Louise was probably never consulted,
Vernon Lee, divining the truth, supposes that the
bride was probably 'in a state of vague exultation,'
nursing the one idea, ' I shall be a Queen.'

By April 11, Louise had reached Bologna. ' At
Loreto the bride was met by a Jacobite dignitary,
Lord Carlyle,' says Vernon Lee. Lord Caryll, not a
peer of the House of Torthorald, is intended. The
Princesse de Stolberg had insisted that her daughter
must marry Charles the very day of their first interview. This meeting occurred (April 17) at Macerata,
in the March of Ancona, where a Cardinal of the
House of Compagnoni-Marefoschi had placed the
family palace at the disposal of Charles. No doubt
the palace was a gloomy barrack, but thither Charles

led his young bride, on Good Friday, of all days in the year. He is said to have been a fond student of foolish prophecies, as of Nostradamus and Merlin. But the 'freit,' or omen, did not warn him : indeed, by the terms of the marriage, he was obliged to bed the bride on the day of their first meeting. On that fatal day Charles writes to Henry that ' ye marriage was made with all ye forms.' Charles wrote the posy for the wedding ring, which, I understand, was a turquoise with a cameo of his own head : [1]

> ' This Crown is due to you by me,
> And none can love you more than me.

Given by C. ye 3d to his Queen, ye 17th April, 1772.' Such is the draft on a scrap of paper.

These were the circumstances of the last Stuart marriage, as far as they can be traced. The young lady so anxious to be a Queen *in partibus* was, on the mother's side, of the blood of Bruce, through that exiled Lord Ailesbury into whose arms fell Charles II., when smitten by his mortal illness. The family was ancient, but poor, the mother was a pensioner of Maria Theresa, and Louise, like Miss Walkinshaw, had been a canoness. Her portraits, at that period, do not represent her as exactly beau-

---

[1] Now, I believe, the bequest of Lady John Scott to the Duke of Buccleugh.

tiful : she has a plump young face, her hair is drawn back high from the brow ; she wears the family jewels that poor Clementina Sobieska wore, and holds a white rose in her hand. Bonstetten represents her as ' of middle height, blonde, with deep blue eyes, a nose slightly turned up, the complexion dazzlingly fair. . . .' Bonstetten, a young Swiss gentleman, had a romantic liking for Louise.

The portrait by Marsigli, engraved and published in England in 1773, shows the new Queen's face as intelligent, but rather heavy. The manner of dressing the hair is elaborate, and unbecoming. A medal, struck on the occasion, is certainly unflattering: an example was bequeathed or given by Louise to Fabre, the painter, and by him to the Museum at Montpellier. A true Queen of Hearts, handsome, intellectual, and simply attired, appears in the engraving of a miniature by Ozias Humphrey, who also did the miniature of Charles, now in the collection of the Duke of Atholl. I have been unable to trace the original miniature of Louise. Her beauty must have been that of colour and intellectual expression, rather than of features. From the first, the wedding was clouded by the refusal of royal honours, eagerly desired both by Charles and his bride. Thus the old Palace of the Apostles sheltered a dissatisfied pair, though, in the houses of Gask and of Bishop Forbes, there was joy

over ' The Queen of Hearts,' and hopes of an heir to
the visionary crown.

Charlotte soon wrote one of her many unavailing
letters :

Sire,—C'est avec le plus profond respect Mon Auguste
Papa que je prends la liberté de vous faire mon complimens
sur votre établissement, et je supplie Votre Majesté d'etre
très persuadés que Malgrés votre oublie, et le Néant
horribles dans lequelles vous M laissés, que cela Ne
m'empecheras jamais de formés tous les vœux les plus
sinceres pour tout ce qui peu faire votre bonheurs, et votre
prospérité ; Ne pouvants rien a'joutés de plus, ayant
épuissés tous les sentiments de mon cœur, dans le nombres
infinies de lettres que j'ay eu l'honneur de vous écrires dont
aucunes n'onts tracés sur vous mon auguste Papa, ce qui
est pour moy une preuves tres clairs de votre abandons
totalles que je n'ai jamais Merité. Mais je vois qu'il faut
prendres mon partis puisque personnes n'oses Même vous
parlés de moy ny vous prononcés seulement mon noms, je
me suis même adressés à Monsieur le principal Gordon,
qui ma parus etre très touchés de mon état d'abandons,
Mais il a ajouttes qu'il ne pouvois pas entreprendre de vous
en écrires dans la craintes de déplaire à votre Majesté, et
beaucoup d'autres m'ont dits la Même choses, de sortes
mon auguste Papa, je n'aures donc pour tout partager
l'honneur que j'ai d'être votre fille que celui du désespoirs,
puisque je suis sans sort et sans état et condamnés con-
séquamment a ménés la vie du Monde la plus malheureuses
et la plus Misérables : je n'ai donc d'autres résources que
de supplié le ciel avec la plus vive instances d'abrégers
mes tristes jours, qui, ne sont que déjas trop remplis

d'amertunes, et j'ay l'honneur de finirs mon auguste Papa
avec un très profond respect

Sire de votre Majesté

La très humble et très obéissante Servante et fille

tres infortunée   CHARLOTTE.

a l'abbaye de Notre Dame
de Meaux en Brie le 27 Avril 1772.

Charles at last replied, through Gordon, Principal
of the Scots College in Paris. He would take
Charlotte into his household, on condition that she
should have no future relations with her mother.
It would never do to have her mother 'anywhere
about.' But Charlotte declined to abandon her
mother. From a letter of June 20, 1773, by the
Cardinal Secretary of State, it appears that Miss
Walkinshaw and Charlotte had come to Rome and
were making themselves inconvenient to the newly
wedded royal pair. They were commanded to depart,
and their rather annoying visit may account for the
singular severity of Charles to his daughter.[1]

Meanwhile Charles wrote as a fortunate bridegroom to his mother-in-law, to Madame de Talmond,
Madame d'Aiguillon, and the Duc de Bouillon. His
habits were reformed, for a while, but, by the end of
1773, Mann reported that his excesses had returned.
He had been seriously disappointed, we have seen,
as had his bride, by the refusal of royal honours.

---

[1] Lord Braye's MSS. p. 234.

Charles wrote to Cardinal Marefoschi : ' it is for the Pope to go before the Catholic Courts ' (in recognising him) ' showing them a good and not a bad example. The sheep usually follow their shepherd, and it is his duty not to disgust them by showing a path of brambles and thorns.' The Shepherd remained unmoved by this pastoral discourse. Charles left Rome for Siena, and his residence there was woven into the odd romance of the ' Comtes d'Albanie.'

In 1847 two gentlemen calling themselves John Stolberg Sobieski Stuart and Charles Edward Stuart published a romance called ' Tales of the Century.' It contained a flimsy allegory of their own pretensions. Their father was James Allen, at one time a Lieu-tenant in the Navy. His father was Admiral Allen. The claimants had for some years given out that James Allen was no son of Admiral Allen, but a son of Charles and Louise : that the child was born at Siena, that the birth was kept secret, that the babe was handed over to Admiral, then Captain Allen, and was conveyed by him to England, and bred to the Navy. This legend was so far accepted that the two heroes were cherished by the Lord Lovat of their day, and occupied Eilean Agais, an islet on the Beauly. Their likeness to the Stuart family was marked, and they behaved with a certain mysterious pomp.

About the time of the publication of their

romance they retired to Austria, later returning to London, where they lived in a dignified poverty, working earnestly in the British Museum library. The younger, the later survivor, died about 1883. Both were men of many accomplishments, engaging manners, and noble bearing. There is certainly some mystery about their father, called the Iolair Dearg, or Red Eagle, in the romance. He lived to a great age, and died in Clerkenwell. From a letter purporting to be his, and certainly, to all appearance, in his handwriting, he gave, about 1829, some kind of countenance to some sort of lofty pretensions. But he seems to have been more interested in the relations of his father's family to the Hays of Errol ; and Sir Walter Scott told Sir Thomas Dick Lauder that, before 1829, he had seen one of the sons wearing the badge of the Constable of Scotland, a post hereditary in the Errol family. To this he could have no sort of right, even if Admiral Allen had possessed a claim, as is vaguely stated, to the Earldom of Errol. The wearing of this badge indicates Errol pretensions as prior to Stuart pretensions. These first peep out when the brethren told Sir Thomas Dick Lauder, in 1829, that their father possessed a copy, on vellum, of a manuscript once in the collection of Queen Mary's Bishop Lesley, of a book called the ' Vestiarium Scoticum.' This manuscript somehow came to the father from, or as part of the property of Prince Charles.

Scott threw doubts on the whole affair, especially as the book contains descriptions not only of High-land but of Lowland tartans at the date of about 1560!

Concerning this book, which the brethren edited later, a minor mystery exists. What is it? Nobody has seen the vellum copy, but a rough copy on paper, of the eighteenth century, said to have belonged to an old Highlander in the Cowgate, actually exists. The style, spelling, paper, and ink are puzzles to experts. Nothing really indicates a modern forgery : nor do the brethren seem to have had the knowledge, skill, or even motive for such an imitation. Mean-while we possess, as against their legend, not only the evidence of internal improbability, but the solemn denial of Charles himself that he ever had a child by his wife, or any child at all, except Charlotte.[1]

Moreover, about 1823, a young English girl was taken by her parents to see the widow of Charles in Florence. She then heard Madame d'Albanie tell her parents that Napoleon sent for her, when he was medi-tating an invasion of England. She was ushered into a large room in one of the palaces, and left alone. Presently Napoleon entered, strode up to her, and said, ' Madame, had you ever a child? ' she answered ' No, Sire,' and he turned on his heel and marched

[1] March 11, 1785, Lord Braye's MSS. p. 236.

out again.[1] We have thus the denials of both Charles and Louise. They never had a child, and to have a child must have been their strong desire : in fact they were married to no other end, and, before the wedding, Charles was making arrangements for 'the Prince of Wales.' His wife had no children, later, by any one. On Charles's death, his brother assumed the shadowy title : on his own death, he bequeathed nothing,—he had little to bequeath,—to any son of Charles. Not one single tittle of evidence, except their personal resemblance to the Stuarts, was ever put forward by the claimants.

I am inclined to think that their legend was based on an anecdote in Bishop Forbes's ' Lyon in Mourning,' which in manuscript was in the collection of their friend, the late Dr. Robert Chambers. According to this story ' a Scots gentleman, son of a noble family, and captain of a ship of war in Britain,' saw Charles at the Opera in Rome. The date of writing is 1774. Charles recognised him for a Scot, sent for him, and, in his servant, recognised a man who had brought him a letter at Falkirk, in 1746.[2] It would be easy for the fancy of the two Allens, who knew the manuscript ' Lyon in Mourning,' to add that the British captain was Captain Allen, and that a royal

---

[1] This anecdote was told to me by a near relation of the lady who overheard the anecdote narrated by Madame d'Albanie.

[2] *Lyon in Mourning*, iii. p. 329.

babe was secretly entrusted to his charge, and brought up by him with his other son, to whom the Admiral bequeathed the bulk of his property. James Allen received only 100*l.*, why, we do not know. In all probability the brothers, though otherwise men of attractive qualities, poetical, good sportsmen, and, in their ' Lays of the Forest,' excellent writers on natural history, were victims of ' megalomania.' I cannot but recognise a strange kind of sincerity in their belief. The phenomena resemble those of hysterical illusion, but how can we account for hysterical illusion *à deux*, for a ' collective hallucination ' ? Many good reasons forbid a further examination of this singular affair. However the Stuart likeness came (and it is closest to James VIII. where it could not be affected, in a photograph taken of the younger brother after death), it did not come from Charles Edward Stuart and Louise of Stolberg. That it came through the Cardinal is out of the question. Perhaps it may go back, as in the case of Admiral Fitzroy, who much resembled the brothers, to Charles II.[1]

---

[1] An article, not wholly accurate (and not by Lockhart), on the *Tales of the Century* is in the *Quarterly Review*, vol. lxxxi. See Mr. Stewart's *Old and Rare Tartans*, and Mr. Groome's article on Charles Edward and John Sobieski Stuart, in the *Dictionary of National Biography*. I have myself seen many manuscripts and notes of the two brothers and of their father. Like Scott I attribute their claim to an over-indulged habit of romantic day-dreaming, and I consider that it acquired the force of actual hallucination. Scott somewhere cites a note from the elder brother's poem, *The Bridal of*

In 1773 and 1774 Charles kept assuring his wife's relations that his affection for her increased with the passage of time. From Paris a certain 'Will Stuart' kept vainly pleading the cause of poor Charlotte. Surely this cannot have been Lord Bute's son, William Stuart, afterwards Primate of Ireland? More probably it is the Marquis de St. James. Early in 1774 Gordon wrote from Paris that Charlotte, despairing of aid from Charles, was determined to marry. Charlotte had made a friend in the Duc de Richelieu, and hoped for a French pension through the Duc d'Aiguillon.

In 1774 Charles moved to Florence: it was later, however, in 1777, that he acquired the Palace Guadagni, or San Clemente, in the quiet Via San Sebastiano. The weathercock of the house still bears the initials C. R. ! The exiled King and Queen were not recognised by the Grand Duke, and were not much in society. Charles, at Florence, in 1775, wrote to Gordon, saying that, if Charlotte married, he gave her up for ever, and meanwhile, would do nothing to help her. She had never offended him, and his conduct was a piece of cruel and senile obstinacy.

Culchurn (1822), dedicated to no member of a Jacobite family, but to the Duke of Argyll. It contains a poem on the House of Hay, an imitation of Flora Macivor's Clan roll-call, in *Waverley*, but said to be taken from an old MS. history of the Hays ; which is impossible. The Errol claim seems to have been uppermost with the two brothers in 1822.

He had quarrelled with and dismissed Lord Caryll (one of the family of Pope's Caryll), for making a trip to Rome. His wife was now left with one lady and two gentlemen. 'What a poor Court that is, you may judge! No subject pretending to be loyal should have left me in such circumstances and situation ; that shows there are very odd people and characters in this world. . . .' The weary old talk about 'subjects' was never abandoned by Charles.

On February 27, 1775, Gordon replied to Charles in the following letter, an exact *pendant* to the last letters of Henry Goring. Gordon gave Charles's heartless message to Charlotte, but, in the very words of Goring, declined to execute such commissions in future :

Gordon to Charles.

27 Feb. 1775.

I communicated to the young lady in question the contents of your letter of the 10th, it tucht her to such a degree that I was sorry that I had spok to her so friely. She seems, since she can have no word of consolation from you, inclined to marry the first who will seek her and has anuff to make her live ; since she is at present of a proper age, and if she were to wait much longer it is probable she would find none. The treatment she has at present is so precarious that in case no match offers she is resolved to go in to a begging order where she will trouble nobody afterwards, if she lives any time, which she does not believe will be the case as her spirits are intirly brock, and the croirant que ma cause est bonne j'espère qu'on me rendra justice, je suis Sire avec un profond dévouement.

L'Humble Moitié de Votre Majesté

Louise R.

Louise was much too clever a woman to tolerate Charles, who, never intellectual, was now suffering depression under an attack of asthma, and a threatening of apoplexy: 'bleedings and emetics' were administered, as he wrote to a physician unnamed. Even had his character been more agreeable, he was no husband for a beautiful and vivacious girl. He tells his doctor that he can hardly sign his name, and often writes one name where he means another. On May 16, 1777, an anonymous writer, in London, sent Charles a violent expostulation about his treatment of his wife. 'You are giving yourself to debauchery, and destroying the health and happiness of an amiable Princess in the same manner as you treated an ordinary woman of fashion, which has never been forgiven you.' Sir Horace Mann's letters constantly report the excesses of Charles, especially when he exhibits himself to the world in his box at the theatre. 'All my countrymen who return from Italy,' says the London letter-writer, 'are surprised that your amiable consort stays with you : there is not a single person who would not go to any length to deliver her.'[1]   He also denounces

[1] Stuart MSS.

Charles for belonging to neither religion, Catholic nor Anglican.

The deliverers of Louise were at hand. In the spring of 1777, Alfieri, a young Piedmontese of genius who had been roaming about the Courts of Europe, came to Florence. He was eccentric and ambitious of fame, was a poet, or, at least, was in training to be a poet. He pursued the Passions, by way of æsthetic education, and, in England, had an intrigue with the beautiful Lady Ligonier. There was a duel and a scandal, and Alfieri was ready to carry off the lady, but she very candidly confessed to another amour—with her husband's groom! This caused a loss of romantic illusions, on Alfieri's side, and his injured heart was now on the watch for a more ideal charmer, an intellectual flame. He found her in the exiled Queen of England.

Louise is described, at this time, by Dutens, author of ' Mémoires d'un Voyageur qui se repose.' Dutens had been a hanger-on of Lord Mount-Stuart's, at Turin, and was now residing at Florence, and in Society there. Of Louise he says, ' Her face, manners, wit, character, and position, made her the most interesting of women. She was of the middle height, had a beautiful figure, a dazzling complexion, very fine eyes, perfect teeth, an air of nobility and sweetness, simple, gracious, and modest. Her taste was culti-vated by the study of the best authors, whence she

Alfieri, as an amateur of married ladies, did not hesitate to make himself agreeable to the husbands whom he was deceiving. Vernon Lee, in her work already cited, asserts, and perhaps with justice, the virtue of the Countess. The question of the real nature of Alfieri's early relations with Louise, under her husband's roof, affects merely her own character : that of Charles is not cleared by any delinquencies on her part. We can scarcely suppose that his acts of brutality are mere inventions, circulated to justify Louise. Alfieri's days were given to poetic work ; tragedies and sonnets welled constantly from his pen. He passed his evenings at the house of the husband whom *il avoit su plaire*, in contemplation of the charms of the Countess.

But the sufferings of Louise now drew to a head. On the night of St. Andrew's Day (November 30, 1780) Charles had deliriously toasted the Patron Saint of Scotland. He then broke madly into his wife's room, attacked her, and is said to have tried to strangle her. Her cries brought the household to her rescue, they were accustomed to such scenes. Walpole, who heard the story from Mann, called Charles's conduct ' beastly.' It was time to make an end. Louise's life was no more safe than that of Clementina Walkinshaw had been. Dutens describes the agents in Louise's liberation. One was Madame Orlandini. She was descended from the great House of Ormond : she was the widow (elsewhere he seems to say the wife) of a General Orlandini and the mistress of the French Minister at Florence. But she discarded him for an Irish wooer, named Gehegan, who had left the English service, and come to Florence in a very poor way. He was 'young, handsome, honest, and *sensible*. His *liaison* with Madame Orlandini was a model of fidelity. For several years they were never seen apart,'—which must have surprised Alfieri.

These interesting lovers, with Alfieri himself, arranged Louise's escape. Madame Orlandini came to breakfast at Charles's house, and suggested that Louise should accompany her to a neighbouring convent, to see the needlework of the nuns. They went out in the carriage, with Charles. Gehegan met the ladies at the convent door, handed Louise out of her carriage and up a flight of stairs ; Louise entered a room, and the door was shut. Gehegan came back, and told Charles that the nuns had been so unmannerly as to shut the door in his face. It was also shut in the face of Charles, who 'pulled, and pushed, and kicked, and knocked.' Finally the Abbess appeared, and remarked that the Countess of Albany had sought asylum in the convent, and would reside under the protection of the Grand Duchess. Charles had to go home in a rage. Mr. Ewald, not understanding Mann's letters, attributes

F F

to Alfieri the *rôle* played by Gehegan. Louise now wrote to Cardinal York imploring his assistance (December 9, 1780). Henry replied with affectionate sympathy. He had long foreseen the necessity of some such step as she had taken. She must know that it had been impossible for him to aid her in her distresses. Nothing could be wiser than her wish to retire to a convent in Rome, the very convent where his mother had found refuge ; a house for which his father had 'une prédilection toute particulière.'[1] Henry would always befriend and advise his sister-in-law. The Vatican would arrange for her safe journey to Rome. Heaven had permitted Louise's sorrows 'to move you to an edifying life,'—which she presently lived with Alfieri ! Possibly, also, Heaven aimed at the conversion of Charles, but Henry thought *that* a most improbable miracle. 'Je n'ose me flatter de cette conversion.'

The Pope, on December 16, also wrote to Louise in the best manner and the most Apostolic, and so Louise drove off to Rome, Alfieri and Gehegan sitting, disguised and well armed, on the box-seat of her coach. They only accompanied her to a certain distance, and, to prevent scandal, Alfieri returned to

[1] Mr. Ewald translates 'when the King my father was under a certain infatuation !' He thus makes Henry accuse James of a passion for Mrs. Hay ! Other mistakes occur in Mr. Ewald's book at this point. He had not read either Von Reumont or Dutens, and misunderstood Mann.

Florence for some time. In February 1781 he went to Naples, for the precise purpose of taking Rome on the way, and seeing, through the convent grating, the object of a flame not only endearing in itself, but, as he calculated, likely to be serviceable to his genius as a Poet. To a British critic Alfieri, with his genius, and his resolute training and education of that faculty, appears much of a Prig, though undeniably a Poet. A young poet lover of another gentleman's wife is very well. But when the lover has perpetually a horti-cultural eye on the cultivation of his talents and fame, through the assistance of his passion, then one can only be sorry for the woman whom he finds serviceable in a poetical way. Louise, later, was, no doubt, happier with her lover than she had been with her husband. In the ' little language ' of the affections, she was Psipsia, and Alfieri was Psipsio : titles of an onomatopoeic sort, derived from kissing.

When the Cardinal came to be possessed of a fuller knowledge of all the circumstances, he ceased to hope that Heaven had designed them as an intro-duction to a *vie édifiante*. In escaping from Charles, Louise had every justification : had there been no Alfieri in the case, her conduct was merely necessary, for her very life was not safe, and Charles's behaviour was a daily insult to any woman. He himself remained unamenable to the conversion for which poor Henry tried to hope. The following letters from Mr. Gehegan are curious, above all when he sends a kind of challenge from Alfieri in Naples. The poet's courage did not shrink from a duel with an old, asthmatic, and apoplectic invalid.

To Charles from C. Gehegan.

Dec. 9, 1780.

Sir,—A report which prevails in town obliges me to take the liberty of writing to you. It has been repeatedly averred to me that you was pleased to say at your table that you would have me shot, were it to cost you half your fortune, for no other reason that I know of than because I had the honour of handing your amiable Consort out of your carriage, and thence up a flight of stairs and in doing so I do not think I have merited your resentment nor can believe you, Sir, could be capable of such low treachery. But in case it were true that you expressed a similar desire I can assure you any body you may employ on such a base errand will be received as he merits and that I shall stay in Florence for some months ready to repel in the most determined manner any similar attempt.

I have the honour, &c.

Dutens says that Charles sent an apology by one of his gentlemen. Gehegan wrote later:

Sir,—It is with the utmost reluctance I find myself obliged to take the liberty of troubling you on nearly a similar affair, to that which I had the honour of communicating to you, Sir, in my first letter. Your experience and knowledge of the world, Sir, will undoubtedly convince you that there is no rank in life, which authorises to use a *Gentleman* ill unmeritedly, or unjustly : if it were necessary to bring proof of the truth of this assertion the duels fought very lately by Princes of the Blood of France with private persons, will be sufficient for that purpose, and you are no doubt, Sir, sensible that nothing can hurt a man of honour more than the imputations of perfidy and treachery : and that the higher the rank of the person who throws such an aspersion the greater is the dishonour and loss of character accruing from it. Many persons who have the honour of dining at your table, say that you are pleased to *speak of Comte Alfieri* in the most unbecoming manner of which he, though now at Naples, has had notice.

It is said, Sir, that you call him a seducer, and attribute to him the separation between you and your most amiable Consort, whereas it is notorious to all Florence, that her state of health and daily sufferings, forced her to that extremity : and that no other person than Madame de Matzan was privy to her design, and it is generally well known that you, Sir, as well after as before, the said separation, often invited him to your house and you yourself must confess, Sir, that this most improbable surmise of yours is without the smallest proof. Count Alfieri, conscious of his innocence, and justly surprised as well as irritated by such a calumny, has prayed me, Sir, as his friend, to know from you whether such a report be true, and if such is your opinion of him ; he being determined if you persist, Sir, in holding this language, to return in the speediest manner to Florence to *Demand Satisfaction* for so gross an injury.

Therefore, Sir, give me leave to request you, Sir, with all due deference, to write me a few lines on this subject, either in disculpation of this gentleman or the contrary, that I may be able to give a proper answer on this matter. I was very happy, Sir, to find that the remonstrances which

I took the liberty to make to you in my former letter, have had the proper effect, and have prevented the measures which my honour would have obliged me to take against you, Sir, whom I was always taught to revere, and respect; for believe me, Sir, I had much rather not exist than live the subject of the injurious language of any man on earth. It will give me no less satisfaction if I am fortunate enough to prevent the very disagreeable consequences which must ensue, Sir, if you persist in speaking so injuriously of my friend Comte Alfieri.

I am, &c.

What answer, if any, Charles may have made to this Lucius O'Trigger is unknown. A duel with an exiled King would have been an excellent advertisement for a young poet, like Alfieri, and perfectly safe, considering Charles's bodily infirmities: not that Alfieri lacked courage enough to fight any husband.

Arrived in Rome the Countess proved that she had no idea of passing an edifying life in a convent, as the Pope had fancied. He kindly gave her leave, 'on any very urgent occasion,' says Mann, 'to use the coaches and servants of the Cardinal York. This was some disappointment to her, as she had hoped that she might have had liberty to take the air when she pleased.' She soon succeeded in getting her own way, Mann writes:

Jan. 23rd, 1781.

. . . The Countess Albanie is treated at Rome with the greatest attention. She has obtained leave to go abroad whenever she pleases without the least constraint. She had a long audience of the Pope in the Sacristy of a Church, Cardinal York treats her with the greatest civility, and had made her the most generous offer, and she goes frequently to dine with him at Frascati, where he commonly resides. He has offered her his house in Town to be attended by his servants and entertained at his expense, though six thousand crowns have been allotted to her by the Chamber of Rome while she remains in that City, but the above offer she has refused, and a house has been taken near the Convent for a cook or other servants, where her table is provided, but she does not intend to stay in Italy; it is said that the Princess Stolberg her mother and the Marquise de la Jamaique her sister are to come to Rome in the spring to carry her to Paris, where she is to live with the former.

Presently Louise left her convent, and removed to the house of the Cardinal, who was fascinated by his beautiful and witty sister-in-law. He reduced Charles's pension by about half, conferring the rest on Louise, who also obtained a pension of 20,000 crowns from France. But the Cardinal's gifts depended on her stay at Rome, and, as she only wished to join Alfieri, she was determined to leave the papal city. Mann was very well informed : the Countess had told a friend, 'in dern secrecy' about the French pension, and the friend instantly carried the news to Mann. Charles, his income lowered, was obliged to reduce his establishment, and to raise a loan of 500*l.* He now lived, says Mann, a regular and inoffensive life.

Meanwhile Alfieri had settled at Rome, where he was allowed to see as much of his lady as he pleased. He must really have had great powers of fascination, for the Cardinal and the Pope looked on benignantly at this idyll of innocent affection. Charles vainly attempted to open their eyes. Mann reports (Dec. 28, 1782) that Charles had sent Prince Corsini to the Vatican with three requests. That his wife might be sent back. That he might receive his full pension of 12,000 (elsewhere ' 10,000 ') crowns : from which 4,000 were deducted for Louise. ' And lastly, that Count Alfieri, whom he accuses of having been chiefly instrumental to her elopment, should be banished from Rome.' The Pope refused to listen, saying that ' as to Count Alfieri, he wished to have many gentlemen of equal merit at Rome.' Prince Corsini fell into general disgrace for acting as Charles's envoy. Thus Charles, left in poverty, ' has totally altered his way of living, and behaves in every respect with proper decency.' Henry justified, to Lascaris, his behaviour about the money, but there is a good deal of variety in the accounts as to the exact sums. He argued that Charles, not being obliged to maintain his wife, ' is richer by receiving only 5,000 crowns than he was before she left him.' Charles did not take the same view of the situation, which was, presently, changed. Mann writes as follows :

March 25th, 1783.

On Saturday I received notice from Count Albany's house that he was dangerously ill, he had been abroad the day before, and had invited company to dine with him the day after : he made the confession (?) yesterday and in the evening the Sacraments of the Church of Rome were administered to him, at the same time that a Courier was dispatched to inform Cardinal York of the very imminent danger in which his Physicians (from whom I receive accounts two or three times a day) then thought his brother to be. . . .

A proof of the serious nature of Charles's malady is his Will, dated March 23–25, 1783. He appoints, as his heir, Charlotte Stuart, 'Duchess of Albany,' then still in her French convent. On March 30 he legitimated his daughter, and the document was signed, in France, by M. Semonin, of the Foreign Office, and witnessed by M. de Vergennes. But Charlotte did not come to her father's house till more than a year later.[1] The Will had been executed when Mann describes the Cardinal's movements thus :

. . . Cardinal York set out from Rome immediately on receiving the notice of his Brother's condition, but being apprehensive of not finding him alive, he stopped at Siena from whence he sent a Courier to get intelligence of him and then came on and arrived here late on Saturday night. He is lodged at a convent near his brother's house, with whom he passes the whole day.

[1] Lord Braye's MSS. p. 235.

Later, Mann writes:

April 26th.

It now appears that during the time that Cardinal York was at Florence Count Albany his brother convinced him of many circumstances relating to his wife's conduct and her *Elopement* from him, of which the Cardinal was not informed, and in which all those who took the part of the Countess had likewise been deceived, that the whole was a Plot formed by Count Alfieri; All this coming from his Brother at a time that he appeared to be in the most imminent danger, made a great impression on the Cardinal, who on his return to Rome exposed the whole to the Pope and obtained an Order from Him to Count Alfieri (who lived in great intimacy then with the Countess) to leave Rome in fifteen days. This was notified to him last week and he was preparing to retire to Venice. . .

Alfieri was obliged to go, and, on March 4, departed for Siena, in a gloomy frame of mind. His lady found a sad satisfaction in copying out his sonnets, 'Sonnetti di Psipsio copiati da Psipsia in Genzano, 1783, anno disgraziato per tuti due.' Genzano, where this inscription was written, is on the shores of the beautiful lake of Nemi, once haunted by

> The Priest who slew the slayer,
> And shall himself be slain.

Louise was ready to make, and did make every sacrifice, to enable her to live where she chose, that is, with Alfieri. Vernon Lee has discovered certain

letters written at this time, by the Countess, from
Genzano, to a friend of Alfieri.   Thus she says, 'Who
knows what will happen, it is so long since the
man in Florence is ill, and still he lives, and it seems
to me that he is made of iron, in order that we may
all die. . . . What a cruel thing to expect one's
happiness from the death of another!   O God! how
it degrades the soul!   And yet I cannot refrain from
wishing it.'   Alas, poor lady!

Her letters to Henry prove that, in the matter
of money, and of diamonds, Psipsia was, for the
moment, nobly disinterested.   She insisted that
Charles was at this time in real poverty.   The letters
of Charles during 1782 contain nothing but protests
against the injustice with which he is treated,
complaints of his poverty, and censures on the
infatuated cruelty of his brother the Cardinal,
especially wounding to 'a heart so sensible as mine.'
His letters were never lucid in expression, and they
become more perplexed than ever.   It may be worth
while to give his letter on the loss of Minorca, which,
says Horace Walpole, interested England no more
'than if the King had lost his pocket-handkerchief.'
Charles shows also that he has been gambling in the
French Lottery, and that he is alive to the struggles
of Ireland.

Charles to Cowley (*Oliphant of Gask ?*).

Florence, March 1st.

There is no poste that comes to me from France unless you had wrote directly to Florence. It seems that a moste violente storm of snow (never heard of before) has filled ye rodes between Rome and Viterbo. Port Mahone surrendered ye 12th Feb. that is certain, with 3,600 men, but no other particulars. The singularity of ye Pop's jurney to Vienna, is confirmed also ; The English having abandoned Port Mahone it is not possible but that Gibiltera must surrender soon ; Jamaica is saide will be attacked and what is there to opose them as it is reported : Poor England.

Yr Sincere friend,　　C. R.

8th, March.

. . . It is assured by good hands that Madras is taken, and ye French also in it, so there muste be a full bankrupt of ye East India Companie. . . .

15th, March.

. . . It is about this time that one draws ye Lottery of ye french India Company, as soon as ye know if any of my numbers are come favorable to me, be pleased to advise me of it immediately : on all sides there continues ye same reports all to ye disadvantage of ye English, it is saide also ye Irish wants to be independante, as well as ye Americans, and it seems their argument is supported by 50 thousand men in Arms, and regimentes. No more about Port Mahone but that they are Prisoners of war it is certain.

Yr sincere friend,　　C. R.

By the close of 1783 his position was sensibly improved. Gustavus III. of Sweden was visiting

Florence. He took pity on the forlorn Royal head, and, going to Rome, contrived a friendly separation between Charles and Louise. By this arrangement, writes Mann, 'the Countess has obtained an amicable divorce *a mensa et thoro*, and liberty to reside where she pleases :

For this single point she has sacrificed every other advantage. She has given up her Pin-money, which by her marriage contract was fifteen thousand french Livres per Annum, as likewise four thousand Crowns (or 1,000 stg.) which the Cardinal since their separation stopped for her maintenance, out of the pension of 10,000 Crowns which the Court of Rome always allowed to their Father, the disposal of which the present Pope left to the Cardinal, who gave his Brother only five thousand, but now the whole is to be given to him, to whom likewise the Cardinal gives up all the furniture in the House at Rome with the Plate and his share of the jewels that were brought into their Family by the late Pretender's wife the Princess Sobiesky, *excepting the great Ruby*, and one of a lesser size, that was pawned to the King of Poland by that Republick, these are to be kept in deposit either to be redeemed, if that State should ever be in a capacity to do it, or to the Survivor of the two Brothers. Among the above things that were portable by land, there is a large Shield of gold which the Emperor Leopold presented to the King of Poland for raising the siege of Vienna, all which were brought here from Rome the beginning of this week, the other effects are to be sent by sea to Leghorn.

Count Albany by the above means will now have a clear Income of ten thousand Crowns from Rome,

besides which he has in the french funds 54,000 Livres
per Annum : The Countess by relinquishing her Pin-
money and part of the Roman pension receives nothing at
present from her Husband's Family, but on the separation
from her Husband the Court of France allows her a pension
of 60,000 Livres and at his death by her Marriage Articles
she will have a Dowry of 6,000 Roman Crowns. By my
former letters I acquainted Mr. Fox with what had passed
between the King of Sweden and Count Albany for whom
His Majesty had actually given orders to a Banker here to
furnish him with four thousand Rix-Dollars, but the payment
of the sum was suspended, first for want of a proper security,
during which time Count Albany fell dangerously ill, and
then His Swedish Majesty having been instrumental to the
afore-mentioned Accomodation, made him judge that
count Albany had not any need of his Assistance. . . . '

Charles was thus relieved from his ' situation si
cruelle, tyrannique, injuste, et si barbare.' Many of
his family portraits were brought to Florence by
John Stewart, his groom of the chamber, who writes
to that effect, on April 24, 1784. The Great Ruby of
Poland, with certain diamonds and pearls, was left
at the Mont-de-Piété in Rome : they were redeem-
able by Poland, but Poland was never in a position
to redeem them, and they were later swallowed
up in the French Revolution. Elcho again dunned
Charles for his famous 1,500*l.*, of course to no purpose.
Charles was dissatisfied with we do not well know
what. He writes to John Stewart (April 24, 1784),
' Je proteste contre la surprise que l'on m'a faite, tant

à moi que à mon très cher frère et cousin, le Roi de
Suède.' He announced his boundless gratitude and
attachment to the Swedish King. We have seen
that, when he thought himself dying, in March 1783,
Charles constituted his daughter his heiress, legitimated her, and styled her Duchess of Albany. He
now began to weary for her presence, in the dull
house where, by a dim light, and with loaded pistols
on his table, he practised on the bagpipes and other
musical instruments.

In July 1784 he sent to Charlotte, bidding her
join him at Florence. She arrived in October, a
tall, strong, good-humoured young woman, whose
expression, in her portrait, is kind and cheerful.
Beneath a kind of silk toque her hair is curled and
hangs in a fringe over her brow. There is no striking
resemblance to either of her parents. Charles received her with delight, covered her with jewels, and,
on St. Andrew's Day, invested her with the Green
Ribbon. On November 16 M. de Vergennes wrote
to ' Myladi Stuart d'Albany,' announcing that Louis
XVI. had granted her father a pension of 60,000
livres, with a reversion in her favour of 10,000 livres
on his death. We have proposals for a medal of
Charlotte, which seems never to have been struck.
One of four designs is that of a tempest-tossed ship,
nearing the English shores, with the Stuart arms on
the flag, and the legend, *Pendet salus spe exigua et*

extrema. The very words *spes extrema* destroy the
myth of the 'Sobieski Stuarts.' The good-natured
Charlotte made the peace between Charles and poor
Lord Caryll, who asks for the order of St. Andrew,
and announces that 'the Elector' (George III.) 'has
more than once declared that if the King were ever
in distress, it would be a real pleasure to him to
assist him.' (March 21, 1785.) These details are
from Lord Braye's MSS.

Charlotte did more : she induced Charles to write
a friendly letter to Cardinal York. Many of her own
letters to him are in the British Museum : she does
her best to reconcile Henry, who had been displeased
by her legitimation, and title of Royal Highness.
From Charles's point of view it seems that, on his
decease, Charlotte would not have been Queen of
England, or ousted Henry IX. The Cardinal, in an
undated Memorial to the Pope, says that he has been
won over by the young lady, and he remained her
kindest friend. Meanwhile, Psipsia had joined Psipsio
at Colmar (August 17, 1784), and the lovers, though
poor, were happy, or would have been happy, but for
certain periods of involuntary separation.

Charlotte was trying to keep her recalcitrant invalid
in order, and ' checked him when he drank too much,'
says Mrs. Piozzi. Her letters to the Cardinal hint at
the difficulties of her task, and at the occasional relapses
of her sire. 'I am so bothered in the head,' writes

Charles himself : his wonderful strength of constitution had for thirty years been overtried : he was asthmatic, dropsical, and 'bothered in the head.' There is a well-known story of how Mr. Greathead induced him to talk about his one hour of glory, and how, when he came to speak of the executions after Culloden, he fell into convulsions. Charlotte entered the room, and said to Mr. Greathead, 'Oh, Sir, what is this ? You must have been speaking to my father about Scotland and the Highlanders. No one dares to mention those subjects in his presence.' In December 1785 Henry induced Charles to return to Rome. There his health did not improve, but there, as elsewhere, he touched for the scrofula, and some of his 'touch-pieces' are extant. Meanwhile, Burns had commemorated Charlotte in the song ' The Bonny Lass o' Albany.' It is improbable that the exiled family ever heard of their greatest Laureate.

It is needless, and it were painful, to dwell on the last sad hours of Charles's decrepitude. His conduct justified the Pope, in congratulating the Cardinal on his brother's conversion to better things, and to a frame of mind more pious. Nursed by his devoted daughter, he resisted the maladies of dropsy, and a threatened apoplexy, till, after weeks without hope, he died on January 31, 1788. His obsequies were performed with all solemnity, by the weeping Cardinal, at Frascati. Thus he who, as late as 1783,

G G

had besought Louis XVI. to undertake his cause, passed away from his unsubdued hopes of Royalty, a year before the tempest shook all thrones, in 1789. His daughter and general heiress did not survive him by many months. The House of Stuart, in the direct line, was now represented by 'a barren stock,' the Cardinal. Such was 'the end of an auld sang,' and, practically, the beginning of the new songs on ' Bonnie Prince Charlie.' The contemporary Lament was left for an obscure Highland bard to chant, in Gaelic verse, that unconsciously reproduces the imagery of the Greek lament for Bion. The King would not have had it otherwise. Untrue to himself, untrue to many a friend, his heart was constant to his High-landers. . . . Farewell, unhappy Prince, heir to such charm, and to such unmatched sorrows ; farewell, most ardently loved of all the Stuarts !

APPENDIX

THE following document is part of a draft of 1759, explaining to the English people the reasons for which the Prince turned Protestant:

Charles's Proclamation, 1759.

The Roman Catholick religion has been the ruin of the royal Family, the subversion of the English Monarchy and Constitution, in the last century, did like an earthquake raise up that fatal rock on which it split. In that religion was I brought up and educated as other Princes are with a firm attachment to the see of Rome. Had motives of interest been able to make me disguise my sentiments upon the material point of religion I should certainly in my first undertaking in the year 1745 have declared myself a protestant, it was too evidently my interest so to doe to leave a doubt with any person. As to the motive which dissuaded me from it, it was no other than a persuasion of the truth of my religion. The adversity I have suffered since that time, has made me reflect, has furnished me with opportunitys of being informed, and God has been pleased so far to smile upon my honest endeavour, as to enlighten my understanding and point me out the hidden path by which the finger of man has been introduced to form the artfull system of Roman Infallibility.

Iff it was greatly my interest when last amongst you to appear to be a protestant, it was surely as much against it after my misfortune and during my Exile to become realy one ; that motive however had no weight with me in a matter of so great concern.

In order to make my renountiation of the errors of the Church of Rome the most authentick, and the less liable afterwards to malitious interpretations, I went to London in the year 1750 and in that capital did then make a solemn abjuration of the Romish religion, and did embrace that of the Church of England as by Law Established in the 39 Articles in which I hope to live and die.

I therefore as a protestant Prince, the Lawfull heir to the crown of these Realms, vested with the full powers of Regent of these Kingdoms, in my Royal Father's name, and in my own, solemnly make you the following promises of redress of grievances already mentioned.

The victory of Hawke in Quiberon Bay nullified these promises.

INDEX

PRINTED BY
SPOTTISWOODE AND CO. LTD., NEW-STREET SQUARE
LONDON